Praise for *Wasteland*

An Indie Next Pick

Recipient of the *AudioFile Magazine* Earphones Award (Audiobook)

"W. Scott Poole's exploration of some of the Great War's consequences for popular art, is fully attuned to the conflict's devastating psychological impact . . . Highly persuasive . . . Poole's general conclusions about World War I's transformation into art, and the process of psychological displacement that accompanied it, are incontestable."

—D. J. TAYLOR, *The Wall Street Journal*

"Thoroughly engrossing cultural study . . . Poole persuasively argues that the birth of horror as a genre is rooted in the unprecedented destruction and carnage of WWI . . . Will make it hard for readers who haven't considered the wartime context for horror's emergence to forget it."

—*Publishers Weekly* (starred review)

"Through books, movies, and more, noted historian Poole traces the roots of modern horror to a singular event that shaped the world forever: WWI. His thesis is that the barbarism of war never fades." —*AudioFile Magazine*

"Elegantly written and cogently argued, *Wasteland* convincingly demonstrates the modern horror genre's origins in the great Dance of Death that was the First World War." —DAVID J. SKAL, author of *The Monster Show: A Cultural History of Horror*

"W. Scott Poole combines smart readings of the horror classics with detailed knowledge of twentieth-century history, art, and literature to dig deep into the serious side of these popular entertainments. I thought I already knew the subject inside out, but *Wasteland* introduced me to fresh facts, new ideas, and surprising connections. This is cultural history of a very high order: intelligent, lively, and wonderfully readable." —CHRISTOPHER BRAM, author of *Gods and Monsters*

"*Wasteland* will appeal to film and military buffs, horror fans, those interested in popular culture and those who seek a better understanding of the escalating violence of the last 100 years . . . A fascinating read."

—BILL SCHWAB, *Missourian*

"Tackling the indescribable horrors of wartime is a delicate but necessary task . . . Beginning with the Great War, [Poole] exhaustively discusses the influences each era's war had on their directors, writers, actors and audiences of the horror genre."

—AHLISSA EICHHORN, *Fangoria*

"*Wasteland* spans multiple nations, dozens of battles, and traces how warfare influenced artists of all crafts. Moving beyond prejudiced perceptions of high- and low-brow art . . . Poole reveals the connective tissue holding together the bones of modern monsters."

—DUSTIN WATERS,
Charleston City Paper

"A fascinating read."

—WAYNE MILLER, Vampires.com

"[A] fascinating new book about how [World War I] reshaped western culture . . . Poole is a very gifted writer."

—GENE WALZ, *Winnipeg Free Press*

"Poole writes with empathic insight . . . His skilled knitting together of a broad range of genres and the spirit of unease permeating them all carries its own salient kind of moral horror."

—CHRIS BARSANTI, *Rain Taxi*

"A sophisticated work of cultural history . . . The book's wide-ranging erudition, strong prose, and clear love and fascination with both history and horror . . . will appeal to a variety of readers."

—JESSE KAVADLO,
PopMatters

"Poole brings a scholar's eye and a devotee's heart to a study of the literary, film, and artistic incarnations of horror from the World War I period to today."

—*Kirkus Reviews*

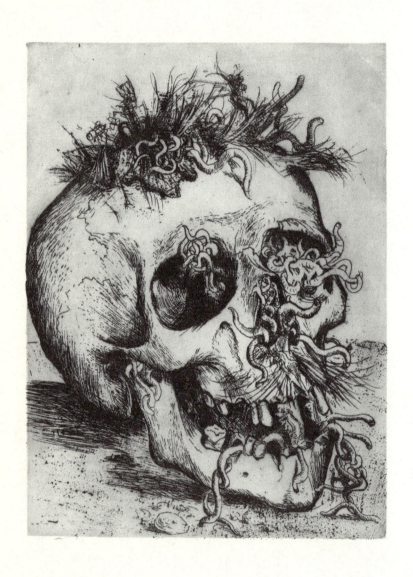

WASTELAND

THE GREAT WAR AND THE ORIGINS OF MODERN HORROR

W. SCOTT POOLE

COUNTERPOINT

Berkeley, California

WASTELAND

Frontispiece: Skull by Otto Dix © The Museum of Modern Art /
Licensed by SCALA / Art Resource, NY

The Library of Congress has cataloged the hardcover as follows:
Names: Poole, W. Scott, 1971– author.
Title: Wasteland : the Great War and the origins of modern horror /
    W. Scott Poole.
Description: First hardcover edition. | Berkeley, California : Counterpoint :
    Distributed by Publishers Group West, [2018] | Includes bibliographical
    references.
Identifiers: LCCN 2018021078 | ISBN 9781640090934
Subjects: LCSH: Horror films—History and criticism. | Horror in
    literature—History. | Horror in art—History. | Psychic trauma—
    History. | World War, 1914–1918—Influence. | War and society—
    History—20th century. | Civilization, Modern—20th century.
Classification: LCC PN1995.9.H6 P64 2018 | DDC 791.43/6164—dc23
LC record available at https://lccn.loc.gov/2018021078

Paperback ISBN: 978-1-64009-266-2

Cover design by Jaya Miceli
Book design by Wah-Ming Chang

COUNTERPOINT
2560 Ninth Street, Suite 318
Berkeley, CA 94710
www.counterpointpress.com

Printed in the United States of America
Distributed by Publishers Group West

10 9 8 7 6 5 4 3 2 1

for Beth

War broke: and now the Winter of the world
—WILFRED OWEN, "1914" (1914)

The Wasteland grows; woe to those who cannot see the
wasteland within.
—FRIEDRICH NIETZSCHE, Thus Spake Zarathustra (1891),
used as an epigram by painter Otto Dix
for Seven Deadly Sins (1933)

And still they come and go and this is all I know—
That from the gloom I watch an endless picture show.
—SIEGFRIED SASSOON, Picture Show (1919)

CONTENTS

WASTELAND

Foreword

Corpses in the Wasteland

There is no document of civilization which is not at the
same time a document of barbarism.

—WALTER BENJAMIN

Writing history seems mostly the preoccupation of dwellers among ruins.
The Great War (1914–1918) represents the literal and figurative ruins of the
twentieth century, the years that caused the sense of exuberance born in the
nineteenth century to sicken and sour. In much of Europe, the sheer number
of the dead swept away a century of sentimental mourning practices in a
matter of months. The war remade the world's map, created new global powers, and brought with these changes some of the seemingly intractable, and
possibly apocalyptic, problems in Asia, the Middle East, Africa, and Russia
that appear to us in every day's news feed.

Behind the words of the freewheeling intellectual and essayist Walter Benjamin, a man who wandered across the broken Europe of the 1920s
and '30s until it became his death, lay another truth. What we admire and
love in our culture—both high culture and pop culture, and even what Mark
Dery calls "unpopular culture"—hides a world of suffering. Everything produced by civilization has written into it the viral code of barbarism. In every
horror movie we see, every horror story we read, every horror-based video
game we play, the phantoms of the Great War skittle and scratch just beyond

the door of our consciousness. Numberless dead and wounded bodies appear on our screens, documents of barbarism coauthored by the Great War generation and all the forces that have fed off them in the decades since.

The world before 1914, just a little over a hundred years ago, seems unrecognizable today. It was a world of creaky empires that had hobbled from the Middle Ages into the modern world—Russia, Hapsburg Austria, the Ottoman Empire. All of them welded together peoples and language groups with little or nothing in common. After the final defeat of Napoleon in 1815, many crowned heads thought the mighty jinn of revolution had been placed firmly back in its prison. Kaisers, emperors, and kings fought short conflicts, made marriage alliances, and negotiated treaties in exchange for tiny territories. Scrappy Great Britain—with its constitutional monarchy, muscular industrial revolution, large middle class, and unmatched sea power—ruled an empire that stretched from the Caribbean to Africa to Asia. America seemed an upstart with a tiny army and territorial ambitions focused on Latin America and the Pacific, regions that had attracted only limited attention among the old European powers.

Signs appeared that this world might crumble. The inability to consider all the ramifications of these signs helps explain why Europe's political culture decided to turn the Old World into flaming wreckage. The Serbian people of the Balkans had developed enormous national pride and grounded it in a partially fictionalized history. They had no interest in becoming another principality of the Hapsburg Empire. The burgeoning economies in western Europe depended more and more on the markets and materials of their colonial possessions, without which they feared economic ruin at home. Russia lost a war in 1905 to Japan, and suddenly a new power appeared on the world stage, one that constituted an utter riddle to most in the West despite its long and fascinating history. The United States had also won a war against Spain, a seemingly decrepit European power. Wars like the short but bloody Crimean conflict and the protracted American Civil War suggested that changes in technology could now kill in the tens of thousands while leaving whole generations scarred and wounded. But a tenuous peace existed while nations and empires played with whole populations as if they were chess pieces. The gamesmanship of the old powers of Europe rigged up a complicated system of alliances, tethered to one another in such a way that one falling into the abyss would drag all the others with it.

In the summer of 1914, the coming of the conflict that at first saw Germany and Austria-Hungary (the Central Powers) fighting against France, Britain, Russia, and Serbia (the Allies) caused an eerie joy to come to the romantically inclined. In this book, we will watch writers and artists and actors and early film directors joining artillery companies, machine gun units, and the infantry. Many, though certainly not all, Europeans spoke of the conflict as an adventure, and probably a short-lived one, in which the grinding routine of daily life would give way to the élan of conflict. Everyone expected to return home a hero. Like a storm breaking the monotony of a hot, dry day, the dark clouds of war thundered across the landscape while a vital rain poured down.

In only a few short weeks, however, horror replaced the so-called war fever of the summer. On the western front, Germany swept through Belgium. German troops came within eighteen miles of Paris, causing at least one million of the city's three million inhabitants to flee. British and French troops fought back the Germans at the Battle of the Marne, but both sides suffered catastrophic losses. Fifteen thousand British soldiers died in just two weeks of fighting. In the east, czarist Russia had some early successes against Austria-Hungary and Germany, invading East Prussia. At the Battle of Tannenberg in August, a relatively small German army under Paul von Hindenburg and Erich Ludendorff handed the Russian Empire a defeat from which it never fully recovered. The fighting enveloped eastern Europe—in Bulgaria, which fought alongside the Central Powers; in Serbia and Romania, both joined to the Allies.

By late 1914, the Germans had been pushed back to defensive positions in France. Both sides began building elaborate trenches, earthworks serving as fortifications, unlikely homes, and burial pits. The no-man's-land that stretched between the armies became a blasted landscape, wrapped in barbed wire, scoured by shelling, and covered with dead bodies that rotted unburied. Men on both sides lived in fetid conditions for months on end without relief. Rats and all manner of other vermin swarmed in the muddy dark. The shelling that signaled an offensive could go on for days, shattering nerves. The night would explode with rifle fire and the rattle of the Maxim gun, the machine gun that shredded the soldiers ordered to charge into the enemy's trenches. Dugouts built for safety resembled the narrator's tomb in Edgar Allan Poe's short story "The Premature Burial" when soldiers choked to death on the earth from their own collapsed defenses.

The trench system horrified observers who saw it for the first time. Valentine Fleming, a British member of Parliament and friend of Winston Churchill, traveled to France at the end of 1914 and wrote of the "absolutely indescribable ravages of modern artillery fire, not only among men, animals, and the buildings within its zone but the very face of nature itself." He described a landscape "littered with the bodies of men and scarified with their rude graves" while the air seemed to explode night and day with "the hideous . . . incessant crash and whistle and roar of every type of projectile" accompanied by "sinister columns of smoke and flame."

Places like the Ypres salient (at the contemporary town of Ieper, in Belgium) became unrecognizable ruins; bodies covered no-man's-land for tens of miles. The Belgian region became one of the most fought-over pieces of ground on earth, with no fewer than three major battles fought there between 1914 and 1918. Germany introduced the use of poison gas at Ypres in early 1915, and the Allies called it savage and inhumane, charging Germany with breaking the rules of civilized warfare. Within months, both sides improved on the weapon and began using it on almost every front, the spectral-looking gas mask becoming as common a soldier's accoutrement as the helmet.

By 1915, trenchworks stretched from the North Sea to Switzerland. Efforts, great or small, to go on the offensive resulted in tens of thousands of dead soldiers and hundreds of thousands of wounded ones. Some soldiers suffered complete breaks with reality, muttering to themselves in a daze, hallucinating, and even suffering psychologically induced blindness. The idea of "battle" itself changed as the trenches became a factory for producing corpses. Before 1914, kings and commanders thought of battles as set pieces that decided the issue in a day or two. By contrast, in the Battle of Verdun, a German offensive that opened in February 1916, fighting continued every day until December, leading to nearly a million casualties. The landscape, once green and lush, remains gored by the war a hundred years later.

The Great War quickly became world war. By the second year of the conflict, the Ottoman Empire, as elderly as the Austro-Hungarian medieval polity, joined in the fight alongside Germany and the Hapsburgs. An Allied offensive in 1915 against the Turkish port of Gallipoli became a nightmare with a large number of troops from Australia and New Zealand entrenched on beaches and dying by the tens of thousands, as much from disease as shelling and machine gun fire. Nothing came of the eight-month conflict except for nearly 300,000 casualties.

Italy entered the fray in hopes of gaining spoils of territory from Austria-Hungary. Japan leaped in quickly alongside the Allies so that it could seize German-held colonies in the Pacific. Immediately after the start of the war, the British in sub-Saharan Africa captured the German colonies of Togoland and Cameroon. German forces waged a guerrilla campaign that likely led to the deaths of more African civilians than British soldiers. Regular British and German soldiers fought throughout the war in South Africa.

In 1917, the United States entered on the side of the Allies even as the red star of revolution rose over Russia. Though it ended the brutal reign of the czars and ultimately took Russia out of the Great War, the Bolshevik Revolution in October 1917 prepared the way for more violence in the form of the Russian Civil War (1917–1922) when the Allies attempted to aid czarist sympathizers and destroy the revolutionary government. Soon, Joseph Stalin seized the direction of revolutionary socialism and became the head of the newly formed Union of Soviet Socialist Republics (USSR).

The United States and its unending supply of soldiers and war matériel sustained the Allies in their final clash with the Central Powers. In the spring of 1918, Ludendorff and Hindenburg launched a massive attack called *die Kaiserschlacht* (the Kaiser's Battle), meant as a giant offensive to end the conflict in France before American troops even began to appear on the ground. Once again, the Germans drove within tens of miles of a panicked Paris, and once again the bitter spirit of the Great War seemingly stopped the advance, grounding a triumphal march in viscera, mud, and blood. Facing the surge in American troop deployment that began in 1918, German hopes for a quick victory in France ended as the Allied forces began pushing them back to their own frontiers. The time had come for an armistice, which was signed on November 11, 1918. The Allied blockade of foodstuffs for German civilians continued, however, and turned the cease-fire into an uneasy peace, marked by the Treaty of Versailles in June 1919. The monster went back in the closet, waiting.

No war fought before 1914 had created so many corpses. Many writers on the war have commented on the mind-numbing catastrophe of twenty thousand British soldiers dying on the first day of the Battle of the Somme in 1916. Historian Martin Gilbert notes further that, on average, the same number died every four days from August 1914 to November 1918. Altogether, forty million people became casualties of the Great War, half of them combatants and half civilians walking the boulevards, tending livestock, raising families, and attempting to live their lives.

The world could not be the same after such bloodletting. By 1922, in Great Britain alone, the government allotted fifty thousand veterans yearly pensions due to shell shock. The government had been parsimonious in applying this designation because, as we will see, there remained doubts about its existence. The numbers of veterans and civilians across the globe who actually suffered unbearable night terrors, severe mental agitation, and even daytime hallucinations that returned them to Verdun or the Somme or the Ypres salient are impossible to count.

We can't disentwine the historical from the horrific. Our monsters are born out of our moments in time. To paraphrase French filmmaker Georges Franju, director of the 1960 horror movie *Les yeux sans visage* (*Eyes without a Face*), discovering history isn't like being decapitated exactly; it's a bit more like having your head slowly twisted off.[1]

What exactly constitutes horror? Being spooked by the dark, and by the dead who might return in it, may have haunted the earliest human consciousness. Ceremonial burial predates all written history; the act apparently represented an effort to placate the corpse so it would not make an unwelcome return. The roots of religion itself may be in this impulse, with gifts to the dead constituting the first ritual.

In fact, much of what we think of as "natural human life" may stem from the terror of death and of the dead. Even sexual desire, and our constantly changing conceptions of gender roles that accompany it, may have much to do with the terror of the dead. The urge to reproduce, once inextricably linked to sex, may have a connection to a neurotic fantasy of cheating death by creating an enduring legacy. You can test the primal strength of this cultural idea by noting how no one questions the rationality of reproduction, even in a world of rapidly dwindling resources. Meanwhile, people who choose not to have children often receive both religious and secular disdain as selfish, the breakers of an unspoken social contract, or simply odd.

Does the fear of death that drives us mean that horror has always been our dark companion, a universal human experience in which cave paintings and movie screens are simply different media for the same spooky message? Not exactly. The idea of death and ruin as entertainment, even something one could build a lifestyle around, appears first in the eighteenth century in novels like Horace Walpole's *The Castle of Otranto* (1764) and Matthew Lewis's *The Monk* (1796). Commentators called this taste Gothic because the interest in ruins and castles called to mind the Gothic architecture of the Middle Ages.

Our contemporary term "goth," used to describe everything from a style of music to black fingernail polish, of course comes from those eighteenth-century goths. The wealthy of that century could fully indulge this new fascination, turning estates into faux medieval manors and forcing their servants, on top of all their other indignities, to appear at parties dressed in robes that made them look like what Clive Bloom describes as "ghoulish monks." It's hard to call this precisely a popular taste, as the novels of suspense that inspired these ideas were damned or banned in some places and very few people had a suitable estate, or enough money or servants, for playing haunted house.[2]

"Horror" in today's sense had yet to be born. The word existed, but it had an appropriately weird history. According to the *Oxford English Dictionary*, "horror" first appeared in the fourteenth century as a synonym for "rough" or "rugged." Over centuries, the term started to carry the connotation of something so "rough," in the sense of "sordid and vulgar," that it caused a physical shudder.

Once Gothic romanticism appeared in the late eighteenth century, the word "horror" showed up in poetry and prose in something close to the modern sense. English Romantic poet Robert Southey's praise of "Dark horror" in 1791 echoed his interest in eerie works in Germany. Even here, the word suggests something a bit sordid rather than spookiness for fun. In a 1798 treatise entitled "On Objects of Terror," English essayist Nathan Drake used "horror" interchangeably with "disgust" and advised artists only to "approach the horrid" rather than actually enter its darkened halls. In Drake's view, "horror" meant physical revulsion, not a good scare. Even into the 1800s, the meaning of the word always suggested the body in a state of intense distress. A medical manual from 1822 used the word in this way: "The first attack [of sickness] commences with a horror."

"The war has left its imprint in our souls [with] all these visions of horror it has conjured up around us," wrote French author Pierre de Mazenod in 1922, describing the Great War. His word, *horreur*, appears in various forms in an incredible number of accounts of the war, written by English, German, Austrian, French, Russian, and American veterans. The years following the Great War became the first time in human history the word "horror" and its cognates appeared on such a massive scale. Images of catastrophe abounded. The Viennese writer Stefan Zweig, one of the stars in the firmament of central Europe's decadent and demonic café culture before 1914, wrote of how "bridges are broken between today and tomorrow and the day before yesterday" in the conflict's wake. Time was out of joint. When not describing the war as horror, the imagery of all we would come to associate with the word appeared. One French pilot passing over the ruined city of Verdun described the landscape as a haunted waste and a creature of nightmare, "the humid skin of a monstrous toad."[3]

The horror of the Great War consumed the lives of soldiers and civilians alike; it sought them out in their sleep, their imagination, and, bizarrely, in their entertainments. The "horror film" had existed almost from the time of the invention of the motion picture itself in the late nineteenth century. But a new kind of terror film manifested in the years following the Great War. The spook shows not only became more numerous; they took a ghastly turn, dealing more openly with the fate of the dead, even the bodies of the dead. Moreover, an unclassifiable kind of fiction began to appear, frequently called "weird" (as in the pulp magazine *Weird Tales*, 1923) because there seemed no better word for it. The public, and its practitioners, began calling it horror fiction. Art and literature pursued some of the same themes, even though at the time a strict division between "high" and "low" culture prevented many critics from seeing horror on canvas or in poetry, and still prevents a few today. British modernist Virginia Woolf wrote that certain feelings proved no longer possible after 1914; a sentiment might be expressed in words, she felt, but the body and mind could not experience the sensibilities "one used to have."

By the same token, new feelings about death and the macabre began to seek expression. The root of these new cultural forms had a specific and terribly uncomfortable origin: the human corpse. Stirring up the primal, perhaps universal fear of the dead, the Great War had placed human beings in proximity to millions of corpses that could not be buried. Worse, many could not be identified, and more than a few did not even look like what we think human bodies should look like. Shells, machine guns, gas, and a whole array of technology had muddled them into misshapen forms, empty matter, if still disturbingly organic. The horror of the Great War, traumatically re-enacted over and over and over after 1918 down to the present moment, drew its chill from the shattered, bloated, fragmented corpses that covered the wastelands made by the war.

My reading of the roots of horror in the Great War is anything but Freudian. That said, Sigmund Freud appears throughout this account as one who not only was affected by the war but also made some interesting observations about how 1914–1918 transformed European culture and consciousness. He complicated his own ideas because of the conflict, conceding that a death instinct may play at least as important a role in how human beings experience life as sexuality and childhood traumas related to it. Thanatos can be as significant, sometimes more significant, than Eros.

One of the ideas Freud entertained concerned how the war changed the subjects that fiction might explore. "It is evident that the war is bound to sweep away [the] conventional treatment of death," he wrote in 1915. While his own sons and many of his students fought at the front, he declared, "Death will no longer be denied; we are forced to believe in it. People really die; and no longer one by one. But many, often tens of thousands, in a single day." Freud hoped, and he expressed it only as a hope, that the return of "primitive" passions, a kind of "bedazzlement" with death, would end when peace returned. He would be mightily disappointed.[4]

One unlikely voice, who indeed had luckily avoided service in the Austro-Hungarian army, helped explain this new, festering reality. Walter Benjamin loved hashish and women too much to get around to writing a proper history; instead, he wrote essays of such beauty and depth that we are still puzzling and wondering over them almost eighty years after his death. He did, during the period that this book covers, fitfully scribble at essays, fiction, personal reflections, and a sprawling unfinished work he called simply "The Arcades Project."

In 1936, four years before his untimely death, Benjamin wrote an essay he called "The Storyteller," in which, amid his meditation on the nature of memory, he said this about the Great War:

> Was it not noticeable that at the end of the war men returned from the bat-tlefield grown silent—not richer, but poorer in communicable experience? What ten years later was poured out in the flood of war books was anything but the experience that pours from mouth to mouth.[5]

Benjamin of course knew about, and often criticized, the vast literature that the war produced, especially those works that talked of the "sublimity" of conflict, praised the "beauty" of unremitting violence, and often shaded over into fascism's dreams of mythic warriors. He wrote the words above about the armless veteran one saw at the café, the cousin who had been at Ypres or Gallipoli and sat silent at family gatherings, sometimes staring off into the middle distance. He wrote of the men who wore masks meant to hide their terrible facial wounds, disfigurements sometimes made even more eerie by the first, halting efforts at combat plastic surgery.

Of these men's experience of war, Benjamin continued:

> A generation that had gone to school on a horse-drawn streetcar now stood under the open sky in the countryside in which nothing remained unchanged but the clouds and, beneath those clouds, in a field of force of destructive torrents and explosions, was the tiny, fragile human body.

These vulnerable bodies—millions of which would be transformed into corpses by history's first fully mechanized killing machine, which we call

World War I—haunt every decade of the twentieth century. Their eyes, filled first with shock and soon with nothingness, became the specters of despairing creativity for a generation of filmmakers, writers, and artists who themselves often went about their work with shattered bodies and psyches. All of the uncertainty and dread that folklore and popular tale had ever associated with automata, the disconcerting effect of a mirror, shadows, and puppets seemed suddenly to become historical reality in the sheer number of millions of dead, millions more permanently disabled and disfigured, and bodies that came marching home like empty husks, the person whom family and friends had known before 1914 having been left in another place.

We must write of such things, Benjamin counseled, "with as much bitterness as possible." For many in his generation, bitterness even proved too weak a concoction.

I hope the air feels thick with static, the smell of an alchemy gone awry, a precursor to what Benjamin once described as a "single catastrophe" that tore history apart like a massive explosion, "piling wreckage upon wreckage." Because not only did single acts of horror happen, they produced a world of horror that we still live in, both in our imaginations and in our daily lives. The artists, writers, and directors who experienced the Great War, most of them directly, never stopped having the same nightmare, over and again, a nightmare they told the world. Meanwhile, like a spell gone wrong, the Great War conjured up a new world, a sort of alternate reality distinct from what most people before 1914 expected their lives to be. It was a dark dimension where horror films, stories, and art became a Baedeker's guide to the new normal rather than entertaining diversions. Monsters had come out of the abyss.

I have tried to write of these things with as much bitterness as possible.

Chapter One

Symphony of Horror

. . . the lovely land of war,
Where the face of nature seems a monstrous septic sore,
Where the bowels of earth hang open, like the guts of
   something slain,
And the rot and wreck of everything is churned and
   churned again;
Where all is done in darkness and where all is still in day,
Where living men are buried and the dead unburied lay.
　　　—GEORGE WILLIS, "Any Soldier to His Son" (1919)

Deathbird

In the spring of 1922, many Germans had one thing on their minds: a film about a ferociously hungry monster with forbidden appetites, a *Totenvogel* (deathbird) that embodied plague, sickness, and decay. The film and its monster kindled the first spark of enthusiasm they'd felt for anything in years.

The dread shadow of *Nosferatu* fell across the world. Directed by F. W. Murnau and guided to final production by Albin Grau, the film—an unauthorized adaptation of Bram Stoker's 1897 novel *Dracula*—premiered on March 4, 1922, at a gaudily advertised special showing in the Berlin Zoological Garden. "What do you expect at the first showing of this great work?" a publicity poster read. "Aren't you afraid?"[1]

Tens of thousands would become afraid, some even obsessed, by the *spukhafte Träume* (spectral dreams) produced by watching this silent film of shadowy effects. In the original prints, Murnau and Grau used color plates to move the viewer from bright day into gloomy night, footlights to make the shadow of the vampire fill the screen, and a score composed by Hans Erdmann that wormed into the ear, even its few lighthearted movements containing ominous undertones.

Murnau and Grau built their vampire tale around the story of a middle-class marriage in the peaceful town of Wisborg. The fictional Wisborg is a nineteenth-century village in an imagined Germany untainted by war, imperial ambition, or the poison of defeat. The opening title card tells us it's the year 1838 and that the film we are about to see is an *Aufzeichnung über das grosse Sterben* (account of the great death) that came to the fairy-tale town. For the filmmakers and their audience, however, "great death" would have called to mind the year 1914.

Murnau and Grau wanted to re-create the pallid romanticisms of their world before 1914 in order to heighten the horror to come. The film's first image, an aerial establishing shot of Wisborg, promises us a visit to a place of peace and solidity. The church steeple that focuses the frame breathes traditional piety over a world untouched by the Great War, or by the vampire's talon.

The film's first ten minutes are meant to assure the audience that a young couple named Hutter and Ellen are the ideal pair, sentimental for one another, living in marital bliss and doing well financially in their bucolic town. We meet Ellen while she plays gently with a cat, bobbing a ball of yarn in front of the frolicking animal and then turning her hand to the domestic work of sewing. Ellen seems gentle and delicate, so much so that we pay little attention to the cat pawing relentlessly at the yarn, pantomiming the feline propensity to torment its prey.

We then see Hutter, like an importunate lover instead of a householder husband, pulling up flowers from the garden for Ellen. The first portent that something may be amiss comes when she cradles the bouquet like the baby the couple clearly do not have. "Why did you kill them . . . the beautiful flowers?" she asks before being swallowed, somewhat unwillingly, in Hutter's embrace. Soon, the film tells us, she will hear "the call of the deathbird" in her soul and welcome the vampire. Unlike the halfhearted affection she gives her husband, she will fall feverishly into the monster's open arms.

First comes love, then comes capitalism. Hutter hears the promise of career advancement from his wizened employer, Knock, an odd little man who clearly has shadowy motives of his own. An intertitle card introduces Knock by telling the audience that he acted as an estate agent "about whom all sorts of rumors circulated." He does seem to know that he's sending the naïve young Hutter into the lair of the monster.

Knock laughs unsettlingly as he tells the ingenu that while he will "earn a tidy sum" for his efforts, they would also cost him "perhaps . . . a little blood." When Ellen first learns of the upcoming trip she appears catatonic with dread. Hutter pays her little mind. After another crushing but quick embrace with the conflicted bride, he rushes off to "the land of phantoms," as Knock called it, while Ellen weeps on the stairs, dressed in widow's black. Hutter appears to have a slight presentiment of danger but nevertheless mounts his horse.

He meets death in the phantom lands in the misshapen form of Count Orlok, Nosferatu. A tower, where Hutter will find himself a prisoner, rears arrogantly against an iron sky. It's what Anton Kaes calls a symbol of Nosferatu's Reich, the realm of death. Hutter will discover that old Knock's insane laughter should have given him much to fear.

Soon after his arrival, Hutter cuts his finger during dinner with the vampire, who himself conspicuously refuses food, in a scene recognizable to anyone who has watched Universal Pictures' 1931 *Dracula* or its numerous iterations. In almost every other variant of this moment, the monster bares his fangs briefly but recovers himself (though Francis Ford Coppola's version from 1992 does feature Gary Oldman's Dracula rather viciously licking a razor). Nosferatu shows no such restraint, grabbing Hutter's hand and sucking hungrily at the cut. Hutter stumbles over himself as he tries to flee.

Why does the creature reveal itself so soon? Unlike the Dracula in later versions of the story, there's little about Nosferatu that makes him seem human in the first place. Rat-faced and impossibly tall, he curls his hands as if they are the very talons of the deathbird the film describes him to be. At that moment in history, not unlike our own, people wanted monsters to show themselves; they had no time for a pretense they could not believe in. Moviegoers had come to see the monster, and the revelation of horror flowed from the screen in a rush of shadow.

Hutter seems impotent in the face of the fate he has brought upon himself. Following his first night in the castle, the sun rises and "the shadows of the night" pass from him as he gingerly investigates the secrets of the place. After an ominous visit from the count the next night, Hutter explores further the following day and discovers Nosferatu sleeping in his coffin. This famous moment in the film seized the darkest part of the Great War generation's imagination. The sight of the undead corpse would likely have evoked all the corpses of the age, scattered across battlefields.[2]

The vision of a corpse existing at some unthinkable intersection of life and death proved compellingly terrifying for this generation. A midnight walk through the early twentieth century reveals a deep and unsettling fascination with the corpse and its various stand-ins. The double, the doll, the wax figure, the puppet all mimicked the Great War dead. They evoked the mechanical automata of the war of steel against flesh that had so completely reminded Europeans of their mortality. Older religious and philosophical verities about the immortality of the soul seemed themselves cadaverous in this terrible new age.[3]

What had the war revealed about the human body and the ancient concept of the soul? People had witnessed too much death and mutilation. Loved ones had not died peacefully in their bed after some encouragingly pious final words. Rather, they had been torn apart, their bodies never found, or they walked about in the trancelike state of shell shock, often scarred, burned, sickened, or blind. *Nosferatu* evoked this terror for a country that had seen more than its share of corpses.

Hutter's encounter with the corpse of Count Orlok doesn't immediately cause him to flee the castle, a clear suggestion that psychological torment has unhinged him. Even after coming to learn that Nosferatu's very existence represents a brutal paradox, a living death, the young Hutter responds to the discovery that he's in death's grip by lying listlessly on the floor of his room, waking to find Nosferatu busily loading boxes full of his native soil for transport to Wisborg, soon to be no longer idyllic.

Several shots later, Hutter has managed an escape from the castle and yet we see him again prostrated, this time in a hospital bed. He appears in a shell-shocked state recognizable to the war-exhausted generation. The nurse attends him as he rises briefly and weakly. "Coffins . . . !" the suddenly animated Hutter screams, and then falls again into desuetude.

Meanwhile, his wife, Ellen, has fallen under the vampire's shadow as well. She sleepwalks, an act that fascinated the early twentieth century, as it seemed akin to a reanimation of a corpse, a human body becoming a marionette moving by an unknown mechanism. Ellen, too, must journey to the land of phantoms, even if she does not leave Wisborg. In one of the most famous shots of the film, she sits on a beach amid cross-shaped grave markers looking longingly out to sea. Her husband, a series of intercuts reminds us, is returning slowly to Wisborg by land. However, she's not waiting for him; something else holds her attention.

Hutter's slow progress and complete loss of strength is overmatched by the fury of Nosferatu's approach. When the monster arrives, a wasting plague follows in his wake. An intertitle card tells us that a "weakened young Hutter" barely made it home. Meanwhile, "the death ship" has its sails filled with the pestilential but virile breath of Nosferatu himself. Unlike her traumatized husband, the monster comes to Ellen at "supernatural speed."

Plague rides on the wings of the deathbird, a fog of disease surrounding the monster presented in the film as some revenant of the bubonic plague, the Black Death of the Middle Ages. Ellen watches from her window, just as she has been watching and waiting through most of the film. She stands at the sill while a town official marks the houses of plague victims with white crosses. The disease spreads, and we wonder if the deathbird's black wings will cover the earth.

The film never explains how or why, but Ellen certainly knows her monstrous lover has arrived. Death on a massive scale has come with him, death as the cinemagoers who filled the seats at the first showings of *Nosferatu* had come to know it. The Dracula of later film iterations dispenses death piecemeal, one neck at a time. The 1922 *Nosferatu*, however, brings a flood of death to Wisborg, just as the Great War had brought to all of Europe what the poet Rainer Maria Rilke called "these days of monstrously accelerated dying."[4]

The vampire, death itself, moves in to an abandoned house across the street from Hutter and Ellen, where one night she sees his phantom image gazing at her from the opposite window. Nosferatu looks longingly at her, framed like an icon by the window from across the street. Ellen turns to Hutter but simply shrugs to see her husband again stretched out on an armchair, somnolent and broken. Then, as Nosferatu starts toward their house, Ellen rouses Hutter; fainting, she tells him to fetch Professor Bulwer (who represents the vampire hunter Abraham Van Helsing from Stoker's novel).

While Hutter hurries to Bulwer for help, Ellen succumbs to Nosferatu, who drinks hungrily, and lustfully, from her, so entranced that he fails to notice the approaching dawn. A rooster crows, and he leaves his place at Ellen's throat and passes the window, where the rising sun dissipates him into a nothingness. His death comes after his, and perhaps Ellen's, consummate act of bliss. She, too, then dies, having sacrificed herself in myriad ways to the creature and leaving Hutter in a miasma of grief.

Nosferatu thus presents a woman who both saves the world from the vampire and allows him to take her, leaving her husband weeping bitterly at the loss. Contrast this with the ending of Stoker's *Dracula*, in which Mina Murray and Jonathan Harker marry and have a child. Indeed, there are three weddings at the end of Stoker's novel, and all of the couples begin lives of bourgeois bliss with the monster safely destroyed.[5]

Nosferatu rose from his crypt in the postwar world at a point when the nineteenth century's often naïve notions could be seen for what they had been. Death claiming so many—recall *das grosse Sterben* from the opening title card—remains the single most important reality conveyed by the film. In this, it shared and shaped its era's understanding of its own reality, which was marked by death in such proportions that human beings could not begin to account for what they had done, what had been done to them, and what the world had become.

Murnau's savage, vicious, patently sensual vampire soon haunted every local *Kino* (cinema) in Germany. Advertising promised it was more than a film: "You want to see a symphony of horror? You may expect more. Be careful. *Nosferatu* is not just fun, not something to be taken lightly."[6]

The creators of this first vampire film certainly did not take its subject matter lightly. Albin Grau was not only a veteran of the Great War but also an occultist who invested the film with its arcane symbolism. He insisted on the point that critics and audiences understand *Nosferatu* as something other than simple entertainment. Before the film's premiere, Grau said it could be seen only in light of the war. The war itself had been, for his entire generation, what Grau called "a cosmic vampire" that had come "drinking the blood of millions."[7]

The Vampire's Shadow over Weimar

Place yourself for a moment in 1922, and imagine a class in a German *Realschule* (secondary school), made up of students between the ages of ten and sixteen. These would have been children allowed to attend school because of their social class and their perceived intellectual ability. Many of these very young Germans had been orphaned by a war in which their country had suffered an astonishing 1.8 million deaths; others returned home from school each day to fathers who were among the 7 million who had survived but had been physically or psychologically mutilated.

These statistics were a shadow that fell across every day of their lives. But on this day—let's say it's a few weeks after the premiere—the children in the class are talking about *Nosferatu*. Whether they discuss the film with enthusiasm or disdain, they think only of the vampire. He is terrifying to look at, with an elongated torso, spidery arms, sharp fingernails, and a bizarre physiognomy marked by pointed ears, ratlike teeth, and thick eyebrows above dark-circled eyes. They say he lives off blood. "He seduces women," one older boy assures the others with an air of someone who has somehow managed to see the film. "He hypnotizes them." The day drags. They are distracted with inner speculation about whether their parents will allow them to see the film that has already given them nightmares.

If their afternoon *Lehrer* (teacher) spent the final grinding minutes of the school day on recent history, the lesson the students received would have been a peculiar one. During most of the Weimar Republic—the attempt at democracy that had begun in 1919 and taken the place of the old imperial Germany—school textbooks did not deal with the defeat of the nation in the Great War. Many did not even mention the humiliating armistice of

November 1918 but instead closed the discussion of the Great War with descriptions of Germany's briefly successful spring offensive (*die Kaiserschlacht*) of that same year.[8]

Of course, the children reading those textbooks surely knew something was amiss. Why had their fathers never returned from the war if it had been a triumphal march toward victory that, somehow, had just ended with no real result? Or, for others, why had their fathers come back so different, their missing limbs, fits of black rage, and tortured wheezing in the night telling a story different from the one their history lessons told?

The dissonance helps explain, in part, why so many of that generation could embrace Weimar's vampire in their teens and then embrace the Nazi Party as they grew into adults. The history they learned in no way resonated with the world in which they lived. Monsters, of both the fantastic and the political varieties, soaked up their nightmares but also gave those nightmares unnatural life.

Adult Germans received similar postwar propaganda from sources more compelling than textbooks. Paul von Hindenburg, field marshal of the entire German army during the Great War and later president of the Weimar Republic, sent a message to his troops on November 12, 1918, the day after they laid down their arms, praising them for their sacrifice and their fortitude in achieving what he and many others chose to see as a kind of victory. "You have kept the enemy away from our frontiers and you have saved your country from the misfortunes and disasters of war," Hindenburg wrote. The German army, he claimed, had "held out for four years against a world filled with enemies" and could march home with "heads held high."[9]

The end of the war brought a brief burst of enthusiasm over the soldiers' return from the trenches. The cessation of the Allied blockade, which had continued into 1919, ended the misery of millions and prevented the spread of the starvation that had already occurred in parts of Germany. The Weimar Republic, named after the German city where the new nation had adopted parliamentarian practices, seemed more secure to many in the German middle class than it had in its earliest months. The economy benefited from a peace dividend before the Allied demand for financial reparations began to take its toll. Democratic reforms expanded the franchise and added women to the voting rolls. But by 1922, the fiction had begun to fray at the edges.

Just as Nosferatu's shadow lengthened over his victims, Weimar's fortunes appeared to be falling under a new darkness.

Weimar Germany had essential structural weaknesses. Antidemocratic forces held positions within the new regime, including not a few monarchists who actually wanted to see the return of Kaiser Wilhelm II from his exile in Holland, where the former emperor spent his days hunting, smoking his pipe, and chopping firewood. Meanwhile, Germany's industrial capitalists hoped to retain the immense wealth and political power they had accumulated under the kaiser.

In 1919, V. I. Lenin, his lieutenant Leon Trotsky, and other Communist leaders in Soviet Russia remained convinced that Germany's Social Democratic Party (SPD) would lead Russia's former enemy to become part of the global workers' revolution. However, the SPD proved to be under the thumb of Germany's capitalists. Worryingly, the hard-line elements of the German army and the dangerously right-wing veterans' groups, some of whom formed paramilitary organizations known as *Freikorps* (free corps), remained tormented by the sting of defeat.

The 1919 "January Revolution," a series of mass strikes under the banner of the German Communist Party (KPD), failed disastrously. The Weimar government and the SPD themselves stood by, or really pretended not to notice, as the *Freikorps* turned the weapons of the trenches against the strikers. The brutal squads of veterans arrested or killed KPD leaders, including the famed Communist theorist Rosa Luxemburg. Her comrades found her bludgeoned corpse in a ditch on January 19, one day after the opening of the peace negotiations in Paris to restructure the postwar world.[10]

Hoping for continued improvement and some sense of stability in the new decade, the German middle classes expressed optimism even as open street battles erupted between partisans of the left and right. However, as the 1920s began, the economic chaos proved impossible to deny and middle-class status increasingly difficult to maintain. Larders became empty, and parlors became silent and sad with the selling of pianos, hand-carved clocks, and other family heirlooms. The men lucky enough to have a job wore suits not from last year but from the last decade. By the end of 1922, the cost of living had increased fifteenfold while the worth of the German mark fell to 7,400 against a single U.S. dollar.

The use of dark, clamoring shadows in *Nosferatu* made the vampire seem like a nightmare that had slipped into the real world, an embodiment of the chaos of postwar Germany. Murnau had set out to film a version of Irish author Bram Stoker's *Dracula* but had failed to receive the rights to the story from Stoker's widow, who guarded her late husband's estate with ferocity and some degree of paranoia.

To get around this problem, Murnau and his colleagues simply changed significant place and character names in the film, setting it in Germany rather than England, making Count Dracula into Count Orlok, and in place of "vampire" using the word "Nosferatu" (which does not mean "vampire" in Romanian but rather functions as an idiomatic expression for the devil or devils). Back in England, Florence Stoker fumed. She also set a battery of lawyers on the case, which eventually resulted in the destruction of Murnau and Grau's production company—but not before the monster stalked the shattered German mind. In fact, the concern over Florence Stoker's legal claims may well have led the filmmakers to create a film out of the darkness of the German experience in the Great War.

Grau should receive much of the credit for the atmosphere of *Nosferatu*. The storyboards, set designs, and message of the story itself came largely from him. He seldom spoke of the film without repeating his image of "the cosmic vampire that had sucked the blood of millions," a war that had produced mountains of corpses. The deathbird Nosferatu—which emerged, like the Great War itself, from the confused history of eastern Europe—turned Germany into a plague-ridden death house.

Apparently more than metaphor motivated Grau's interest in such matters. During his time among the Austro-Hungarian forces fighting in Serbia, he heard a farmer tell the tale of a recent vampire outbreak in the village where Grau had been stationed. Local panics over such tales had been a phenomenon of Balkan village life for hundreds of years, though they had become especially common during the eighteenth century (despite that time being described by historians as an age of reason). A confused Austro-Hungarian official in 1725, for example, informed his superiors that he'd allowed Serbian villagers to dig up a grave and incinerate the body to prevent it from becoming a revenant and spreading disease and death in the neighborhood.[11]

The Serbian farmer's tale was just one version Grau told of his introduction to the vampire myth. In a much more dramatic retelling, included in an essay about *Nosferatu* prepared for a German film magazine, Grau described how, while clipping one another's hair—a delousing technique common on the eastern front, where the louse-borne disease typhus remained a perennial threat—he and four of his companions began telling stories. A Romanian member of the group insisted to his comrades that he knew from his own experience that tales of the vampire contained more than a little truth. His father had been buried without the benefit of priest or a proper church ceremony, one of the many ways that Balkan folklore explained the creation of the undead. (Other possibilities included, but were not limited to, dying impenitent, dying while attempting to commit a murder, or dying by one's own hand.) The young Romanian soldier, Grau claimed, carried on his person a document attesting to the fact that authoritative witnesses found his father's tomb empty one night, prompting the villagers to wait until the creature returned to its grave in the daylight hours to stake and burn the body. "That night," after he and the others heard the Romanian's story, Grau insisted, "we didn't sleep a wink!"[12]

This sounds like a bit of the carnival barking that plays such an essential role in the culture of horror. The tendency toward ballyhoo is found even in contemporary horror films that claim, shamelessly, that the "events you are about to see are based on a true story." Grau's essay turns serious, however, when he writes, once again, of the vampire-like nature of war. The story of his sleepless night waiting for the icy touch of the undead reminded him not of a fantasist nightmare, but of the "suffering and grief" the Great War produced, its "monstrous events that have depleted the world."[13]

Grau's interest in vampires may or may not have begun in Serbia, but he had an indisputable fascination and involvement with the occult, an obsession born from his desire to understand the nature of *das grosse Sterben* and its meaning. He had a great deal of company. The séance became a pastime of the German middle class after 1918, so much so that Thomas Mann wrote about such meetings as common affairs. Grau placed alchemical symbols throughout *Nosferatu*; they are especially notable in the bizarre real estate contract signed by Count Orlok. Far from a standard legal agreement, the document bears a number of so-called Enochian symbols. Contemporary occultists cobbled together this cryptic mystical language from the fakes and forgeries of early modern grimoires. Books dealing with the occult, and many authors proffering magical books, made the image from *Nosferatu* of Ellen reading *The Book of Vampires* immediately recognizable to its first audiences.[14]

The English occultist Aleister Crowley, who is described by his most recent biographer as "the twentieth century's most infamous magician," made his way into this milieu after the Great War in hopes that his allegedly mystical *Book of the Law* would place him at the head of Germany's Ordo Templi Orientis, a magical society in which Crowley had been involved for a decade. Albin Grau had a close enough association with the group to read the German translation of Crowley's *Book of the Law* when it appeared in 1924.

Grau showed a special interest in Crowley's tendency to proffer dark prophecy to his followers. Indeed, Crowley, who referred to himself as "the Beast" of the book of Revelation, made images of a world in ruins part of his shtick when it fit the audience. Grau seized on this dark vision with all the pessimism born of war and described Crowley's message as portraying a "primitive world order" like "the darkest days of Atlantis." The vicious bloodletting of the war in the Balkans had made Grau more than ready to believe in a world in ruins, a world where Nosferatu and his plague reigned over all.[15]

Murnau did not share Grau's occult interests. He had, however, like his collaborator, discovered in the Great War a chilling sense of disquiet, the shadow of the cosmic vampire passing across his heart. Drafted at age twenty-six, he survived the Battle of Verdun, a struggle that lasted close to a year and cost over 700,000 casualties. He then served briefly in the newly inaugurated German *Luftstreitkräfte* (air force) before a crash in Switzerland made him a prisoner of war in 1917. His capture likely saved his life, keeping him out of the lethal spring offensives of 1918.

These experiences alone might have provided the inspiration for the greatest horror film of the 1920s. But Murnau's suffering also had an intensely personal quality. In 1915, the war took Murnau's onetime lover and friend Hans Ehrenbaum-Degele. The twenty-five-year-old poet and composer died on the eastern front in the bloody onslaught at the Narev River, today in Poland, in which huge numbers of Russian troops, some armed only with bayonets or clubs and engaging in what a contemporary historian called "berserker warfare," enveloped and stormed a German fortification. Murnau had been conscripted, but Degele had joined the army of his own accord after publishing his first collections of poems. Thus, not unlike Hutter in *Nosferatu*, Degele had rushed off into the darkness, volunteering for the kaiser's army and sending Murnau poetry with lines such as "Dig thy Grave deep soldier! / Perhaps one day peace will be born . . . and everything will shine again."[16]

For Murnau and Grau, the personal experience of terror under the shelling of the Central Power's enemies led them to connect grief, trauma, mysticism, and perpetual mourning with vampire lore, the possibility that the dead refused to stay dead, that the carnage of war did not represent a single historical catastrophe but a new apocalyptic epoch that no armistice could end. Something had been born that, as Grau so often repeated, fed off the blood of millions. Crowley's dark Atlantis began to rise from the chaos.

The Roots That Clutch: Horror and the Great War

Now, in the twenty-first century, one hundred years after the armistice that ended the Great War, horror reigns. Vampiric yearnings, bodies writhing with demon hosts, blood fetishes, and hordes of zombies or singular reversals of the natural order fill not only the big screen but also screens of all types and sizes. Even ghosts, seemingly so old-fashioned in the digital age, have attached themselves to the Western world's central nervous system, resonating with artists, writers, and filmmakers who desire to scare us to death.

Why? Not only do we consume enormous amounts of horror, but we read and write a great deal about why we think it matters. In the last decade, a large number of books, essays, and online posts have been written to suss out our morbid interests. Often these writings rely on what you could call the mirror argument. That is, horror in film and fiction reflects the anxieties of the present moment and, in an overused phrase (I've used it myself), mirrors the era's deepest fears.

Mirrors, as we will see, are actually more dangerous than this. Horror films and fantasies are more than mirror images of our anxieties. They have a history that intertwines with the sadness of the world and with the fear the world's sadness provokes.

To borrow the words of T. S. Eliot, who will join us on our cemetery walk, "What are the roots that clutch, what branches grow / Out of this stony rubbish?" What are the roots of horror in the monster-crawling wasteland of the modern world? Do grisly novels and gruesome movies simply push whichever of our buttons are most prominent at the moment? Does it make what we regard as the real world less frightening by introducing us to alternate realities that are even darker?

Horror in fiction and film began its danse macabre in the wake of the Great War. Such a cataclysm had never been seen before in human history. The Napoleonic Wars (1799–1815) had lasted more than fifteen years and appeared world-changing in their importance. Fought in sprawling set-piece battles and on the world's sea-lanes, they had an extraordinary scale. But casualties had remained relatively low, given the technology of cannons and muskets; moreover, the world had looked in 1815 a lot like it had in 1799. The crowned heads of Europe tried their best to pretend the French Revolution had never happened and, after Napoleon's deadly escapades, redrew the map of Europe along familiar dynastic lines.

The Civil War in the United States had stunned Americans and Europeans alike with its savagery. Shiloh, Antietam, and Gettysburg produced a startling number of casualties as cannons unleashed shrapnel on charging human bodies—the first large-scale use of such a technique. The new rifled musket increased accuracy and produced mass slaughter, making necessary the first tentative steps toward trench warfare around Petersburg and Richmond, Virginia, in 1864–1865. This terrible war produced its own heritage of horror in the late-nineteenth-century American interest in murder, the strange obsession with the display of battlefield corpses in the photography of Mathew Brady studios, and the horror fiction of Union veteran Ambrose Bierce.

But nothing like World War I had ever been imagined; it could not have been, since no precedent for such violence existed. German and French forces fighting over the rubble of Verdun in 1916 alone produced more than half as many deaths as the entire American Civil War. More *civilian* casualties caused by the Great War in Africa occurred than in the American conflict. To this number must be added almost a quarter of a million military casualties among African troops conscripted from the European powers' colonial possessions. The British army suffered more than twice as many casualties in a single day of the Battle of the Somme than in the combination of Shiloh's two days and Gettysburg's three.[17]

The optimism of the middle and upper classes in nineteenth-century western Europe made the sudden eruption of the most lethal war in human history especially astonishing. A British merchant, banker, or other member of the professional classes in London in early 1914 prospered in the metropolitan center of a worldwide empire whose navy ruled the oceans and whose economic muscles flexed on every continent. A German of the same class agreed with the philosopher Georg Wilhelm Friedrich Hegel that "the German soul" represented the apex of human history, the most civilized country on earth, and perhaps, despite its naval limitations, the world's most powerful military.

The stillborn hopes of the nineteenth-century bourgeoisie lay on the ground wrapped in bloody cerements in the autumn darkness of 1914. The conflict humbled Germany and its allies, while Britain's exploitation of millions in Africa and Asia became increasingly obvious and untenable. When the war finally ended, the plans the Allied powers hatched at Versailles to continue to cannibalize entire continents for labor and resources actually accelerated the final collapse of British imperial power later in the century and, though none could imagine it at the time, created conflicts in Asia and the Middle East that today threaten the very possibility of a human future.

The primary combatants—along with British Commonwealth countries such as Australia, Canada, and New Zealand and the colonies in Africa and Asia—dealt with the cataclysmic changes wrought by the conflict for much of the twentieth century. No one could guess these long-term effects, and even the results of the immediate cultural and geopolitical changes did not register with most people. What much of the world did experience was a psychological paroxysm when confronted with the war's almost unimaginable death toll.

Nearly ten million soldiers died in the Great War, and another eight million noncombatants—and these are conservative estimates that likely fail to account for the real death toll. The brutal new battlefield technology created a landscape of corpses. The Maxim gun, high-intensity shelling, and mustard gas brought death and disfigurement to an entire generation. New battlefield medical practices allowed men to survive wounds that in the nineteenth century meant certain death. This sent millions home from the trenches permanently mutilated. The official count of all the military wounded has generally been placed at twenty-one million. The veterans who suffered permanent psychological injury from the carnage they witnessed and participated in are impossible to number.

The statistics are generally well-known. Historians Stéphane Audoin-Rouzeau and Annette Becker have written that such numbers quickly become unreal as our minds seek to dam up the flood of despair they induce. So think of it in slightly different terms, they suggest. If we look deeper into the raw math of the body count, we find that, for example, France lost 900 soldiers *every single day* of the four-year war, and Germany 1,300.[18]

Horror became an outlook on life rather than a new entertainment amid the sheer number of dead. Film historian Lotte Eisner called the obsessions of cinema during Germany's postwar years "the haunted screen," partially because the films used supernatural evil, betrayal, revenge, and morbidity as their subject matter. Across the continent, poets and painters, particularly those associated with the surrealist school, used their imaginative powers to explore Gothic themes, the distortion and dismemberment of bodies, and, always, death in its most visceral forms.[19]

This new culture of horror drew on antecedents from the nineteenth and early twentieth centuries. In the United States, some of the first short films produced by the Edison Company showed actual public executions and, in at least one case, a lynching. The same corporation released the first cinematic version of Mary Shelley's *Frankenstein* in 1910. In this iteration, the Monster emerges from a scouring bath of chemicals, perhaps foreshadowing the poisons that would make their appearance in the Ypres salient in 1915. Universal Studios, later acclaimed for creating the golden age of American monster movies, produced a short film called *The Werewolf* in 1913, though the film's use of supposed Native American legends made it more an example of the silent era's expropriation of Indian life than a horror film.[20]

Robert Louis Stevenson's 1886 novel, *The Strange Case of Dr. Jekyll and Mr. Hyde*, proved to have a continual draw for directors, beginning with a short (under ten-minute) version in 1911 and again in 1920. The more famous Rouben Mamoulian version, starring Fredric March transforming into a nearly lycanthropic Mr. Hyde, did not appear until 1931.

The Great War had definitively shaped a desire for the creators of horror to do more than entertain, to thrill and chill. There was something confrontational about the way artists, writers, and filmmakers produced horror. They seldom had any kind of obvious political conclusions they wanted drawn from their work, but they almost always wanted their audiences to come face-to-face with death in new and disturbing forms that mocked the bourgeois cheer of much of prewar Europe. People who felt directly addressed by this new horror culture seemed to want the same.

The experience, memory, and meaning of the war proved very different for Americans than it did for their European allies. America entered the war late, joining Britain, France, and the other Allied powers in April 1917. Mobilization took time, and the American troops did not begin to make their presence felt on the battlefield until 1918. Even though the war was in its final shudders, more than 100,000 American soldiers lost their lives and veterans returned shell-shocked by their brief experiences, primarily on the western front.

Life at home remained much the same while American soldiers went "over there" in the words of the popular song. Industrial magnates, described at the time as "war profiteers" and "merchants of death," made millions by selling munitions to both sides of the conflict. This fact played such a prominent role in America's entrance to the war that critics of President Woodrow Wilson saw him as Wall Street's representative abroad. Senator George Norris of Nebraska charged Wilson with attempting to "put a dollar sign on the American flag." Six senators voted against the declaration of war, and fifty representatives stood against it in the House.[21]

The war proceeded nevertheless and opened the way for the U.S. government to initiate what we now call the national security state. Under the Espionage Act, passed in 1917, the Wilson administration imprisoned former Socialist candidate for president Eugene V. Debs, who had garnered close to one million votes in 1912 (at a time when the electorate only included about fourteen million). His crime had simply been to speak against American entrance into the war. (The Espionage Act, which was never rescinded, was used prominently in 2013 against National Security Agency whistle-blower Edward Snowden.)[22]

Wilson later became known for the idealism of his approach to international affairs; in his own words, he sought to "make the world safe for democracy." In truth, the desire to ensure that the United States played a major role in shaping the postwar world remained at the forefront of his mind. Wilson warned a group of prominent visitors to the White House in February 1917 that, "as head of a nation participating in the war, the President of the United States would have a place at the peace table." Following the Paris Peace Conference of 1919, Wilson claimed that America had become known as "the savior of the world." Future developments—barreling toward the world like a freight train—revealed how unwarranted the president's crowing enthusiasm had been.[23]

The men who fought the war were, of course, not the same as the governments that waged it or the public that supported it. American veterans found themselves heavily commemorated in the first few years of peace, and then forgotten. Veterans have been praised for their sacrifice and used as symbols of national pride by some of the very politicians who allow their postwar lives to descend into disaster. (The 2003 invasion of Iraq and the 2001 invasion of Afghanistan provide recent examples.)

In 1917–1918, smiling American doughboys (infantrymen) appeared in the *Saturday Evening Post* and other popular periodicals after the declaration of war. Usually the magazines showed them sitting peacefully in camp, but even when shown charging, they still appeared with a grim smile. American businesses, too, used them to advertise soap, cigarettes, fountain pens, and toothpaste.

Although an enormous number of World War I memorials still stand in small towns across the United States, most are of indifferent quality. Remembering the doughboy as the epitome of honor and sacrifice, rather than as an actual human being, became the order of the day. This attitude toward soldiers is manifest in artist Cecilia Beaux's 1919 comments in *American* magazine. Memorials, she suggested, must be built at "a minimum price" while exhibiting the simple beauty of the American ideal of the soldier. Beaux believed, and local committees who actually funded and built monuments apparently agreed, that monuments should memorialize a kind of platonic ideal of American manhood rather than a reflection of the suffering of the wounded or the even the memory of the dead as anything other than an unexplained sacrifice. "We are a busy and cheerful people," she wrote. "We shall not become morbid over our dead."[24]

The Great War veteran certainly counted as old news when the stock market collapsed and the banks closed in 1929. After several years of struggle, American veterans, their families, and other supporters joined together in a 43,000-person-strong protest to demand payment of wartime bonuses. The so-called Bonus Army marched on Washington in 1932. The United States had promised a payout of cash certificates, essentially bonds, that veterans had been given for their service. When President Herbert Hoover ordered the secretary of war to clear the tent city the marchers had erected, heavily armed soldiers under the leadership of Douglas MacArthur stepped in.[25]

Americans thus proved themselves ready to remember an idealized version of the men who had fought the war while forgetting the actual people. At least in the minds of the politicians and the general public, the veterans represented a demographic small enough to forget. Such a mind-set has made the costs of the war, perhaps the experience of war itself, difficult for the United States to fully grasp.

This very different experience of the Great War caused Americans to come later to the horror film and its themes than their European counterparts did. Still, an American interest in nightmare fictions began in the 1920s and, notably, centered on body horror (a specific type of horror that deals with destruction, degeneration, or violation of the human body) and the psychological torments with which American veterans, if not the larger public, would have been so familiar. The American horror tradition in the 1920s grew from two sources. First, the personal obsessions of director Tod Browning and actor Lon Chaney came together to capture the dark underside of American life in film, unleashing a sinister Mr. Hyde in response to the cheerful yet moralistic Dr. Jekyll of most of the nation's mainstream popular culture. Second, the émigrés who arrived in the United States immediately after the Great War brought Europe's ghosts with them. From them, the United States would have its own haunted screen.

If we removed these two influences, horror in the American tradition of this era would have been the pastime of the marginalized. American film in the 1920s dwelled heavily on light romance and comedy with action films. Although American folklore was replete with monsters, supernatural horror probably would have found little purchase in popular culture without European influences. The horror-fiction magazine *Weird Tales*, for example—which started publication in 1923 and remained the only pulp magazine publishing such stories until its rival *Strange Tales* appeared in 1931—had a small circulation in relation to other pulp magazines of the era, tiny in fact when compared to competitors that churned out westerns, detective tales, and romance.[26]

A few practitioners of the dark arts would begin to change this lack of interest in horror, working their alchemy on the dross of the Great War. Children and adults watching horror flicks at a Saturday matinee in the late 1920s and throughout the 1930s encountered some of the most radical artistic movements in Europe. Time and again, Hollywood would attempt to make horror as escapist as, and perhaps more escapist than, many of its other genres. But modern terror could not forget the trenches. Writers who worked in obscurity in those decades slowly entered the American consciousness. The social and economic events that followed the Great War, unwinding its consequences like the opening of a shroud, eventually negated the happy public pronouncements of "the American dream" and "the American century." The telling of an American horror story became possible, inescapable.

A World of Terrors

We are becoming more aware of the Great War as we crawl out of the wreckage of the twentieth century into yet another new world of gods and monsters. The Great War has received significant attention due to its centennial in 2014. The subtext to the commemorations has been a growing awareness on the part of scholars and activists that the global chills and fever of the past hundred years are largely traceable to the madness of the summer of 1914, when the major powers of Europe showed a fervent determination to cover the earth in corpses.

Compounding the misery, as if a civilization chose twice to commit suicide, the first fateful redrawing of maps and reallocations of power and of peoples set the stage for the rise of fascism, the efforts by European powers to hold on to their African and Asian empires, the willingness of the United States to expend blood and treasure to aid them, and even the construction of what Westerners began to call the Middle East—during which the Allies carved states out of the dead Ottoman Empire, moved entire populations against their interest and will, and unleashed the same kinds of ethnic and national hatreds in western Asia that had turned Europe into a slaughterhouse.

The new colonies, now called mandates (as if this appellation represented a new, friendlier version of the old imperialism), included the region of Mesopotamia partitioned off and renamed Iraq. The British ended the war in control of Palestine, a region made up of an overwhelming majority of Palestinian Arabs. Some Muslim and some Christian, they accounted for close to 90 percent of the population.

In November 1917, British foreign secretary Arthur Balfour asserted the empire's support for "the establishment in Palestine of a national home for the Jewish people." What became known as the Balfour Declaration grew out of a confusing mélange of anti-Semitism (a Jewish homeland, some hoped, would rid England and Europe of Jewish people) and the belief that Jews could handily administer their own state while the Arab peoples already there lived in a state of semibarbarism. One British official in the India office said, for example, that the Arabs lived like "red Indians."[27]

In the next thirty years, with the United States looking on approvingly, Britain also created the new state of Pakistan. This decision helped legitimize a virulent form of religious nationalism that finds expression in today's right-wing Hindu-nationalist Bharatiya Janata Party in India, certainly one of the legacies of Britain's inability to cease interfering even after granting independence to its former colony. Pakistan, an American client state since the Cold War, has also become home to a powerful religious fundamentalism, dangerous to its own people as much as to the larger world.

The new world order that emerged from World War I represented a slow-acting poison running through the relations between peoples and cultures. In 1919, the long-term consequences of this poison were not yet apparent, but the physical and emotional wounds were readily so. Horror as an art form, as escape, as a rendition of what had just happened, became the only possible response for a world that could not stop screaming. Horror served as critique of the war, as a way to remind Americans and Europeans of what war meant.

Horror also underscored the moral hypocrisy that followed the armistice. Woodrow Wilson's seemingly progressive Fourteen Points—a statement of principles to be used in the peace negotiations—ironically help prove the point. Although using the language of national self-determination and democracy, Wilson and the United States provided support to a British military intervention on the side of conservative, counterrevolutionary forces in the Russian Civil War (1917–1922). France reasserted its control over Southeast Asia and its colonies in Africa with American compliance and aid.

The Allies' desire to maintain and even extend their overseas empires had consequences that long reverberated. In France, a young Ho Chi Minh—who had grown up in French Indochina, traveled extensively, and become engaged in anticolonial activism—brought a petition to the Paris 1919 meetings. He believed that Wilson actually meant what he said about allowing peoples to create new, democratic states. Wilson refused to even see the young reformer. In the decades ahead, Ho, heavily influenced by the Chinese revolutionary Mao Zedong's interpretation of Marx, waged a decades-long war for Vietnamese independence first against France and then the United States.

A young Mao himself, a student in Beijing introduced to Marxism in 1918, joined protests against the 1919 Paris Peace Conference. "So much for self-determination," he said of Wilson, calling the Allies' behavior "shameless." Wilson, in the eyes of Mao and Ho, seemed to have no clear path or plan beyond mouthing progressive ideas that brought plaudits from the crowds even as he aided America's allies in their continued subjugation of Asia and Africa.[28]

The shadows cast by the Great War attenuated the armistice. The Italian Communist leader Antonio Gramsci, imprisoned in 1926 along with thousands of other leftists and trade union leaders in Mussolini's Italy, said the years after the Great War represented a moment between old and new when "morbid symptoms had begun to appear."[29]

Did the war even end in 1919? Bloodletting on an enormous scale continued into the early 1920s. The Russian Civil Wars raged until 1922, and a Polish-Soviet conflict caused 250,000 casualties between 1919 and 1921. The Balkans also exploded in a war between Greece and Turkey that created 200,000 causalities in the four years after the Treaty of Versailles. Romania invaded Hungary to seize lands and help overthrow the Communist government that came to power in 1919. Regions that had never known anything like ethnic or nationalist tension—Palestine, Iran, and the new states made up by Allies such as Iraq, Jordan, and Syria—suddenly became hearth regions for endemic violence that would grow over the century. By the 1930s, war had come to Asia and Africa because of the military ambitions of Japan and Italy.[30]

We continue our contemporary lives in this morbid half-light. Our fictions are less projections of our anxieties and more explorations of our cultural life, which is bound up with the monstrous world unleashed by the massacres of 1914, the mountains of dead the coming years produced, and the peace treaty that brought no peace.

Sigmund Freud suggested that the return of the dead constitutes the most primal and profound fear of humanity. "There is," he wrote in 1919, "scarcely any other matter upon which our thoughts and feelings have changed so little since the very earliest times . . . the belief that the dead man becomes the enemy of his survivor and seeks to carry him off."[31]

However, I doubt that even Freud could have predicted our current insistence on screening and rescreening death in the horror film. We spend many of our entertainment dollars on fantasies about characters who are in love with the resuscitated or unquiet dead in ways that may have made Freud rethink his entire conception of repression. It's been said that, of all the things Freud proved prescient about, he would never have imagined the physical dreamscape of Disneyland. Neither could he have predicted the horror business. But what else could have come of the terrible new world created a hundred years ago?

The Rage of the Golem

Albin Grau hired screenwriter Henrik Galeen to pen *Nosferatu*. Galeen had, in 1915 and 1920, worked with famed German actor, director, and Great War veteran Paul Wegener to produce scripts for two tales about a creature from the Jewish folklore of Eastern Europe: the mythical golem, a monster of mud and clay whose very existence threatens the world.

By the beginning of the Great War, the fable of the golem had a history of four centuries behind it, stretching back to the ghettoes of Poland but most closely associated with Prague's Jewish quarter. In its most canonical shape, the story tells of the famed Rabbi Judah Loew ben Bezalel of Prague, who created a hulking figure from the silt and clay of the river Vltava as a protector of the Jews, supernatural insurance that their community would continue to live under the Holy Roman Emperor Rudolf II.

Prague's Jewish quarter, a ghetto that had been walled off from the rest of the city since the medieval era, had been transformed in the nineteenth century during a brief period of liberal reform in the Austrian Empire that included a "Jewish emancipation" and the end of an extraordinary list of proscriptions. After the old ghetto walls came down in the 1850s, stories about the golem became more common, in something of an expression of nostalgia for the life in the Jewish quarter. They also became more frightening.

In many of the new tales, Rabbi Loew invests his creature with life either by placing under its tongue a slip of parchment bearing the secret name of God or carving on its forehead the Hebrew word for truth. Although serving his master and the Jewish community for a time after his creation, the golem eventually becomes uncontrollable. His rampage entails the destruction of the Jewish community itself, the very people he'd been created to protect. The stories further suggest that, if not stopped, the powerful creature will actually bring ruin to the entire cosmos. To prevent this, Rabbi Loew must remove the parchment or scratch out the Hebrew letter *aleph* from the golem's forehead so that the word "truth" becomes "death."[32]

This story, fashioned like the golem himself out of the native soil of Mitteleuropa, ceased to be simply folklore and became part of mass culture during the Great War. Paul Wegener produced no fewer than three films about the golem between 1914 and 1920. Austrian writer Gustav Meyrink's novel *The Golem*, first published in serial form in 1913–14 and then in book form in 1915, became a runaway bestseller. Maya Barzilai has called it "the *Da Vinci Code* of its day" and notes that a paperback pocket edition appeared for distribution to soldiers in the trenches.[33]

The golem story became freighted with meaning during the war years because of the suggestion in the tale that this creation could lead to apocalypse, capturing the sense that the war had created just such a monster. The story's occult elements may also have resonated with the era's fascination with the supernatural and the thin places between worlds. Israel Joshua Singer, a Jewish writer from Poland and the older brother of Nobel Prize winner Isaac Bashevis Singer, saw both tendencies in the monster's popularity. He called the Great War a "gigantic global golem . . . that has risen on clay feet and set out on its path, knocking down everything that stands in its way." He wrote of a world in which both collaborators and victims were part of the great monster. "Every one of us," he claimed, "has become a small bit of clay in the large golem."[34]

The sense of the war as a monstrosity that had escaped the control of its own creators may account for the popularity of both the tale of the golem and *Frankenstein*. Henri de Man, socialist politician and Belgian veteran, described the war as "the secret dread of those that created it" and a machine that moved on its own. We might think of war in the abstract as "a campaign" in which "one leader pits his will against that of another," wrote German author Rudolf G. Binding. "But in this war both adversaries lie on the ground and only the war has its will."[35]

Paul Wegener's own experience of the Great War found its way into *The Golem: How He Came into the World* (1920), the only surviving film in his trilogy. Wegener—who co-wrote, directed, and starred in the film—felt he, too, had become a creature of clay and mud, and the victim of sorceries he could not fathom or control. He volunteered for the German army at age forty. Already well-known as an actor by 1914 (the year in which his first film in the Golem series appeared), Wegener arrived on the front lines in October. He soon faced his first experience of heavy combat and became one of only four in a forty-nine-member squad to survive the baptism of horror. He won the Iron Cross, though he was allowed to leave the army at the rank of lieutenant in 1915 due to severe trauma. In letters from the front, Wegener regularly described himself as suffering from "a nervous fatigue of the heart muscle" or "an acute nervous heart weakness."

Wegener frequently spoke of life in the trenches as being spent covered in clay, an instrument and an object of horror. He wrote a journal, published in 1933, in which he described whole days spent "seething in the clay." In his dreams he could hear the "screams of the wounded" but also woke up with no stronger sensation than a primal joy at being alive, "a disgusting joy" he guiltily told himself.[36]

In the 1920 film, the Golem (played by Wegener) is born of mud and dark magic in a misguided attempt to protect the Jews of Prague. To animate his creation with a "magic word," Rabbi Loew raises a demon called Astaroth, who appears as a spirit of violence and vengeance.

We first see Wegener's Golem as a laborer whose experience is not unlike that of a soldier of the trenches. (Wegener had been a "canal worker" during the war, building fortifications.) When Rabbi Loew's assistant Famulus tries to turn the Golem into an avatar of his jealous vengeance, the worker becomes a weapon.

The Great War lurks in the film as its true monster. Although a political crisis may have made Rabbi Loew feel as though he had no choice but to create the Golem, he ultimately loses control of his creation. This theme resonates with Wegener's own sense of the meaning of the war. Soon after his combat experiences, which won him Germany's highest military honor, he described the war as a combination of "senseless murder" and "boredom . . . positively absurd with no end in sight." His letters called the war "the most monstrous, dumbest and atrocious thing" and he became a critic of German war aims almost from the time he left the army.

The Golem ends on a note of humane pathos. In his rage, the now unbound monster smashes the walls of the ghetto and seems on a rampage that, as in older legends of the creature, will end in cosmic destruction. Wegener chooses to affirm a deeply human value in his monstrous reflection on the meaning of war. A little girl sees the Golem as a playmate rather than a monster. This enables the Golem to bring to heel the spirits of violence and horror erupting inside him. He lifts the child, seemingly menacingly, but it's a playful embrace. She removes from his chest a magical talisman that contains the magic word bringing him to life and, unlike an earlier scene in which Golem fights Rabbi Loew's effort to do this, a more pliant Golem accepts his mortality and sinks into oblivion.

Artists found it difficult to find hopeful endings in their stories of monsters unleashed on the world in 1914. In fact, another filmmaker, a British veteran of the trenches, reimagined the scene between child and monster in gruesome fashion.

Kafka's Labyrinth

Postwar Prague produced much more for the horror genre than Meyrink and Wegener's popularization of the golem legend. Though mapping a very different part of the nightmare lands than many in the early twentieth century, the German-Jewish writer Franz Kafka dealt with themes of body horror that continue to appear in unlikely corners of horror film and fiction.[37]

Kafka has, of course, never really been viewed as a horror writer. For some literary critics, to do so would reduce him to being a genre writer, generally not a compliment. Such a view, along with trying to draw a line between high and low culture that's impossible to defend, dismisses the unclassifiable nature of so much of what horror fans consume. It would further ignore how Kafka worried at ideas that have become formulaic for lesser horror writers who have absorbed his themes of alienation, ruin, torture, and madness, even if they haven't engaged specifically with his work.

Kafka was born in Prague in 1883, and the city shaped every bizarre angle and absurdist symmetry in his conception of the world. He spent much of his life in a multiethnic city within a multiethnic empire. "Multiethnic" meant nothing like the modern term "multicultural," however, and plenty of cultural antipathy existed in Kafka's hometown and in the Czech lands of the Hapsburg Empire more generally.

Two years before his birth, anti-German riots had broken out in the normally peaceful city, much of the violence directed against German-speaking Jewish business owners who had prospered after the end of the ghetto. During the writer's lifetime, the Czech-speaking majority openly displayed a generalized dislike for Germans living in Prague, a prejudice intertwined with anti-Semitism, given that most Jews spoke German. Kafka himself wrote his fiction in German.[38]

In the region that, following the Great War, became Czechoslovakia, anti-Semitism did not take the same form it did in other eastern European states after the fragmentation of the Hapsburg Empire. Kafka, like others in the Jewish community, still keenly felt alienated in the city of his ancestors. Although he considered himself an atheist, he became actively interested in cultural Judaism in his twenties, associating with a Yiddish theater group in 1910.

The entire German-Jewish community shared this sense of isolation, so we cannot attribute Kafka's own simply to the fact that Jews often found themselves treated as strangers in their centuries-old homeland. Psychological descriptions are also inadequate. It's true that his deeply conflicted relationship with his family and his inability to form lasting relationships with women—something he passionately desired but couldn't achieve—did increase his sense of isolation. "I lack all aptitude for family life except, at best, as an observer," he wrote in 1913.[39]

Kafka the man remains as much a mystery as his work. He did build a close relationship with one sister, Ottla, and maintained a lifelong friendship with literary companion Max Brod. Sometimes reclusive and convinced he would die alone, Kafka also went through stages of frequenting brothels, drinking heavily, and traveling occasionally. Efforts to break out of his isolation often led quickly back to despair and anxiety over his writing. But again, like the isolation he experienced as a Jew in Prague, none of this serves as an adequate explanation for the kind of writing he produced. Max Brod said of his friend that the invisible powers that moved the world suffused his understanding of reality. Walter Benjamin, who never met but deeply admired Kafka, wrote that the world represented for the author a series of "indecipherable communications." In response, Benjamin concluded, Kafka "made parables for himself."

Whatever the reasons for it, Kafka became a theremin vibrating weirdly to the times. He had the ability to join his own personal suffering, both physical and psychological, to the profound suffering of the age. The sensibility that allowed such a connection perhaps accounts for the odd combination of nihilism and empathy that appears throughout his fiction.

An observer of his times, Kafka had no sense of attachment to the empire or the emperor. His politics—he had an interest in socialism that grew toward the end of his life—made him wary of the idea of a war for imperial prerogative. He received his conscription notice in 1915, but his employer, a workers' insurance company, helped him receive a deferment by classifying Kafka as an "essential civil servant."

Although Kafka luckily avoided conscription, it's impossible to divorce his work from either the war or the complex political and cultural formations of the Austro-Hungarian Empire as it hurtled toward its sudden death in 1918. Emperor Franz Josef, eighty-four in 1914, soon watched the decimation of his armies in the field; he lived in justifiable paranoia that revolution might shatter his rattletrap empire. In 1915, regiments raised in Prague staged two protests at the front itself, including one regiment carrying a banner that read, "We march against Russia, but we don't know why."[40]

The outbreak of war in August 1914 coincided with Kafka's first flourishes of writing, which were also among his most terrifying. On August 6, five days after seeing off his conscripted brothers-in-law at the train station, Kafka described himself watching with "a malignant look" a "patriotic speech" by the mayor of Prague. "These parades," he wrote bitterly, "are one of the most disgusting accompaniments of the war."[41]

News of the war remained almost universally bad for Austria-Hungary on the eastern front, as meaningless a slaughter for both Allies and Central Powers as in Belgium and France. Germany did make enormous advances in the east as the kaiser's army slammed like a mechanized tidal wave over the Russian military, the czar's huge but antiquated army unable to cope with this suddenly modern form of warfare. Still, losses on both sides had been unthinkably high and signaled the catastrophe to come.

Austro-Hungarian troops had far less success trying to move against the Russians and the Serbians than did their German allies, and they quickly became bogged down across a 175-mile front. The hammer of war shattered the psyche of the infantry from the first weeks of the conflict. On August 23 near the village of Krasnik (in today's Poland), a young Austrian soldier named Friedrich Feuchtinger recalled a drummer boy, even his role in the regiment a relic of outworn notions of war, walking with "bloodshot feverish eyes" as their regiment came under Russian shelling. "I look at him once again," Feuchtinger recalled, "see his eyes widen and his mouth open; blood runs from it and he calls a throaty 'Mother,' then sinks down dead."[42]

During this period, when it became clear that the kaiser's and the emperor's assurances of a quick victory deserved nothing but scathing disdain, Kafka began work on his most dreadful horror tale and then launched into one of his most disturbing parables. Even those who resist including Kafka in the horror genre might find a chill running down their spine while reading certain of his works.

"In the Penal Colony" (1914), a short story, examines the theme of bureaucracy taken to its naturally illogical conclusions while also presaging the next four years of European slaughter. "It's a remarkable piece of apparatus," reads the opening line. A character identified only as the Officer in this place without names looks in "admiration" at the infernal machine of punishment, and he expects the Explorer to agree. Seeking to provide a demonstration, guards walk the Prisoner, hobbled by chains, toward the thing described in close detail by Kafka as an advanced type of industrial machinery. The automaton can "go on working continuously for twelve hours" and even if the sadistic mechanism slows in its work, "it will only be a small matter that can be set right at once."

In a world of smoke and furnaces and bellows, the machine gleams with modernity, brutalism apparent in every aspect of its design. The story reads like a prophecy of the terrible machines that efficiently broke skin and bone on battlefields across the world. The Officer takes enormous pride in this mechanism, having the Explorer watch as the unlucky Prisoner is strapped into its steel claws. For Kafka, the Officer stands in for every haughty Austro-Hungarian military functionary he had seen marching about with troops of conscripts since the war began. He wears a "tight fitting full-dress uniform coat, amply befogged and weighed down by epaulettes." He expounds on the machine invented by "the former commandment" with enthusiasm. We soon learn the machine's purpose: it harrows the skin of the convicted with a thousand needles, writing their sentence onto their bodies in acid as they scream in pain for hours. (The victims become Clive Barker's "books of blood," and Barker himself seemed to channel elements of the story in his surrealist horror fiction and cinema.)

Written soon after "In the Penal Colony," Kafka's well-known novella *The Trial* (1915) gives us one of his most memorable protagonists: "Someone must have been telling lies about Josef K., he knew he had done nothing wrong." Yet K. has been arrested and doesn't have any idea why. The arresting officers do not explain anything to him or display any interest in his crime or, more important, his innocence or guilt. His trial will stretch interminably: in fact, part of the terror of the novella comes from the possibility that it may have no actual end; the trial may have been an end in itself. K.'s inability to know his crime has an almost supernatural effect of turning him into a criminal. The novella combines absurdism with paranoia and claustrophobia. The setting could be Prague, but it's not exactly Prague. It's the Prague of the wasteland, a dead city and a city of the dead. Human beings exist on an empty landscape that has become a wasteland, with events they do not understand deciding their fate.

Around the time Kafka began writing *The Trial*, in late April 1915, he watched a member of a Hussar regiment on a train and saw in his saber, uniform, and demeanor nothing but a cause for mockery. "He smiled a great deal in every direction," Kafka noted, "a really unwitting meaningless smile." Kafka saw the rictus of death in the Hussar's insouciant grin.[43]

In 1915, Kafka set aside *The Trial* and published another novella, *The Metamorphosis*, the story of Gregor Samsa, who wakes one morning to find himself transformed into a verminous bug. The story's grotesqueries are sometimes described as a kind of magical realism, but readers can find in it a dark magic. Kafka combined both physically unsettling descriptions of Gregor's struggle with his insect body and the sense of utter and complete alienation from the experience of other human beings. The final paragraphs are nearly dizzying in their effect, an unhappy ending that manages to distill all unhappy endings that have ever been.

Kafka kept a rich literary diary starting in 1910; he ceased writing it in 1917 and did not resume until after the end of the war. Dark masterpieces continued to come from his pen over the next few years as he labored in near anonymity.

The Skull and the Corpse: Avant-Garde Horror

Fritz Lang, born in 1890, remembered his hometown of Vienna as "a confectionary city of a fairy tale." Turn-of-the-century Vienna's intermingling of the baroque and the bohemian gave it a dreamlike quality. Lang remained obsessed with cities of dreams, and of nightmares, throughout his career.[44]

The future filmmaker's difficult relationship with his family complicated his love for his native city. He performed poorly in his *Realschule* and, to his father's disgust, academic failure forced him to withdraw. His father very much wanted him to become an architect, seeing this as a natural continuation of the family's success. Some have claimed that this would have had the director following in his father's footsteps, although it appears that, according to Lang's most reliable biographer, his father actually ran a burgeoning construction business. The family, Lang himself simply said, lived a "thoroughly bourgeois" existence.[45]

Lang's failed experience in the *Realschule* should not mask what appears to have been a wide, if undisciplined, imaginative and intellectual curiosity. An adolescent Lang snuck into the room of the family's attractive maid as an adolescent, hoping to see her undressing. He found instead a pile of penny dreadfuls—sensational mass-market novels—with titles like *The Phantom Robber*. He combined his penchant for reading pulp crime magazines with studying the works of the existentialist philosopher Kierkegaard while pursuing his interest in the works of Gustav Klimt, one of Vienna's most complex artists. Attracted more and more to painting, Lang also became enamored with the decidedly different, though equally challenging, art of Austrian expressionist Egon Schiele.

Klimt's art drips with sexuality, sensual surfaces, and the glittering self-possession of upper-class Vienna women. Though perhaps its effect might be a bit dulled today by endless reproductions of *The Kiss*, Klimt's style proved highly influential, inspiring, for example, Lang's earliest films, particularly *Die Nibelungen* (1924) and *Metropolis* (1927). Schiele, known for his nudes, also produced grittier portraits combining some sense of social realism with life on the Viennese streets. Though he died young during the influenza pandemic in 1918, Schiele remained a continuing influence, joining the dime novels and the philosophy in Lang's later explorations of crime and horror.[46]

Lang left Vienna in 1909 at the age of twenty-one to become an art student in Paris. In the brief biographical sketches that he wrote or had publicists provide to would-be interviewers, this portion of his life remained shadowy. In fact, he frequently offered hopeful biographers with a number of contradictory facts. We do know that he returned to Austria in 1914 to take part in some of the bloodiest fighting on the eastern front. After a short apprenticeship in film in the years after he returned, he would begin telling stories of monsters, many of them the shadows, doubles, and automata that whispered the secrets of the dead.

Artists rushing off to the front only to return with visions of horror became a common experience of the war years. German painter and etcher Otto Dix claimed that he and his generation had thrown themselves head-first into "an insane exercise of four years."[47] Born in 1891, Dix had shown a talent for painting and printmaking during his youth in Germany, being apprenticed to a master painter at the age of fifteen. Like a number of other artists influenced by the avant-garde, he set aside his paints and canvases in the summer of 1914. He first joined a field artillery unit assembled at Dresden. In 1915, he requested a transfer to a Maxim gun unit and survived the Somme, two years on the eastern front, and the final German spring offensives of 1918.

The decision to give himself to the "insane exercise" forever haunted Dix's mind and art. He never forgave himself or the world. The horrors he witnessed fevered his nights. Dix repeatedly dreamed of crawling through shell-ruined homes, once happy and filled with laughter, now ghastly with the stink of the grave. The nightmares found their way to his canvas. Between the end of the war and the Nazi accession to power in 1933, Dix's oeuvre portrayed a world of disfigured and damaged veterans, skeletons charging through a fog of mud and blood, and a Germany ultimately unable, or unwilling, to face what it had become as it tried to lose itself in the vibrant and outré popular culture of the Weimar years.

The relationship between surrealist nightmares and the birth of modern horror has generally been ignored. For many, surrealism belongs simply to the strange world of "modern art," too challenging to understand even if it's given grudging respect. Salvador Dalí remains the surrealist who has been given the most acclaim, his 1931 *Persistence of Memory* becoming a standard poster for college dorm rooms. Ironically, given his popularity, Dalí's work represents some of the most radical, if also most accessible, of the surrealist dreamscapes. Many of his works are, like surrealism itself, the landscape of nightmare.[48]

The work of the avant-garde had, by 1920, bridged the trauma of war and the world of the horror film. André Breton, who wrote the *Surrealist Manifesto* (1924), had his life profoundly altered by his own experience of the

Great War. Born into a petit bourgeois family in Normandy, Breton studied medicine and psychiatry before 1914 and then served in a neurological medical unit in Nantes in 1915. Here he witnessed firsthand the effects of war trauma, the shell shock of soldiers from the front, most soon forced to return or face the accusation of malingering.

While working at the hospital in Nantes, Breton befriended a fellow devotee of experimental literature, Jacques Vaché. The antisocial, monocle-wearing Vaché has been nearly forgotten today. However, his *Lettres de guerre* (*War Letters*), published in 1919, heavily influenced Breton and the surrealist movement more generally, with his description of the trenches as a monstrous compendium of blood and bodily fluids, rain "pissing like vinegar" and the sun "sprinkled with acid" when it looks on the cataclysm below. Vaché committed suicide by overdosing on opium soon after the war.

Horror offered the surrealists the grammar for the new language they sought to create. The form offered a way to represent shell shock in both its literal and metaphoric manifestations. Surrealists developed a deep fascination with the work of Freud, whose essays on the nature of trauma and nightmare began to appear in the 1910s. Freud's three sons, Martin, Oliver, and Ernst, all served in the Austro-Hungarian army. Martin spent much of 1915–1918 in an Italian prisoner of war camp. Observation of the global bloodletting forced Freud to broaden his definition of trauma beyond infantile sexuality and early, repressed memories of Oedipal obsessions. A death instinct—which included both horror and allure—lay submerged and waiting in our swamp-like unconscious, a greater threat than our sexual repressions.

Surrealist art, heavily influenced by Freud, in turn influenced the first horror films. The earliest masterpieces of horror, including *Nosferatu*, *The Golem*, and *The Cabinet of Dr. Caligari* (1920), all drew on surrealist themes. Carl Theodor Dreyer's haunting *Vampyr* (1932) self-consciously sought to put surrealism and other modern artistic movements onto film stock. Dreyer commented on his passionate interest in modern art at the time of making *Vampyr*. The monster masterpieces from Tod Browning and James Whale that emerged from Universal Studios drew implicitly on avant-garde art even as they disdained any discussion of "intellectual influences," knowing it would seem absurdly pretentious to do otherwise, in the "that's entertainment," jazz-hands world of 1930s Hollywood.

The war created the mise-en-scène for horror outside the visual arts. A new kind of poetry also breathed the war's pestilent air of horror. Often cataloged under the very broad category of literary modernism, it resurrected not only the bloody terror of war but also the same worlds of nightmare and trauma that artists and filmmakers visited in this time of monsters.

T. S. Eliot had no firsthand experience of World War I, though not for lack of trying. He attempted to enlist in the U.S. Navy in 1917, but recruiters immediately rejected him for physical limitations, including a rapid heart-beat and a past hernia. He spent the war years becoming the protégé of Ezra Pound and making an unfortunate marriage with Vivienne Haigh-Wood (who may have slept with mathematician and essayist Bertrand Russell during her honeymoon with Eliot). Eliot taught at a variety of tony British schools until taking a position at Lloyd's of London, an occupation at which he proved surprisingly adept, given the seeming paradox of poet as successful banker.

In 1917, while failing to join the war effort, Eliot wrote "The Love Song of J. Alfred Prufrock," a weary anthem of modern malaise that would become his second-best-known poem. He began work on his masterpiece, *The Waste Land*, after the Great War. The poem, though seldom seen in these terms, constituted as much a symphony of horror as *Nosferatu*: Both appeared in 1922. Both imagine a world poisoned by violence. Corpses come back to life, and the drumbeats of an ancient primal desire for destruction are at the heart of both film and poem. In both works, an undefined plague ravages the world and death calls into question all human ties and relationships.

Eliot completed *The Waste Land* while recovering in a sanitarium after a complete mental break brought on by his revulsion at the state of the world and, more intimately, his failing relationship with Haigh-Wood. Deeply controversial among its first readers, indeed often despised for its pastiche of street speech, classical imagery, and Asian religious concepts, the poem represents the opposite of an instant classic. Barely understood by most when it first appeared, the poem slowly gained a reputation for its ability to take the temperature of the world shattered by what men had done, and had had done to them, in the trenches.

The imagery of *The Waste Land* is macabre: hooded figures march in throngs across a bridge of death, a submerged corpse has pearls in place of eyes, waste places suggest the apocalyptic landscapes that today we associate with everything from zombie films to video game series such as Fallout and, notably, Wasteland.

The Waste Land's imagery clashes with, while also making more dreadful, moments such as the sad, pathetic, joyless sex between office workers and the nonsense blather of pub talk suddenly silenced when patrons wander haunted streets, forced out of the light and comfort of a fire and a pint. A child's nursery rhyme, an old folk tune born out of the terror of the plague years, makes for a grim soundtrack running throughout the poem. Eliot would have heartily despised the comparison, but it has a not dissimilar effect on the reader to Wes Craven's infamously creepy "1, 2 Freddy's Coming for You" from the *Nightmare on Elm Street* series.

Eliot eventually retreated from this wasteland of terrors as best he could. In the 1920s, he sought psychic relief in a conversion to Anglo-Catholicism, a High Church version of the Christian faith that seemed to satiate his need for mystical experience, a need he'd earlier sought in Buddhism just as Albin Grau had explored the occult.

Eliot's dabbling with darkness did not stop with his conversion. He may have ended his terrifying poem with a repetition of "Shantih"—the Sanskrit word for peace—but nothing about the 1920s promised peace from the terror the Great War had unleashed. In the years to come, Eliot's friend and mentor Ezra Pound helped pull his protégé farther into the darkness of the twentieth century, reawakening in the staid Eliot the irrational horrors that made him explore the wasteland in the first place.

The War and the Weird Tale

"What is this Shantih! Shantih! Shantih! Anyway," American horror writer H. P. Lovecraft snidely commented in a letter to his own young protégé, Frank Belknap Long. Lovecraft never tired of making fun of Eliot, to the point that the vastly successful writer became a kind of obsession with him. Though he deplored Eliot, Lovecraft read and reread him; wrote a parody of his work for an amateur journal; went to hear him speak when the poet came to New England; and, a year after reading *The Waste Land*, tried his hand at writing a prose poem that delved into the same dark emptiness.[49]

The lives of Lovecraft and Eliot represented a peculiar set of contrasts and comparisons. Like Eliot, Lovecraft had attempted to join the military in 1917 and had been rejected as a poor physical specimen. Both men despised much of what had come with what Lovecraft called "mongrel Mechanamerika," an America that had exchanged art for the clanging machinery of industrialism—and allowed entirely too many immigrants to come to its shores for Lovecraft or Eliot to stomach.[50]

Lovecraft's lucky failure to make it to the trenches, however, did not keep the shadow of the Great War from his work. Two of his earliest tales, "Dagon" and "The Temple," deal with inhuman terrors that may swallow "war weary" mankind when the time is right. Moreover, his more famous stories, mostly written between 1926 and 1936, evoke monstrosities that will cause human beings to "flee into the peace and safety of a new dark age." Such pondering came from his reading, among others, of German historian Oswald Spengler's two-volume *Decline of the West* (1918, 1922), a work that pessimistically suggested that the Great War had represented the explosive collapse of the values that had guided the West since the Middle Ages and precipitated a creeping growth of darkness and decay.

Lovecraft's "Nyarlathotep" (1920)—a prose poem never professionally published in his lifetime—captures the emptiness and fear of the war's aftermath. The work describes "a season of political and social upheaval" that has spread across the world. He writes of "a sense of monstrous guilt" settling heavily on humankind, a reference to the combination of grief and panic that both veterans and the watching world felt about the war's terrible carnage.

Into this social and metaphysical wasteland, where "out of the abyss between the stars swept chill currents," comes Nyarlathotep, the "crawling chaos." Lovecraft's own inveterate Anglo-Saxon racism made Nyarlathotep appear "out of Egypt . . . swarthy, slender, sinister," but in some sense the thing embodies an almost perfect incarnation of fascism's lure. He holds the world in a combination of astonished rapture and despair. Lovecraft imagines him as a combination of a reality television star, political demagogue, and Nikola Tesla. Nyarlathotep plays tricks of psychology on the crowd while showing them the wonders of electricity. People watch and listen in obsessed horror.

Lovecraft ends the experimental fiction with a vision of universal decay and death, his own wasteland much more terrifying than Eliot's in many respects. The "season of political and social upheaval" forces human beings to recognize themselves as living inside a vast, multidimensioned corpse, "this revolting graveyard of the universe" from which arise "the muffled, maddening beating of drums, and thin, monotonous whine of blasphemous flutes from inconceivable unlighted chambers beyond Time."

Lovecraft's vision certainly wears a darker hue than even Eliot's, but the resemblances between the two are hard to ignore. The very notion of a prose poem bears the stamp of modernism. The "terrible city of unnumbered crimes" in Lovecraft seems much like Eliot's "Unreal City." Both include a march of the unquiet dead victimized by the wasteland.

Both men retreated into peculiar versions of conservatism that made each susceptible to the dark prophecies of fascism's crawling chaos. Eliot's Anglo-Catholicism shared much of the generalized anti-Semitism of the 1920s and '30s, even showing up now and again in his poetry. Lovecraft professed a philosophical pessimism while believing that the meaninglessness of the universe meant that tradition, history, and racial mythology offered human beings a tiny raft on the "black seas of infinity." Lovecraft sometimes admitted that he knew his own beliefs about this were "illusory," a trick that the mind plays on itself to ward off suicide.[51]

This rejection of any kind of meaning or pattern in the universe did not keep him from remaining committed to a systematic set of ideas borrowed from the pseudoscientific racism concerning human differences born in the nineteenth century. Significantly, and in contrast to what some of his apologists have claimed, Lovecraft made explicit use of racism in his fiction. In the 1920s he would have words of praise for Mussolini and, while seeing Hitler as faintly ridiculous, believed that Nazism in 1933 offered a reasonable option for the German people. It's very difficult for modern readers to understand how Lovecraft did not see in such figures an incarnation of his own Nyarlathotep, a crawling chaos emerging out of the despair of these years.[52]

The Great War had offered both Eliot and Lovecraft a vision of apocalypse. Indeed, Eliot and Lovecraft seem part of an echo chamber of a world gone mad in dreams of its own desolation. Eliot's waste land feels like Lovecraft's revolting graveyard of a universe that in turn chills us like the death plague of Nosferatu's coming. These images twitch and gibber beside Crowley's dark Atlantis, which so disturbed Albin Grau. Lovecraft's "city of unnumbered crimes" appears again in the horror that Kafka conjured in *The Trial*. Down these same twilight streets and purple dark alleys walks Josef K., obsessed with the secret of his trial and desperate for knowledge that we sense will bring him nothing but despair and death.

Writers who had already mapped the wasteland received attention for the first time. Few have heard of the Welsh author Arthur Machen, and it's too bad. He wrote some of the most disturbing horror fiction ever written, before anyone called it horror fiction. Born in 1863 to the family of a High Church Anglican minister, Machen had a lifelong interest in an idiosyncratic blend of Christianity, Celtic mythology, the Holy Grail, and the faerie folk as creatures of terror. (Imagine a Tolkien without the pedantry or a C. S. Lewis without the theological dogma who writes well about horror rather than badly about centaurs and magic wardrobes.)

Machen had his most prolific period of writing tales of the bizarre between 1890 and 1900. All dealt with the idea of ancient evil surviving into, and sometimes thriving off, the industrial present. During this decade he wrote his best-known stories, "The White Powder," "The Black Seal," and "The Great God Pan," the latter described by Stephen King as a tale that's always inspired terror in him. The literary establishment mostly ignored Machen except to question the moral qualities of someone who could write "The Great God Pan," a reaction that must have been a hoot for the puritanical, if peculiar, Machen.

Machen the horror author offers a profound contrast to Lovecraft and Eliot, though both admired his work. He appeared to have had a lifelong attachment to the Anglo-Catholicism he inherited from his clergyman father, a comfortable but serious faith that never came to him as a cataclysmic crisis of conversion, as it had for Eliot. He led a bourgeois life with marriage and a number of children. His first wife, Amelia Hogg, whom Machen affectionately called Amy, died of cancer in the twelfth year of their marriage. Not being particularly solitary by nature, Machen married the stage actress Dorothie Hudleston in 1903 and lived with her for much of the rest of his eighty-four years in conventional happiness.

The Great War led Machen to turn again to writing horror fiction. The dark times of 1914–1918 had the effect of giving him a literary respectability he had not previously experienced. Reviewers would fall over themselves in praise of him during the 1920s, Edmund Pearson writing that he surpassed Poe. Much of Machen's early work saw republication throughout the decade and became a source of much-needed income. Many collectors began paying hundreds of pounds for the limited editions of his early work, transactions from which he saw not a copper farthing.

Outwardly, Machen's life may have not displayed any signs of dramatic crisis or louche behavior. His stories of the 1890s, deeply influenced by the decadent movement in literature, lead the reader to imagine him the absinthe-drinking bohemian he most certainly was not. His mystical interests, somewhat similar to Eliot's, did allow him to write a new set of tales that shed a spectral light across the trenches. Around the time of his first wife's death, he developed his lifelong interest in the Holy Grail that led him to at least the shadowlands between religion and the occult. The grifter occultist Aleister Crowley, though held in contempt by Machen, became convinced that the author's stories channeled the same "magikal" worlds he had tried to hawk in his own incomprehensible teachings.

When 1914 came, Machen had been banging out copy for London's popular *Evening News* for four years. He found journalism pretty thoroughly distasteful, but he had no other means of income beyond some dwindling family bequests. His literary renaissance began with a patriotic ghost story in 1915, probably among his worst tales and one he perhaps came to regret. It contributed to—and Machen worried it had created—one of the most enduring supernatural legends of the Great War. He would also write a novella in the war years that offered a mysterious allegory for the meaning and aftermath of the conflict itself, a story of a terror that leached out of the wasteland of the war. Not surprisingly, most people liked the militaristic ghost story.

A Monster in the Trenches

The Great War gave a monster born out of the revolutionary turmoil of the nineteenth century a new and terrible life. A young second lieutenant who served in the British army in Flanders would one day reanimate this monster, who became the most iconic symbol of cinematic horror in the twentieth century.

James Whale's war had been a desperate one, an extension of the miseries of his early life in the West Midlands town of Dudley. His father, William, worked as a blast furnace operator at the ironworks while keeping pigs in an alley behind the family's tiny house. Both William and his wife, Sarah, actively engaged in the work of the local Methodist Church. Young Jimmy, who was born in 1889 and discovered both his artistic bent and his attraction to the same sex at an early age, must have found his family's strict Methodism and economic difficulties more than stifling.[53]

James Whale received the nickname "Jamie the Gentleman" for his occasional mimicry, some of it mocking, of the British upper classes. His interest in the arts first manifested in an aptitude for drawing. As a young adolescent, he took a job working for a cobbler, sometimes making a few extra coins by bringing in old shoes and selling the brass nails for scrap. He pocketed a small portion of his earnings while giving the rest to his parents for the support of himself and his three siblings. The small amount of money he managed to save went toward his tuition as a night student at the Dudley School of Arts and Crafts beginning in 1910.

When the war began in August 1914, Whale did not immediately enlist in the British army but instead went to work at Harper and Bean, a producer of munitions and vehicle parts. At night he volunteered for the YMCA, which built and maintained barracks and canteens.

Few, if any, saw Whale as a shirker for not joining the army. In fact, it's a myth that war fever swept an entire generation of British men into uniform in a burst of nationalism and hatred for the enemy. A massive number of volunteers—nearly one million—did seek to enlist in the first five months of the war, but that number accounted for just 30 percent of the total of men in Britain eligible for the army. Men who felt invested in the concept of "the nation," Britain as a force for civilization through its imperial system, first joined en masse. Fully employed skilled workers and a significant portion of the middle class made up the majority of these enlistees.[54]

Most continental powers had long instituted conscription and so managed something like full enlistment long before the British. In the United Kingdom, a parliamentary debate ensued over conscription, and the policy did not become formalized until 1915, essentially after the British army had been bled white by the unexpected ferocity of the early campaigns.

Once Britain did embrace universal conscription, the only policy that allowed for a modern nation-state to wage war on a scale required by the conflict, Whale sought a place in the officers' corps. The son of a working-class family certain to be drafted in any case, Whale trained in the evenings with a group of cadets and received his commission in the summer of 1916, becoming a second lieutenant in the Worcestershire infantry regiment.

Early in his time as a soldier, Whale experienced what counts as some lucky breaks, at least in the context of World War I. In 1916, his battalion arrived late at the Battle of the Somme, so he did not endure the disaster of July 2. He did endure the mud and blood of the trenches, the shrieking of shells, and the incredibly dangerous raids and patrols required of young officers.

Whale's battalion mobilized to take part in a diversionary maneuver against German lines near the French city of Arras that turned into a battle costing 160,000 British casualties, but it arrived at the front just as the attack ended. The British command then sent the battalion to Flanders. There Whale saw his worst fighting of his war. He took part in General Douglas Haig's ill-conceived attack at the Ypres salient, where German troops captured him. They held him prisoner for the final eighteen months of the conflict, a situation that likely saved his life. During his time as a prisoner of war, he and his fellow officers staged amateur theatrical productions in an environment of relative comfort given the treatment of POWs in most modern wars.

Following the war, Whale spent a decade both acting in and directing a number of small productions. In 1919, he met actor Ernest Thesiger, a fellow veteran who'd had far more horrific experiences in combat than Whale and who went on to star in two of his horror films. Thesiger was, like Whale, openly gay to friends in Hollywood and the theater. Unlike Whale, he chose to marry a woman, both for social reasons and, more significantly, to avoid the possibility of being jailed under Britain's laws against same-sex relationships that remained on the books (frequently enforced) until 1967.

In 1928, Whale became fascinated by a stage play written by fellow veteran R. C. Sherriff called *Journey's End*, a claustrophobic tale of the Great War with little plot and action, much of it a conversation taking place in an officers' bunker while the sounds of shelling and machine gun fire explode and rattle in the background. Whale saw in the play not only his own experience but also the experience of a generation.

Journey's End became a surprise hit on the stage, earning Whale critical acclaim and the opportunity to become part of the burgeoning American film industry. He worked with Howard Hughes on the "talkie" portions of his controversial war epic *Hell's Angels* (in which several stunt pilots died during filming). Whale had the opportunity to coauthor and direct a film version of *Journey's End* in 1930. Universal Studios, whose 1930 adaptation of Erich Maria Remarque's novel *All Quiet on the Western Front* had garnered significant acclaim and box office receipts, also hired Whale to direct a tragic love story called *Waterloo Bridge*, about a doomed affair between a sex worker and a British officer.

In 1931, Carl Laemmle Jr., son of the founder of Universal Studios, convinced his father to produce a film version of the classic work by Mary Shelley, *Frankenstein*. Oddly, given the success of the studio's war-era films, the elder Laemmle worried that the topic would prove "morbid" and that "people don't want that sort of thing."

"Pop," the son wearily assured his father, "they do want that sort of thing."

Having convinced his father of the money to be made in the horror business, the younger Laemmle asked James Whale to direct the project.

He proved the perfect choice.

Horror did not suddenly spring to unnatural life in the years after 1918. The folktales of Europe and early America were filled with monsters of the forest and frontier. Mary Shelley and Bram Stoker imagined Frankenstein's Monster and Dracula—the two faces of death that historian of horror David J. Skal called "the dark twins" whose stories haunt us still—in the nineteenth century. Not even cinematic horror began with the Great War, although the sheer weight of diabolical celluloid unleashed on the world after 1918 makes it seem as if it did.

However, something did change after Ypres, Gallipoli, the Somme, and Verdun. On a geopolitical scale, the world would not suddenly be set right: the "war to end all wars" ignited a round of conflict that became increasingly savage and that was part of the path to what we now call World War II. The victorious Allies' efforts to restructure the world created the framework for enduring conflict. Fascism's iron tread; the unremitting violence across Europe, Africa, Asia, and Latin America between 1918 and 1939; the Cold War; the Vietnam War; the Arab-Israeli conflict; and modern terrorism rooted in a revolt against Western modernity and imperialism all began with the efforts among the Great War victors to make the most of the spoils.

After 1914, the world changed, and so what frightened us changed. Horror became our most fundamental approach to the world. Too much death and suffering, on a scale unimagined before, unhinged us. The piles of bodies, an entire generation wiped out, could not be forgotten. Much of the entertainments we consume—romantic comedies, action flicks, reality shows, and superhero franchises—are efforts to hide from these realities. Horror, even in its most escapist mode, brings us to the edges of the last century's wastelands.

The malignant, festering wound of the Great War holds our attention still. Like a series of images in a nightmare detached from sensibility and chronology, the smoke, mud, blood, and dismembered bodies of the trenches flicker behind the images in our films, the color and tone of our art, and the need to read books that unsettle us deep into the night. The horror that has come to nest in the center of our culture grew out of this history. It's a horror that paralyzes us like a night terror even as it has become part of a multibillion-dollar entertainment industry.

The corpses in the wasteland of past and present haunt us. We are still in Eliot's land of the dead, imprisoned in Kafka's penal colony, running from the unexplained rage of the golem, listening to Lovecraft's drumbeat of horror, and shivering in the chilly shadow of Grau and Murnau's Nosferatu. We cannot awaken from history.

Chapter Two

Waxworks

Well might the Dead who struggled in the slime
Rise and deride this sepulchre of crime.

—SIEGFRIED SASSOON,
"On Passing the New Menin Gate" (1928)

Marching Corpses

Death offers the only way out of the clutches of history. But what happens if
the corpse returns? What if bodies behave in ways that violate physical laws?
What if they come to avenge themselves on the living?

French director Abel Gance began filming the silent movie *J'accuse* (*I
Accuse*) even before the armistice of 1918. In the late summer of the war's final
year, after the slaughter of the German spring offensives, Gance gathered
two thousand French soldiers on leave to shoot the penultimate scene. Most
of these infantrymen had recently manned the fortifications near Verdun,
where, for nine months in 1916, French and German forces fought continuously over the four-hundred-year-old fortress city with little effect other
than almost 800,000 casualties. Close to 1 million soldiers died for this salient on the western front during the course of the Great War.[1]

A 1938 remake of the film opened with stock footage from the French War
Department intercut into images of a small group of soldiers that includes the

protagonist, poet Jean Diaz, crawling through the rubble as shells rain down on them. A dove floats in a putrid pool of water, and when the camera pulls back, we see that a shell has struck a large stone crucifix. Christ's corpse now hangs upside down as the soldiers move past, one of them seeking to save the dead dove to eat later. Although the action and the tinting of the film suggest daytime, shadows crush the world under heavy darkness. Trees reach toward an empty sky like gnarled hands. In scenes that are supposed to take place out in the open, we feel we are in a collapsed trench dugout.

Gance had ventured to make the first and most explicit effort to connect the story of war to the emergence of horror. His intention becomes clear at the film's end when the dead rise and shamble toward a French village inhabited by civilians who in the filmmaker's imagination had been unaware of the sacrifices their men had made at the front. The soldiers come out of the ground to accuse the villagers and return to their graves only when the terrified villagers accept the accusation, or at least understand what the men of France have suffered. Like many films that dealt with war in this era, the violence prosecuted against noncombatants remained unexamined, unseen, or, in the case of *J'accuse*, a source of terrible irony.

The soldiers who acted out their own tragedy in Gance's epic, many of them fresh enough from the carnage that they could display their bandaged wounds, did not know they would become part of the most memorable scene of the first horror film of the postwar world. Neither they nor their director knew that the vast majority of these walk-on actors would return to the front to die in the final three months of the war.

J'accuse, in both its iterations, represented something of a confused mixture of the thematic elements from Great War horror and romance. Melodrama plays out against the backdrop of combat when the character of François Laurin eagerly enlists in 1914 but worries, with good reason, that his wife, Edith, will not remain faithful in his absence. She is, in fact, already having a love affair with the young poet Jean. Before he joins the French army, François sends Edith away to live under the watchful eyes of his parents. This fateful decision leads to her capture by the enemy, with the clear suggestion that the German soldiers rape her. The violence Edith suffers reflected the reality of the war for millions of noncombatants and so, paradoxically, appears in a film that accuses civilians of not understanding the soldiers' plight. Battered and abused, Edith returns to her village with a daughter born from the assault.

The misogynistic elements of the film not only include the perennial obsession over feminine betrayal but also draw on specific worries about control over women's sexuality during the war years. An entire genre developed around the fear that women on the homefront would not remain faithful. Paul Leni, soon to become one of the great horror filmmakers, directed the 1921 German silent film *Hintertreppe* (*Backstairs*), which featured a veteran, believed dead, returning home and killing the man his fiancée has fallen in love with, mutilating him with an ax. When the young woman discovers what has happened, she commits suicide.[2]

In *Drums in the Night* (1922), German playwright Bertolt Brecht tells a similar tale with a very different conclusion, one much influenced by Brecht's emerging Marxism. The play features a lover traumatized by the war and by the discovery of his beloved's homefront engagement to a wealthy war profiteer, with little distinction made between the horrors of each experience. The wronged veteran makes what's presented to theatergoers as the saintly decision to forgive his affianced even though it's questionable whether she needs his forgiveness, given that he's been missing for four years and her family pressed her into the engagement. The two are reunited but only amid the blood and flames of the Spartacist uprising, Germany's failed 1919 socialist revolution.

J'accuse perhaps helped create this particular kind of homefront drama, though anxieties already felt by men during the war provided a major impetus. Gance's film tries to salve men's worries in a peculiar way. In the first act of the 1919 version, we see the development of what's known in popular American flicks today as a "bromance" between François and Jean after both men serve together in the trenches. Jean tells his friend they are fighting a kind of "duel," but it's with fate and not with each other. François demands to know whether Jean loves his wife. He receives Jean's heartfelt confession by replying that he hopes his own death will allow Jean and Edith to find happiness. Bizarrely, the moment when the two men confess their mutual love for Edith may represent the most romantic moment in the film. The scene reads as if they are revealing their love for each other, and subsequent events reveal that this is more or less what they are doing.

The bond between the two men prepares the way for the tragedy, and the supernatural element, of *J'accuse*. A German shell mortally wounds François. Jean returns to his village, insane with grief, and alternately reads from and tears up his poetry while calling forth the dead of all nations. Some critics have written that Gance portrays Jean's trauma in a kind of hallucinatory vision, and this can be seen in the 1919 version. The 1938 film, however, suggests a terrifying suspension of the laws of nature. The corpses of French and German soldiers rise from their graves and begin to march home.

Gance's assistant director in the original version of the film, the poet Blaise Cendrars, appeared as one of the mutilated living dead. Cendrars, who had been part of the opening wave of modernist poetry before the war, fought on the Somme from late 1914 to February 1915. During the fighting at Champagne in the fall of 1914, he had been badly wounded and lost his right arm. In one of his most famous poems, "The War in the Luxembourg" (1916), he writes of young children in Paris's Luxembourg Gardens digging trenches in their sandboxes and asking for the latest newspaper instead of the fantastic stories of Jules Verne. In *J'accuse* he helped bring together the fantastic and the horrific in a way few had ever done before.

The corpses that come from the ground are in various states of decay. Images of the army of the dead are intercut with scenes of mass panic as people flee. Viewers today, particularly of the 1938 version, might be startled by how much these scenes resemble the apocalyptic situation of the contemporary zombie film that, at the beginning, almost always shows us a montage of mass panic, images that signal society's breakdown. Gance gives us just such an image of a society in free fall during 1919.

Gance did not really know what to do with the dramatic idea of a zombie army coming forth to the horror of the living. He showed the gored veterans rising and marching and then returning to their graves. Nevertheless, we learn much from *J'accuse* about the meaning of the Great War and its influence on horror. It represents the first moment that a director considered the possibility that the return of the dead could become an act of social criticism.

The theme of the living dead as a plague that forces human survivors to reimagine their world has become central to the contemporary zombie genre, so much so that social satire seems notable in its absence. This trope has become a staple of modern horror cinema, with George A. Romero's

Night of the Living Dead (1968) and the rest of his oeuvre often being copied. Most films that have attempted to deal with zombies in serious fashion (I obviously do not speak of the 2008 *Zombie Strippers* and the other efforts to cash in on America's most popular early-twenty-first-century monster) developed an essentially formulaic set of rules for dealing with the zombie apocalypse.

This paradigm for survival, in post-9/11 America, has resulted in an ideologically confusing set of zombie fantasies. The template for dealing with the undead became such a deeply ingrained part of modern American horror culture that Max Brooks's parody manual, *The Zombie Survival Guide* (2003), became a bestseller. Brooks followed up with *World War Z: An Oral History of the Zombie War* (2006), which models itself on both Studs Terkel's *"The Good War": An Oral History of World War II* (1984) and a variety of post–Vietnam War memoirs.

The success of Brooks's work seems to echo the original effort by Gance to connect the suddenly living dead to the realities of war. Romero's film appeared just months after the 1968 Tet offensive—a major campaign of the Vietnam War—and featured a cemetery covered with commemorative flags in the year that American troop totals in Vietnam reached their highest levels and causalities mounted.

The popularity of Brooks's zombie fictions burgeoned after the 2003 invasion of Iraq. In an odd twist, Brooks became a frequent and popular speaker at conferences of military leaders. According to journalist Spencer Ackerman, Brooks became "a cult hero" in the American military. Ackerman added, "I've found his books on practically every forward operating base I've been on in Iraq and Afghanistan."[3]

Gance's shot of soldiers clawing their way out of their own graves remains a grainy negative image lurking behind many films of the post-9/11 era. Romero's 2005 *Land of the Dead*, his finest work since *Day of the Dead*, offered audiences a great film and a thinly veiled allegory of both the growing divide of class inequality in America and the George W. Bush administration at war. In Romero's film, human survivors have come under the limited protection of the walls built around luxury condominiums called Fiddler's Green. However, only a tiny number of the living, all wealthy and white, are allowed to live in the high-rise, which includes a mall, restaurants, and various entertainments that make the apocalypse seem far away. The rest are relegated to a kind of "slum city," where most, though not all, are black or Latino.

Romero himself said that Bush's secretary of defense, Donald Rumsfeld, served as a model for his chief villain, Kaufman (played by Dennis Hopper). Indeed, Kaufman wages war against the zombies outside the walls not because they threaten Fiddler's Green, but because he needs a distraction while providing the wealthy on whom his power depends various consumer goods collected by the raiding parties made up of desperate tent-city dwellers. Blowback comes in the form of a zombie proletarian army that marches on Fiddler's Green. The zombies have learned, under the guidance of a self-aware zombie revolutionary leader, to use weapons and work together.[4]

No such critique of the prevailing economic order appears in *J'accuse*, although many on the left during the Great War and later took note of the vast profits reaped by the owners of heavy industry in Europe and America. Gance was slightly influenced by French socialism at a time when socialist movements in Europe appeared to be nearing a moment they could challenge the capitalist order. The war decisively changed the socialists' stance, with much of the leadership of the left joining the nationalist fervor that accompanied the beginning of the war. Gance's limited interest in such matters blunted his interest in the revolutionary possibilities of his corpses on the march.

Romero's films, in contrast, are examples of how later efforts to resurrect a zombie army onscreen contained a more forceful social critique. But *J'accuse* became the first tentative march of the mutilated demanding justice. Famed horror director Joe Dante appears to have been directly influenced by Gance's film in his 2005 feature *Homecoming* (made for Showtime's *Masters of Horror* series). In Dante's harrowing tale, a Republican president leads the nation in an unnamed but divisive war in the Middle East. During the election, one of his speechwriters tells a grieving mother, "Believe me, if I had one wish, I would wish for your son to come back because I know that he would tell us how important this struggle is." The president (with a personality equal parts Bill Clinton and George W. Bush) begins using this line as part of his boilerplate campaign speech.

The president gets his wish in the fashion of "The Monkey's Paw." The war dead rise and march to vote "for anyone who ends this war," as one of their grave-choked voices explains. The undead soldiers do not want human flesh or the thanks of a grateful nation. They simply want a useless war to end.

Abel Gance's rising undead army—an extraordinary idea in 1919—conveys a message that contains more ambiguity than the often on-the-nose zombie allegories made during the early twentieth century's "war on terror." In fact, it's possible to view *J'accuse*, particularly the 1919 version, as a parable about how the people of France did not support the war enough, as the walking-dead veterans simply return to their graves after they are satisfied that their sacrifice has been properly honored. The film's theme of marital infidelity, that inescapable trope in the cinema of the Great War, became a symbol for the larger question of whether the nation had been faithful to the cause of its soldiers. The dead came back to make sure they had.

At the same time, the film's willingness to confront the viewer with the war dead remained open to other interpretations in exhausted Europe. By 1938, Gance's message had become, whether he admitted it or not, a clear warning. The director told an interviewer that he had no interest in politics, but he added, "I am against war because war is futile. Ten or twenty years afterward, one reflects that millions have died and all for nothing."[5]

J'accuse barely found an audience in the United States. Viewers, and at first even American distributors, seemed convinced that the film carried a clear pacifist message. Pioneering director D. W. Griffith took a liking to the film and ensured that it received distribution through United Artists. Its bleak message found little reception in a nation eager to put the war behind it. The American public had no desire to think of a living corpse, and certainly not an army of angry corpses, or the questions such a fever dream posed.

Are You Caligari or Cesare?

The murderous folly of the Great War had chilled western Europe to the bone, and the new, gruesome entertainment of the horror film became neither escape nor catharsis but rather a repetition of trauma. Telling these stories sometimes had the effect of ripping the scab from the wound so that it never became healthy, or grieving until grief became an end in itself. At times, the stories included social criticism. In all cases, the horror film included a long, angry procession of unquiet corpses.

Not everyone would agree, or at least believe, that horror films carry so much weight. "You are reading too much into the movies" is a fairly common response to such claims. "They're just entertainment." This idea of course has its own history and, paradoxically, it begins with a writer who thought that the films made after the Great War did contain coded messages about the era. He saw in them a dangerous message that explained the path from Germany's defeat in 1918 to its resurgence as a threatening power twenty years later.

Siegfried Kracauer left Germany in 1933, emigrating to Paris the same year that Adolf Hitler became the German chancellor. After the beginning of World War II and the invasion of France, he fled for the Spanish border with the renegade essayist Walter Benjamin in the summer of 1940. Unlike Benjamin, however, Kracauer found a way to make it to the United States, where a Rockefeller Fellowship awaited him in the spring of 1941, thanks to his fellow exile the philosopher Max Horkheimer. New York City's Museum of Modern Art offered Kracauer a position that involved studying the German films made between 1918 and 1933, a task he hoped might yield some clue as to what had become of his homeland.

The book he produced in 1947, *From Caligari to Hitler: A Psychological History of the German Film*, has had an enormous influence on film criticism. Perhaps more important, it's had a deep influence on the way the average person thinks about movies, even if they've never heard of the admittedly obscure source of their ideas. Of course, the book's pugilistic title made it clear that scholars and audiences alike could not view film as simple entertainment. Movies carried political import, not simply reflecting the times but also embodying the horror of the times. Overall, the book denigrates film, and filmgoers, in such a way that it lends credence to the ideas that entertainment means industry rather than art and that all film represents an escape from reality. A critic influenced by such views today might say, for example, that the offbeat comedy *Mall Cop* (2005) is not much different from François Truffaut's drama *The 400 Blows* (1959), while the complex television crime drama *The Wire* and the tacky reality show *Celebrity Apprentice* exist in a continuum of mindless satisfaction. It's a dour view of popular culture that many fans paradoxically hold when they demand that films "leave out the politics" or say that they "just want a good show."

Like a movie fan who might be a little suspicious of "reading too much" into film, Kracauer spoke of films as a commodity, primarily a means to make money. The movies, he believed, are just entertainment and so they are simply mirror images of the culture that produced them, flexible and flaccid in the messages they convey. He did not think that this made them, as his friend Walter Benjamin believed, possible instruments of revolutionary change. Instead, as artifacts of mass culture, they put dissent to sleep, enervated their audiences, and legitimized the existing order. Had he lived in our era, he would have seen in the phrase "Netflix and chill" the bottomless swamp of this cultural morass.

Films that appeared in Germany between 1918 and 1933 had, Kracauer insisted, "deep psychological dispositions" that led the German people to "surrender to the Nazis." He seeks to account for Hitler's success in terms beyond politics, economic collapse, and the general structural weaknesses of the Weimar regime. No, something more terrible had been lurking in the shadows, a set of motifs finding expression in the dream life of film, or really the nightmare life of film. Antonio Gramsci had been right: in the ruins of the Old World, "morbid symptoms" had appeared. The people of the Great War's aftermath found themselves in the time of monsters, and the monsters filled their screens. This had desensitized them to the real monsters that emerged among them.[6]

Kracauer began his survey with *The Cabinet of Dr. Caligari* (1920), frequently if incorrectly called the first horror film. It's still a good place for Kracauer, and us, to begin since it staged many of the themes that would obsess the genre in the early years. The human body as an empty husk, a figure who combines the mad scientist and the magician, and even the city as a nightmarish wasteland all appear in the film. *Caligari* garnered more than its share of critical attention in Germany and abroad. In some intellectual circles, the French term *Caligarisme* came to stand in for the sense of loss, doubt, and existential desperation of the postwar generation.

The larger public responded to *Caligari* only in a limited degree. The movie's confusing advertising campaign may have been partially to blame. The slogan used on posters—"You must become Caligari!"—repurposed a line from the film, but no one knew what this could mean. The film did not carry the same shock value as the later *Nosferatu*, and word seems to have gotten around that the ending had been a bit of a letdown. Director Robert Wiene's decision to conclude the film as he did offers something of a tale within itself.

The film version of *Caligari* opens with a framing story absent from the original script. We see the character of Francis sitting on a bench in what seems to be a hospital. An old man sitting beside him, perhaps another patient, has been babbling about "the terrible fate of all life." Jane, the film's female lead, walks by as in a trance. "What she and I have experienced is yet more remarkable than the story you have told me," Francis says to the old man. Francis's response comes across as a rather confusing non sequitur that might have tipped off a vigilant cinemagoer that something was a bit off. The old man has been talking about the nature of life, not telling Francis a story.

Following this prologue, we see a wizened Dr. Caligari attempting to receive a permit for his hypnotist act in an imaginary German town called Holstenwall. The town official refuses and ends up the first murder victim in a film soon filled with corpses.

But even before the killings begin, the set itself erupts into a violent, surrealist nightmare. Buildings hang at impossible angles, and rooms tilt in dizzying fashion. In this dreary dreamscape two young students, Alan and Francis, become the focus of the narrative. They attend the town fair, where it becomes clear that both are in love with Jane. Joined by her, they visit the tent of Dr. Caligari. A peculiar kind of séance takes place in which Caligari takes questions from the audience and poses them to the allegedly sleeping Cesare; he's waxen in heavy pancake makeup, lost in a shadowy haze between devilish puppet and living corpse. In this state, Cesare supposedly brings messages from the land of the dead at Caligari's command. Alan asks when he will die, and Cesare replies, "Before dawn." Police later find the young student stabbed to death, just as the town official had been.

Francis becomes convinced that Caligari ordered the zombie-like Cesare to kill for him. While he searches for proof, Jane becomes the next target of Caligari's murderous homunculus. Although Cesare pulls a knife to slay her, he instead kidnaps her and, in one of the most famous sequences in the film, leads Francis and Jane's father on a chase through the night terror of the set.

The police join Francis in investigating Caligari, who escapes into an insane asylum. Wiene chooses to close the cinematic version with the device of having Francis revealed as a patient in the very asylum where he believes he has tracked Caligari. Dr. Caligari is, in fact, the lead physician and director of the asylum, where Francis lives out his delusions, and we learn that the film we have just watched has simply been a trip through Francis's madness.

The screenwriters, Hans Janowitz and Carl Mayer, had a very different vision of *Caligari*, one that would have made its subtext clearer to audiences, perhaps too obvious in the eyes of the director. The original story had been born one night before 1914 and, during the war, had ripened into a terrifying vision meant to condemn the willingness of the masses, not to "become Caligari," as the confusing advertising poster said, but to become Cesare. The zombie-like Cesare, and the people of Germany, had been somnambulists under the control of their own Caligaris in epaulets during the previous decade.

On that strange night, Janowitz, a Czech poet living in Hamburg before the beginning of the war, had seen an interesting young woman and followed her to a Hamburg town fair in 1913. Losing her among the festive multicolored tents that spread across the Reeperbahn, still today the center of nightlife and entertainment in the city, Janowitz heard what sounded to his probably inebriated ears like ephemeral, ghostly laughter in the trees. But from the bushes emerged the shadow of a man, suddenly looming up in the darkness and just as quickly fading back into it. In the eyes of the poetic Janowitz, the darkness seemed to reabsorb the phantom. He returned home, never having seen his love interest.

The next morning, the local news reported that someone murdered a young woman named Gertrude at the town fair the previous night. The press described what had happened to her as "a horrible sex crime." Although he had no foundation outside his own imagination, Janowitz became obsessed with the idea that the beautiful young woman he had hoped to meet had been the victim. His fixation on this notion became so intense that he attended the funeral, where, again with little real evidence, he believed he saw the shadow from the foliage. His nightmares told him this had been the shape that murdered Gertrude.[7]

Janowitz's murderous shadow in the night later became Cesare, but only after four years of war. Janowitz served as an infantry officer for most of the conflict and emerged a confirmed pacifist. The war then helped him mold his peculiar experience from 1913 into a tale of horror.

Carl Mayer, who shared Janowitz's antiwar sentiment, collaborated on the project. Mayer himself had worked to convince an army psychiatrist that he was unfit to fight. His brother, however, had died in the infantry. Around the time he began his collaboration with Janowitz, Mayer had fallen in love with the actor Gilda Langer, herself mourning the loss of a fiancé on the western front.

The framing story Wiene added to the film dissolved the tale into a dream and robbed it of its piercing metaphorical power. In the original script, Caligari and the director of the local asylum are indeed the same person, but Caligari actually has been committing crimes through the agency of Cesare, a corpse brought back from the netherworld by its master. When Francis confronts Caligari with these facts, his mask of sanity slips away and the film concludes with the doctor a patient in his own asylum.

Janowitz and Mayer had, Kracauer claimed, sought to communicate their vision of German society's obsession with authoritarianism with the film, the two confirmed pacifists revealing in Caligari's control over Cesare the willingness of the German people to follow their leaders, as if hypnotized, into the maelstrom of war. They had been sleepwalkers who went about their deadly business unconscious of the consequences. Authoritarian leaders turned citizens, marching in lockstep, into somnolent killers.[8]

The film critic Kracauer believed that the beginnings of the German film industry had chewed up the screenwriters' original vision and turned *Caligari* into a product that reaffirmed the audience's desire to accept and never question authority. The fearful possibilities of loss of control, the image of the lumbering Cesare moving murderously through the night on Dr. Caligari's errands, did chill the first viewers of the film. But, Kracauer insisted, the ending reaffirmed the need of the masses for the control of strong leadership. Social authorities might sometimes appear like villains, but in reality the masses are much more likely to suffer a fever dream, a delusion of overweening power, than to truly confront a mad Caligari who could bend them to his will.

In fact, although the writers did not get what they wanted in the film, the message they hoped to send may have been simpler—a message about their own obsession with the idea of the corpse and *das grosse Sterben*.

The film sets, already bizarre, would have been even more surreal if Janowitz and Mayer had had their way. They had hoped to hire Czech engraver, artist, and author Alfred Kubin to design their wasteland and their living corpses. Kubin's work matched well the aesthetic that the authors hoped to achieve, given his fascination with mechanical puppets and his ability to reimagine the narrow, dreamlike streets of Prague as a fantastical landscape. Kubin had written a strange, semiautobiographical fantasy novel, *The Other Side* (1909), of which Lotte Eisner writes:

> He describes his wandering through the dark streets [of Prague], possessed
> by an obscure force which led him to imagine weird houses and landscapes,
> terrifying or grotesque situations. When he entered a little tea-shop, every-
> thing seemed bizarre. The waitresses were like wax dolls moved by some
> strange mechanism.[9]

Kubin's obsessions with landscapes of horror and waxen death dolls suited the era's terror of the corpse and the battlefield, as well as the tendency of both realities to transform waking life into a dream.

In 1920, Weimar Germany looked back on its brief flirtation with revolution one year earlier. Though few in the middle class voiced the sentiment openly, many felt some gratitude for the brutal tactics of the right-wing *Freikorps*. Perhaps the nation had not become a social democracy and indeed barely held on to the democratic reforms it had managed since 1918. But at least the Germans had kept the Bolsheviks from the door and the authorities ruled with a firm hand. Had they become Caligari? In fact, they had become Cesare.

Kracauer had been certain that *The Cabinet of Dr. Caligari* predicted both the rise of the authoritarian personality and how the forces of fascism would seize hold of this pathology for its own ends. Just as the continent had become a sleepwalking murderer in 1914, it continued to act as a death

doll in a world of fantasy and nightmare, answering the call of the authoritative voice. The people of Germany, he thought, had been willing to see
themselves and others locked away in a madman's cabinet or in an asylum as
madmen themselves. All for their own safety.

From his vantage point, Kracauer had more than enough reason to voice
suspicion about German film. His tendency to see authoritarianism everywhere, while understandable, doesn't account for the Caligari screenwriters'
own obsessions, centered more on the murderous automaton Cesare than on
the question of authoritarianism. Death itself and the reanimated corpse are
at the center of their vision of the film and the version seen by audiences.
Neither man could leave behind the Great War. Rather than predicting Nazism, they told the story of the great death.

The Dark Carnival

Kracauer had surprisingly little to say about the popular *Nosferatu* despite his
thoughtful discussion of director F. W. Murnau's work as a whole. He did
write that Murnau had "the unique facility of obliterating the boundaries of
the real and the unreal," a comment that resonates with the film's relationship to the Great War in which, many soldiers claimed, reality and fantasy
blended under the constant strain of shelling and the debilitating anxiety of
the trenches. However, for Kracauer, the dread shadow of Count Orlok hovers over the period after 1919 in a different, almost mystical way. He refers
to the 1920s as a time when "the German soul" found itself "tossed about in
gloomy space like the phantom ship in *Nosferatu*."[10]

Kracauer's political orientation may explain his lack of interest in writing about the first vampire film. By 1930, he had read much of the work of
Karl Marx. This led him that year to write a frighteningly prescient book,
The Salaried Masses, in which he claimed that Germany's new white-collar
workers would prove especially susceptible to Nazism. History, unfortunately, bears out his thesis. Lower-middle-class white-collar workers joined
in an unlikely alliance with the wealthiest industrialists to become the back-
bone of Germany's Nazi Party.

Much of the German left saw *Nosferatu* as precisely the kind of entertainment that desensitized the people to political concerns. Socialist critics of the film complained vociferously about moviegoers taking *Nosferatu* seriously, even as they couldn't themselves avoid discussing it at length. The leftist *Leipziger Volkszeitung* (Leipzig People's Newspaper), for example, insisted that the film distracted the working class by enshrouding them in a "supernatural fog." In fact, the paper saw it as part of a larger effort by the ruling class to keep the people "sufficiently stupid for capitalist interests."[11]

Marxist worries about the popularity of such films may appear overwrought today. We'd do well to remember that these critics wrote in revolutionary times, when hundreds of millions of people had been either utterly terrified or passionately inspired by the 1917 people's revolution in Russia that, ever so briefly, looked like it might spread across all of Europe after the climactic end of the Great War. In the early 1920s, a turn from revolutionary fervor to fantasy in German entertainment seemed to them to mark the final collapse of their hopes, particularly after the bloody failure of the Communist uprisings that followed the war.

Moreover, the Marxist criticism did not simply focus on a single popular film that had seized the public imagination. The workers, the *Leipziger Volkszeitung* claimed, faced what amounted to "a supernatural epidemic" in the world of entertainment. The paper argued that the new taste for horror represented a new kind of capitalist propaganda and that the proletariat would do well to stay at home rather than give their money to the film industry "and the phantom Nosferatu can well let himself be devoured by their own rats."

Notably, even those who castigated the film for its allegedly lurid and escapist nature could not help but see it as intimately tied to the bloodletting the world had recently inflicted on itself. Marxist critics admitted that "this dangerous nonsense about spiritualism and the occult" had been eagerly consumed by "millions of disturbed souls" victimized by the war and its consequences.

Kracauer and his fellow leftists would feel right at home among today's film critics. The horror genre continues to receive criticism as an adolescent pastime, nihilistic in its premises with limited expectations of its own audience. Even in the golden age of Universal Studios monster movies, critical reviews of horror films tended to use the opportunity to dismiss them with a bit of snark. *The Hollywood Reporter* in November 1931 couldn't help but praise the direction of James Whale in *Frankenstein*. The reviewer also couldn't bring himself to write with unadulterated praise of a "spook" film. He opined that Universal Studios had either "the greatest shocker of all time—or a dud."[12]

More recently, Robert Perrucci and Earl Wysong, in their book *The New Class Society: Goodbye American Dream?* (1999), described horror, along with action films, as one of the perennial "escapist genres." Carol Clover—who wrote an entire book asking second-wave feminism to think in more complicated fashion about slasher films (*Men, Women, and Chainsaws: Gender in the Modern Horror Film*, 1992)—agreed with famed film critic Robin Wood that horror films are inherently disreputable.

The allegedly escapist and formulaic quality of horror continues to attract fans in droves—and still elicits attention and exegesis from intellectuals. Hundreds of think pieces on the zombie phenomenon alone are currently in existence. All essentially ask what it means that zombies have become a national obsession over the last several decades and particularly since 9/11.

Nosferatu rose suddenly from his crypt in the years after the Great War to the same kind of questioning and criticism. Why do people care about these horrible things? Why do they need them? Even the harshest critics of what Murnau and Grau had wrought felt compelled to talk about the new craze for the supernatural in relation to the Great War, at that time the most catastrophic event in terms of the loss and degradation of human life that anyone could begin to imagine.

Perhaps rather than Kracauer's claim that it offered an escape from history, the horror film allowed (and still allows) audiences to talk about trauma in an oblique way? The power of horror that allowed for the expression of the darkest of shell-shocked impulses certainly proved irresistible for the talents of the avant-garde after 1918. The painter turned director Paul Leni produced a horror fantasy film entitled *Waxworks* in 1924, a prologue to the nightmares he soon helped bring into the world. His vision began in Weimar Germany but ended up, and ended too soon, in Los Angeles.

Leni's *Waxworks* continued the themes of *Caligari* by reintroducing the terror of the reanimated corpse, the husk brought to life to live out a terrible past in the present. He produced the film in the aftermath of the Nazi Party's failed Beer Hall Putsch. In fact, the film screened in Germany while Hitler, imprisoned for only nine months for his part in the attempted overthrow of the Weimar government, feverishly mapped out the sadistic fantasies he planned to unleash on the world in what became *Mein Kampf.* The dreamy atmosphere of *Waxworks* echoed both the morbid half-light of 1914–1918 and seemed to forecast the things that had slithered into history with the rise of fascism.

Henrik Galeen, screenwriter for both Paul Wegener's first (and now lost) golem film in 1914 and *Nosferatu*, also wrote the screenplay for *Waxworks*. The film opens in a carnival, a space for frivolous amusement that had increasingly begun to take on dark undertones. During much of the nineteenth century, the traveling circus placed "freaks" on display in the sideshow, a series of tents that ran along the side of the big top, which housed the three-ring circus. At one time, such entertainments had a certain degree of middle-class respectability conferred by the reputation and popularity of nineteenth-century American showman P. T. Barnum. Barnum saw his work as educational and even scientific. He had, for example, included temperance lectures as part of the program at the famous Barnum's American Museum, at the corner of Broadway and Ann Street in New York City, giving his entertainments the strongest of bourgeois credentials.

By the beginning of the twentieth century, the traveling carnival had begun to fall into disrepute. Medical authorities began to question the representation of human oddities as entertainment. This criticism emerged less from physicians' humanitarian impulses than from the professionalization of their own discipline. A new generation of doctors saw human abnormalities as part of their own bailiwick rather than a source of entertainment.

Increasingly, the respectable classes viewed the sideshow as a working-class entertainment run by dangerous, socially marginal carnival workers (carnies). Films such as *Caligari* sealed the deal, preparing the way for the fully embodied "dark carnival" of Tod Browning's *Freaks* (1932), the threat-laden atmosphere of the traveling show in Alfred Hitchcock's *Strangers on a Train* (1951), and Ray Bradbury's 1962 novel *Something Wicked This Way Comes*. Today, and it's difficult to explain without this background, many people still find the sound of carnival music eerie and suggestive of something dreadful.

Leni's carnival is, like Robert Wiene's in *Caligari,* a nightmare dimension in which a young poet in this age of disillusioned poets takes a job from a showman. The poet will work in service of the dark carnival, writing narratives for each of the empty-eyed figures in the showman's wax museum. In the cavernous tent the waxworks begin to move and act out the dreamlike tales of horror the poet imagines. These dark imaginings revolve around tyrants inflicting torture, and in the final sequence the writer imagines himself and his love interest, the showman's daughter, chased by a waxen but suddenly living Jack the Ripper. The line between the poet's imagination and what's really happening onscreen remains fuzzy, as does the boundary between a shell-shocked generation's experience of watching the film and their history.

Kracauer viewed *Waxworks* as yet more evidence of the German tendency toward authoritarianism. He found in the film "the collective German soul" that had long been "wavering between tyranny and chaos." Citing a number of other examples of tyrannical personalities portrayed on film in the era, he saw the cinematic obsession with these figures as part of the fascist sensibility that placed Mussolini in power in Italy and created similar powerful political movements in much of Europe, most prominently, of course, in the rise of National Socialism in Germany.[13]

Doubtless these films did express European anxieties about an entire nation's willingness to follow political and military leaders into the maelstrom of war. Certainly veterans had reason to question why they had, again and again, gone over the top of the trenches into the blasted lunar landscape of no-man's-land at the sound of a whistle, losing arms, legs, and blood while leaving the corpses of their comrades behind.

But Kracauer presses this interpretation of early horror, and of German film in general, too far. There's not enough evidence, for example, that the world understood that their somnambulist obedience had helped produce the outrages of the Great War. The true terror for this generation remained the terror of the dead, most specifically the terror of lifeless corpses hanging cruciform in barbed wire, lying shattered across hundreds of fields of fire, or filling the rat-infested trenches and floating, bloated and purpling, while the rain fell in torrents. Implicit in films like *Caligari* and *Waxworks*, and explicit in *J'accuse* and *Nosferatu*, the loss of the dead combined with the inability to properly and fully mourn and forget them, lurked in the shadows on the screen.

We can see this sensibility in Leni's choice of uncanny terrors. The waxwork had a long history by the 1920s in the genealogy of death, religion, science, and what we today call body horror. The marionette and the shadow play are images of terror with ancient roots in human religious beliefs. Creating an image of a thing living or dead has, from the earliest ages of human religious consciousness, endowed that image with the properties of the sacred. At the same time, the uncanny power of such images has led to warnings in Judaism, Protestant Christianity, and Islam about the dangers of "graven images," the worry over idolatry.

These strictures point toward the terror you feel when an image's empty eyes look back at you or when they *seem* to do so but cannot. In most monotheistic traditions, nervousness over the making of idols masks the deeper terrors of the empty image, the possibility that it can become inhabited by the horror of the world, demonic shadows filling a space meant for the divine. Perhaps even worse, human beings have feared that they contain a nullity, that behind their own eyes waits an utter nothingness. The idol, the image, the puppet, the automaton, and the homunculus might suddenly become the simulacrum of the corpse.

By the beginning of the Great War, emerging Western secularism, coming in fits and starts since the eighteenth century and always accompanied by feverish fundamentalist reassertions of belief, had taken the terror of the empty image into the realm of entertainment. In *The Secret Life of Puppets* (2001), Victoria Nelson describes this process perfectly when she notes how the Egyptian mummy of late antiquity transformed in twentieth-century horror films "from a divine body within an organized religious belief system to an organic demon." Nelson adds that what we are seeing in this process amounts to a full retreat from the concept of the human soul in the Western imagination.[14]

Creating the false body in wax has a history longer than film. Waxworks as a form stretches back before its appearance in traveling fairs and film. The fashioning of the wax image always had its grotesque side, with the Catholic Church's use of often unintentionally terrifying wax saints holding the alleged relics and remembrances of their own martyrdom: teeth, bones, even hearts. The making of images to work sympathetic magic, hexing people or freeing them from just such a curse, had a long history in the folk traditions of Europe. The making of so-called poppets in England existed long before the notion of the voodoo doll and may have contributed to it when Europeans came in contact with the Africans they enslaved in Haiti and the rest of the Caribbean. Whatever the origin, the magical practice shows a relationship in the human mind between the doll and the dead.

One did not have to believe in magic to make such a connection. Medical students throughout Europe had, for several centuries, used finely crafted wax figures for anatomical study. Modeled frequently as young and female, often designed so that on the outside they seemed like exquisitely beautiful women caught sleeping, the figures sometimes contained as many as seven anatomically correct layers that students could fold back to reveal the mysteries of the body. These began to appear in the Renaissance, but the eighteenth century became the golden age of what some called "anatomical Venuses" but that medical students more commonly called "slashed beauties" or "dissected Graces." The attention given to the modeling of perfectly formed breasts and hips, as well as delicate lips, eyes, and hair, make it impossible to ignore sexual fetishism as an element in their creation.[15]

A public passion for the wax figure continued to grow in the eighteenth century. Swiss physician Philippe Curtius, whose medical training prepared him for the modeling and sculpting of anatomically accurate figures, became the first entrepreneur of such shows in France. Although he began his exhibition at a fairground, his wax displays proved popular enough with all classes to allow him to open his tony Salon de Cire, which included his Caverne des Grande Voleurs, where he made use of fake blood to portray his scenes of crime and murder.

The depth of meaning that accrued to the figure in wax can be seen in the degree to which politics affected, and almost destroyed, Curtius's career. His assistant, Marie Grosholtz (1761–1850), better known by her married name and entertainment moniker, Madame Tussaud, modeled the severed heads of the guillotine's victims during the so-called Reign of Terror that followed the French Revolution. In Curtius's waxworks, models of the decapitated heads of Louis XVI and Marie-Antoinette shared the same display space with executed revolutionaries such as Robespierre and Marat.

Although the portrayal of beheaded political figures at first provoked surprisingly little partisan controversy, Curtius's wax figure of the Marquis de Lafayette almost lost him his business and his life. Lafayette had briefly been seen as a heroic figure in France until he led counterrevolutionary forces in 1792 and then fled to Austria. Public outcry led Curtius to offer a public apology to the National Convention for continuing to display his wax Lafayette and, in an act that showed the degree to which waxworks had come to incarnate the figures they represented, Curtius saved his own skin by publicly guillotining the waxen traitor outside the Salon.[16]

Madame Tussaud took over Curtius's operation after his death. The experiment in entertainment became an international phenomenon after the French Revolution. Tussaud moved her waxworks to England in 1802 and over the next half century transformed it into perhaps London's most popular entertainment, with many imitators in Victorian England and the United States. The British royal family in wax remained a perennial favorite, but so did the portrayal of crime, assassination, and torture. Customers passed through a candlelit labyrinth featuring blood-drenched crime scenes and the acts of tyrants, poisoners, and murderers as they left the attraction. *Punch* magazine first used the nomenclature Chamber of Horrors in 1846 for what Tussaud called The Adjourning Room.[17]

Although Tussaud herself died in 1850, the waxworks remained a popular attraction at the beginning of the Great War. In fact, during the first flames of war fever, Madame Tussaud's Wax Museum featured special displays of all the dynastic figures involved in the conflagration. Kaiser Wilhelm's wax image suffered so much abuse from angry crowds that it had to be removed, although it, too, would rejoin the other monarchs later in the war. War maps, shell fragments, and other relics of war joined the display. The museum's proprietors seemed to realize early that the war would provoke a taste for the macabre, a counterintuitive desire to remember the conflict, even by the returning veterans and soldiers on leave, who often thronged the attraction from 1914 to 1918.

France had its own Chamber of Horrors, which grew in popularity in the aftermath of the nation's tremendous losses in the Great War. The French public mourned without end, becoming especially expressive at mass burial sites such as Douaumont, a fortification at Verdun turned into an ossuary that contains the bits and pieces of perhaps 100,000 unidentifiable German and French corpses. The French also flocked to the Théâtre du Grand Guignol, which had opened in Paris in 1897 and presented criminal scenes, images of mental illness, and the macabre supernatural. Since the theater was located in a former convent, cherubic angels still peeked out of the shadows at the grotesqueries onstage.[18]

The earliest of what would become known as special effects played an essential role in the Grand Guignol, including staged monstrosities, gallons of fake blood, and highly believable bodily mutilations. The shadow play took a step beyond Tussaud's. Instead of waxworks, live actors became dead bodies, showing the audience that even if corpses had no souls, they had plenty of blood and entrails.

The Great War actually increased the French public's fascination with such gory spectacle. In fact, audiences demanded that the Grand Guignol make a more explicit connection with the war. The popularity of *J'accuse* alone suggests that they had some desire to contend with the death puppet, the eidolon of the Reaper.

Camille Choisy, who owned the Grand Guignol at the end of the war, proved happy to oblige this taste for horror. Even as France suffered millions of casualties, Choisy incorporated fake poison gas attacks and startling explosive charges that mimicked the shelling of the trenches. The use of surgical instruments, influenced by the horror stories of combat triage at the front, became instruments of torture and death in Choisy's productions. The popularity of the theater and its ghastly fare endured in France into the 1920s—an adaptation of *Caligari* played there in 1925.[19]

Tussaud's, meanwhile, began to lose its appeal in the early 1920s. Waxworks in general declined in popularity, as did the sideshow and the circus. Historians of popular entertainment have tended to see the rise of film as the undoing of these other entertainment forms. Although it's impossible to deny the influence of the new art form, it's also true that in the case of the waxworks, the scale of death in the Great War fully awakened the primordial terror of the corpse. Both the dead body and the waxwork made it difficult to imagine the possibility of an eternal soul.

Waxworks, and the unsettling questions they raised, seemed to incorporate all the eerie elements of the war's transformation of the human body into an icon of death and mutilation. They are inanimate bodies, shells with no ghost, blank except for the nightmares that the audience imposes on them. The waxworks guide audiences into the darkest of uncanny valleys, the dead eyes of the figures mirroring nothing. They are puppets that call our personhood into question in exactly the same way the corpse calls into question what we have convinced ourselves of concerning the possibilities of the afterlife.

German horror films dealt with this concept again and again with *Caligari*'s Cesare being only the most well-known corpse-puppet, standing in for the mounds of the lifeless created by shell and Maxim gun. But the horror of this idea, a horror that destroyed optimistic hopes for a human soul animating the fleshy pulp of the body, became the defining feature of postwar horror films. We see it in Nosferatu's ability to empty both Ellen and Knock, and Hutter himself, of their allegedly natural desires and fill their empty husks with desire for him. Indeed, the vampire glides through the world nearly incorporeal, fading to ethereal nothingness in the sunlight, as would be expected of one that comes from the land of phantoms. Ellen, in contrast, stays behind as a lifeless puppet, a figure of terror as well as grief.

Mummies and Dolls

We find the terror of the corpse in some unlikely places during and after the Great War. Ernst Lubitsch, born in Berlin in 1892, fled in the 1930s to America, where he made comedies such as *Ninotchka* (1939), starring Greta Garbo and famously advertised as the film in which "Garbo laughs!" In 1940, a year after his infant daughters somehow survived the sinking of the SS *Athenia* by a Nazi U-boat as they made their way to America, Lubitsch made the classic comedy *The Shop around the Corner* with Jimmy Stewart (remade in 1998 as the crowd-pleasing, maudlin *You've Got Mail*). Lubitsch made the world laugh in the midst of war and exile.

But even he did not escape the wartime obsession with the dead. Long before his exile in America, Lubitsch directed *The Eyes of the Mummy* in Oc-

tober 1918, when the death toll of the spring offensives was becoming known
on the home front and the German army teetered on the edge of collapse.
At the same time, civilian deaths in Germany mounted from the worldwide
influenza epidemic and the British blockade.

Lubitsch chose a strange tale to tell in the midst of chaos. He mixed
orientalism, exacerbated perhaps by the awareness of the fighting on the Ottoman front, with a story of violent passion, supernatural curses, and death.
Like other German movies in that era, it reflected the growing interest in
mesmerism, featuring an Egyptian woman named Ma who attempts un-
successfully to escape the hypnotic power of Radu, a vicious and mystically
powerful archetype of the "exotic" East. Ma also embodied the European's
sensualized notions of the colonial world. The character was played by Pola
Negri, an excellent Polish actress heavily sexualized in the silent era.

British archaeologist Howard Carter's account of the opening of Tut-
ankhamen's tomb in 1922 helped spark a widespread interest in mummies,
his 1924 lecture tour of the United States creating what has been called Egyp-
tomania. This would eventually result in Boris Karloff's classic turn as *The
Mummy* in 1932. However, German archaeologists had been robbing graves
in Egypt since the 1880s. Most famously, the representatives of a historical
museum in Berlin essentially cheated Egyptian authorities out of the famous
bust of Nefertiti on the eve of the Great War in 1913. Thus, a cultural fascination with the "oriental" world (a term that appears again and again in *Eyes
of the Mummy* in describing Egyptian customs) already had a long pedigree.

The film holds together surprisingly well today, despite being available
only in badly degraded prints with contemporary music that seeks to sound
like the lost orchestral setting used by Lubitsch. Negri's character, Ma, peeps
through an ancient aperture in the tomb of an Egyptian monarch, her gothic
double named, confusingly but appropriately, Queen Ma. Negri, as the "eyes
of the mummy," represents not only orientalist fantasy but also the primordial death doll. The audience, from Ma's first scene, must have watched the
film with near certainty that she would die. When Ma marries a German
painter, Radu's jealous rage causes him to so viciously sling a blade into a
portrait of her, yet another Gothic double, that the act feels like a murder.

Lubitsch continued to worry the idea of the death doll, even when working in a genre other than horror. His 1919 comedic fantasy film, *The Doll*,

keeps the darkness at bay, but only just barely, with a few laugh-out-loud moments. The film tells the story of a young German named Lancelot whose nervous disposition and sexual repression keep him from living up to his legendary namesake or indeed from agreeing to marry. We see Lancelot's terror of sex rather clearly in a scene that features him running from forty possible female suitors who have taken part in a Weimar-era *The Bachelor*–style contest arranged by his father.

When Lancelot seems to find an answer to his problem, the film begins to take on the surrealist quality of the era's horror culture. A group of monks (anxious to get part of his fortune) point Lancelot to a dollmaker, who builds lifelike female automata. Lancelot has the idea to substitute one of these dolls, built "primarily for bachelors" the film cagily tells us, for a human wife. Hijinks ensue, and Lubitsch takes the edge off the whole affair by playing up the romantic and farcical possibilities. (The "doll," whom Lancelot weds, is actually the dollmaker's real-life daughter.)

The Doll, however, cannot entirely escape its roots in the morbid imagination of the German Romantic writer E. T. A. Hoffmann, one of whose short stories provided the basis of the tale. Hoffmann's "The Sandman" (1816) had its character fall in love with an automaton and presumably have sex with it while disdaining his thoroughly human betrothed. The story had obsessed Freud and became part of the basis of his idea of the uncanny since it posed the question of what exactly constituted the difference between the mechanism of an automaton and the mechanism of flesh, blood, and organs. Lubitsch's *Doll* may have scored some laughs, but it had an uneasy relationship to an era that saw the human body pour out its entrails like so many scraps of clockwork.

Some of the comedy of *The Doll* works by what in central Europe, particularly in Czech culture, goes by the name of *smutný vtip*, roughly translated as "the sad joke." The dollmaker's apprentice, who looks ten years old, repeatedly attempts suicide by drinking paint and leaping out of windows. This plot point would not be a knee-slapper in the best of times but was certainly not one at a moment when Great War veterans committed suicide at an alarming rate. The automata themselves lead us into skin-crawling territory, particularly given the film's suggestion that they are created primarily to provide sex. Lubitsch, the comedy director, created a work that did not stray far from Hoffmann's shadowy imagination and indeed looks ahead to the uncanny, empty-eyed bodies that existed on the razor's edge of the living and the dead.

Germany's haunted screen surely deserves all the attention it can get in a study of why horror emerged after 1918. But the phenomenon also grew outside of Germany. Italian horror cinema, whose golden age most fans would rightly place in the 1960s and '70s with the works of Dario Argento, Mario Bava, and Lucio Fulci, also shows a fascination with the corpse and the questions it poses for the living. But this began in the years after the Great War and not with the blood, sex, and gore of Italy's infamous *giallo* (yellow) films. (The term referred to cheap paperbacks with yellow covers that dealt with psychological horror, mystery, and lots of bloody murders.)

Prior to the war, Italy had been part of a defensive alliance with Germany and Austria-Hungary, but it sat out the conflict until 1915, when it joined in the fighting along with the Allies. Although their country sided with the victors of the Great War, many Italians across the political spectrum declared the effort a *vittoria mutilata* (mutilated victory). The country had lost 600,000 dead and suffered a major military defeat at the Battle of Caporetto. The desire to escape the horror and humiliation of war paradoxically resulted in an effort to proclaim the glory of warfare in many quarters. Filippo Tommaso Marinetti, part of the futurist movement in Italy and a coauthor of *The Manifesto of Futurism* (1909), wrote that his movement sought to "glorify war," which could cleanse Italy of its "gangrene of professors, archaeologists, tour guides, and antiquaries." The vision of the steel and fire of modern war as a purifying force combined with a fear of a Communist revolution along the lines of what had occurred in Russia and almost occurred in Germany. Doom came to Italy as a result.[20]

Italian director Eugenio Testa's *Il mostro di Frankenstein* (*The Monster of Frankenstein*) appeared in 1920, perhaps the only film in the long history of films associated with Mary Shelley's novel to properly distinguish the creature (the Monster) from the creator (Dr. Victor Frankenstein). Unfortunately, we know almost nothing about the picture. No prints seem to have survived, and there are only two still shots available. All we know for certain is that it dealt with the terror of the corpse: the reassembled death puppet built of a pile of bodies.

Mussolini's National Fascist Party came to power in 1922, two years after this lost version of the Frankenstein story was produced. The regime made the country unfriendly to horror cinema, in part because the Fascists understood that such films confirmed the primal fear of death. Light soap operas, comedies, and war films that focused on the bravery of Italian soldiers remained welcome, winning awards such as the Mussolini Cup at the Venice Film Festival, founded in 1932. Death in battle could be celebrated; the meaning of death and certainly the brave soldier transformed into a corpse had to be excluded.

But the corpse kept walking.

Shadow Kingdom

The Russian Marxist novelist Maxim Gorky, on seeing his first film in 1895, famously described himself as having entered "the kingdom of shadows." Many of the most important creative minds behind the postwar film compared their work to the raising of ghostly specters, with Murnau calling film "the shadow of life." Numerous artists and writers did the same. They seemed compelled by the idea of ghostly shadow in which the dead could live on. But the kingdom of shadows forced upon its subjects the possibility of the vengeful dead, the hungry dead, or, perhaps most terrifying of all, the empty dead, the corpse, the dead as void.[21]

A new idea by the producer of *Nosferatu* offered a powerful example of the terror of human beings as empty puppets rather than ensouled beings destined for eternal life. Albin Grau had the germ of the notion that became the 1922 Arthur Robison silent film *Warning Shadows: A Nocturnal Hallucination.* The techniques and themes Robison used reveal the era's need to explore the twilight between the real world and the nightmare, the no-man's-land of the traumatized mind, mesmerized by the violence of history.

One of the first truly psychological horror films (one finds it hard not to imagine what a Hitchcock remake might have been like), *Warning Shadows* brought together the terror of the body as puppet with the male anxieties over the faithfulness of the war bride that seemed to appear everywhere in Euro-

pean fictions of the era. The film's unnamed characters, who move in hallucinatory sequences as if in a trance, appear as little more than marionettes.

The film imagines a coquettish wife of the German upper classes who,
outrageously, invites her suitors to a dinner party. The guests include one
simply referred to as "the Lover," suggesting that he may have succeeded already in his intentions. Her jealous husband, known simply as "the Count,"
sits by furiously while his wife flirts with her paramours. Robison intimates
that the whole narrative will explode in violence.

Magical realism invades the tale with the appearance of a juggler and
hypnotist who, preternaturally sensing what is about to occur, puts the entire
party into a deep trance. They enter the world of dreams, indeed the world of
nightmare trauma, where their shadows, puppet-like eidolons of their true
selves, act out all their passions. The shadow world emerges as both the playground and the battlefield of the Freudian id. All of the characters' desires,
from lust to revenge, rage freely. The Count, playing his rivals against one
another until they stab his unfaithful wife to death in a fit of jealousy, cli-
maxes the nightmare. Realizing what they have been led to do, the suitors
defenestrate the Count, brutally murdering him.

The film so successfully muddies the line between hallucination and
reality that we forget that we've been party to an infernal puppet show. The
hypnotist awakens the six characters, and us, from the group therapy session of marionettes, part séance, part Freudian psychoanalysis, and all shad-
owplay. The dream world has shown the participants the outcome of their
actions. The wife's admirers leave in shame, and she consents to play the
loving, faithful spouse. In heavy but well-wrought symbolism, the film ends
with all shadows disappearing; the natural light used by cameraman Fritz
Arno Wagner in this scene suggests both new beginnings and the end of the
nightmare of passion and violence.

Wagner had also filmed the famous shadows in *Nosferatu* and seems
to have been responsible for the idea of the vampire extruding his power
and bringing death by enveloping his victims in his monstrous silhouette.
Wagner had wide experience with photography by the time he entered the
German film industry, working for a time on newsreel composition in New
York. He had gained experience in photographing violence and death during
his reporting on the Mexican Revolution in 1913. He enlisted in the German

army at the beginning of the war but suffered a terrible wound; he survived to work first with Ernst Lubitsch (prior to *Eyes of the Mummy*) and then F. W. Murnau.

Wagner's interest in the shadowy worlds of trauma and nightmare emerged from his brief but chilling experience with an elite German Hussars cavalry unit. The German army featured 110 cavalry units at the beginning of the war, mostly used for scouting and screening the disposition of troops. Some German and Austrian horse soldiers saw slightly more direct action on the eastern front against Russian Cossack troops. Similar units in the British army made a brief return when the German front broke and collapsed into retreat in late 1918.

Wagner had been discharged by 1915 when he wrote an oddly uninformative account of his wartime service for *Leslie's Illustrated* entitled "Ten Weeks in the German Army." Wagner's description of his tour of duty simply describes rather than romanticizes the cavalry, perhaps the one European military unit that sustained its reputation for gallantry past the early months of conflict. (Even the romance of the cavalry did not last; the final major use of mounted troops on the western front came perhaps with the Battle of Verdun, during which, on one day in March 1916 alone, seven thousand horses died from shelling.) During his long career, Wagner spoke little about his service, or his injuries, after this single short article. His reflections on the violence of war appeared wholly onscreen.[22]

The shadow of war had enveloped the world. Its influence appears even in the work of a Danish director who had little direct connection to the Great War, although the culture of horror it produced affected him profoundly and brought death to the screen in a storm surge of dark energy. Made in 1932, a decade after *Nosferatu*, Carl Theodor Dreyer's film *Vampyr* extended the terrifying concept of vampirism into the realm of dream. It evokes Murnau and Grau's "land of phantoms" even more successfully than they themselves had done in 1922. Dreyer's images overwhelm his narrative, and the film, an opera of death, offers a truly bizarre mixture of jump scares, occult lore, morbidity, and even an implicit eroticism that, anecdotally, still has an inexplicable effect on viewers today.[23]

Dreyer maintained a lifelong fascination with what suffering did to the human being and the message the corpse delivered to the living. In the minds of many cinephiles, *Joan of Arc* (1928) remains his masterpiece, but its close examination of the psychology of martyrdom often proved too much for contemporary viewers and certainly for today's audiences. *Vampyr*, in contrast, continues to work in its subtly disturbing fashion across the decades.

The plot of *Vampyr*, to the degree that plot matters much in the film, concerns a young man named Allan Gray, who has come to brood incessantly on occult lore, very much in the manner of a Lovecraft protagonist. (Oddly, the character, played by actor Julian West, looks like Lovecraft, but at the time the author remained buried in obscurity, so there's no chance Dreyer would have known of him.) We are introduced to the tall and wan Gray by an intertitle card that calls him a "dreamer for whom the line between the real and the supernatural became blurred." His wanderings have taken him to a place never fully identified. It's been suggested that it's Transylvania, vampire country since Stoker made it so in 1897. In truth, it's purposefully a no-place, a phantasmagoria, in line with Stoker's own decision to place his vampire warlord at home in "the land beyond the forest." We know only that Gray has found his way, by means not fully explained and for reasons unknown, to a village overlooked by a castle. (Incidentally or not, in addition to *The Trial*, another of Kafka's uncompleted works is *The Castle*, published posthumously in 1926. Dreyer later showed an interest in Kafka's work, his bleak 1943 film *Day of Wrath* described by one critic as bringing together the themes of Kafka and American writer Nathaniel Hawthorne by using an early-modern witch trial as a metaphor for the Nazi occupation of Denmark.)[24]

A series of mysterious events leads him to two young women, Gisèle and Léone, the latter of whom has been bitten by a vampire. Gray allows the village doctor to use him for a blood transfusion meant to save Léone. Exhausted, Gray falls asleep, then wakes to find the doctor, who has become the vampire's slave, trying to poison Léone. The doctor flees (taking Gisèle with him), and Gray follows them to the castle, where he falls into a dream-state in which he watches himself in his own coffin. He awakes with the knowledge that he must drive a stake into the heart of the vampire.

The shots in which Gray observes himself in his own coffin are among the most memorable in the film. Dreyer had the idea of placing a small windowpane that allowed the camera to show us the waxen face of Gray's corpse while also giving the audience a shot of the corpse's view through the pane glass. The coffin bobs on the water, splashed across the pane, as the camera allows us to look through death's own eyes.

Eventually, Gray destroys the vampire, Léone recovers, and the doctor dies in an unlikely accident when hundreds of pounds of flour fall upon him and suffocate him in a mill. This absurdist moment opens the way for a kind of escape by Gray and Gisèle, who depart the castle in a boat (not unlike the one in which Gray has seen his corpse, his own death doll, floating), cross a river in dense fog, and walk through a mist-filled forest where sunshine starts to come in through the trees. The final shot of the film cuts back to the mill, where the gears grind to a halt.

On the set of *Vampyr*, Dreyer described the fear he hoped to generate in his film. He wanted us as viewers to experience the feeling that we are sitting in an "ordinary room," all the lighting as expected and the furniture in place with nothing that seems intended to provoke the uncanny. "Suddenly we are told that there is a corpse behind the door," he said, and "the atmosphere has changed." The light will pale while the very quotidian qualities that made the room seem almost dull take on a sinister quality.[25]

The German public apparently wanted the heroic, sacrificial death matched with unending grief that closed *Nosferatu* rather than the resolution of *Warning Shadows* or Dreyer's "corpse behind the door." Whereas Murnau's Count Orlok had been popular, box office receipts marked both *Vampyr* and *Warning Shadows* as failures. Wagner himself admitted of *Warning Shadows* that, at the time, only "film aesthetes" had any interest in the film while it "made no impression on the general public." The trauma of war, as Freud himself had noted, wanted to replay itself over and over again rather than seeking resolution in the light of common day.[26]

The fact that audiences took little notice of Dreyer's *Vampyr*, which only decades later became a recognized classic, had more to do with politics than subject matter, although the subject clearly did not suit much of Europe's mood at the time of its release. The film had been distributed in Germany in May 1932. In less than a year, Paul von Hindenburg named Hitler chancellor of Germany, the Reichstag burned under mysterious circumstances, and the head of the Nazi Party seized emergency powers with either the support or the silent acquiescence of the majority of Germans.

German audiences wanted to see themselves in a quite ordinary room, not in Dreyer's pale chamber with a corpse behind the door. German censors edited the film to inexplicability even before Hitler consolidated power. An unhappy audience in Vienna rioted on its premiere. History would return them to the land of the phantoms, death's own kingdom of shadows.[27]

Broken Faces

The United States also rejected the kind of nightmares directors and screen-writers sought to show to Europe. When, for example, *Caligari* came to the States in 1921, it found some limited success at the box office and earned praise from a number of important critics. Nevertheless, some of the more popularly written reviews described it as "morbid" and attributed this to its "continental" origins without making any direct reference to the reasons continental Europe might have been in a morbid state of mind.[28]

In addition to unfriendly critics, *Caligari* also faced a hostile public in at least one American city. In May 1921, about two thousand patriotic peo-ple in Los Angeles marched to express their disdain for the German-made *Caligari* at the old Miller's Theatre on South Main Street (whose owner also managed the more famous Alhambra). The American Legion organized the protest, which apparently got somewhat out of hand as night fell, leading local police and the naval provost (since some sailors on leave took part) to appear on the scene. Little seems to have happened, however, beyond a few fistfights and some egg throwing.[29]

The feeling of some American veterans about the rather small number of German films coming to U.S. theaters does not seem to have significantly affected the success of *Caligari*. Anti-German sentiment did not remain strong in the 1920s; the era's very public racism and xenophobia turned in-stead on African Americans, Jews, and the increasing number of Catholic immigrants from Italy and eastern Europe.

Americans enjoyed comedy, romantic drama, and sometimes a mash-up of the two when they went to the theater. Still, the partnership in crime and bodily mutilation horror that developed between American director Tod Browning and actor/special effects maestro Lon Chaney suggests that some Americans, perhaps especially veterans, wanted something more than light fare. It is also likely that hundreds of thousands of civilians with strong family ties to old Europe had more awareness than their fellow citizens did of the human suffering the war had produced in Europe and around much of the rest of the world.

Browning had been born in Louisville, Kentucky, in 1880. Fascinated by sideshows and stage magic from his earliest years, he literally ran away to join the circus at age sixteen. He would spend much of the next two decades performing across the Midwest. Browning's most infamous performance, a supremely eerie prefiguring of *Caligari* and his own directorial management of Universal's *Dracula*, was a bit known as "The Hypnotic Living Corpse." This act involved not only a Cesare-like engagement with rural audiences but concluded with his living burial in a wooden casket, a full six feet underground, with ventilation tubes occulted from the audience and milk pellets in his pockets to help sustain life.[30]

Browning's big chance in the movies came after the outbreak of the Great War when a fellow Kentuckian who'd had some success in two-reel comedies brought Browning in for a small role. His sense of showmanship and what could sometimes be a commanding personality—he had been a carnival barker as well as a working act—put him in the director's chair by 1915. An automobile accident in the same year, caused by Browning's excessive drinking, gave him lifelong injuries (their nature and extent remain a matter of speculation).

After a two-year blacklisting, a sort of professional punishment for his alcoholism, Browning returned to directing, now making dark tales that reflected his own life experience while gathering the black shadows of the postwar world. While working on one of the earliest gangster pictures, *Outside the Law* (1921), Browning met a young Lon Chaney for the first time. David J. Skal has written at length about the significance of this partnership for the roots of American horror, describing how between them they found a chilling formula that united the grotesque subtext of the circus sideshow with Chaney's makeup skills to "give convincing shape to Browning's dark vision of physical limitation and disfigurement."[31]

Browning and Chaney worked together while America's '20s roared with bathtub gin parties and while, simultaneously, a much more conservative

America ballooned the membership of the Ku Klux Klan and allowed for the draconian antics of the early FBI hunt for sympathizers of the Russian Revolution, with immigrants from eastern Europe and most everyone on the left perceived as probable Bolsheviks or anarchists. Neither the director nor the actor had deeply held political convictions, and neither had much direct connection with the Great War. Yet they created a funhouse hall of mirrors that brought America's seediest impulses to light and that reimagined the wounds of war for an America convinced it would never again enter a European conflict.

Before his collaboration with Browning, Chaney had begun the portrayal of physical disfigurement in the 1919 film *The Miracle Man*, a now lost picture that made him a star. Both his growing artistry with makeup and his ability to contort his body in bizarre fashion appear again in the 1920 film *The Penalty*. Playing the character Blizzard, a double-amputee crime lord who rules the San Francisco underworld, Chaney brought incredible menace to the character.[32]

The Penalty also speaks to the times with allusions to the Red Scare and the anti-immigrant fervor of the era. Blizzard uses immigrant gangs in his plans for domination, alluding to the notion that white nationalists remain fond of today, of the alleged criminality of recent immigrants and new Americans. However, Blizzard also comes across as a surprisingly sympathetic villain, a gift that Chaney frequently displayed. This nuances what could have been a simplistic nativist nightmare.

Browning and Chaney joined their macabre talents in a 1925 film for MGM titled *The Unholy Three*, which featured three criminal circus performers (including a dwarf played by the famous Harry Earles, later to star in Browning's controversial 1932 *Freaks* and in *The Wizard of Oz* as part of the Lollipop Guild). Chaney appeared as a deranged ventriloquist, another version of the séance medium, the mesmerist, and the hypnotist figures that became symbolic of an era of mental confusion and torment.[33]

Somewhat surprisingly given the mood of the country, *The Unholy Three* earned both critical praise and hefty box office receipts. The influence of *Caligari*, and the whole catalog of postwar horror, appears in the film with the introduction of the carnival and ventriloquism to the narrative. Both alluded to the era's unspoken anxiety over the unreality of what had happened to the world since 1914. The carnival had begun to evoke a shadowy world of primal violence, while the ventriloquist—throwing his voice in such a way that he seemed to split himself in two—suggested the double and the death doll.

Chaney and Browning repeated this formula again and again in the 1920s with films like *West of Zanzibar*, *The Road to Mandalay*, and *The Unknown*. Chaney's career included playing the part of a hunchback twice, an amputee twice, and a scarred and disfigured person at least five times.

A few film historians have seen in Chaney's surprising success a kind of Horatio Alger tale that Americans couldn't help but find attractive. Chaney's net worth and studio salary impressed the public, but so did, it's been claimed, his ability to shape-shift, to become anything he sought to be, just as the "American dream"—a term coined in a rather optimistic American history textbook in 1931—said all real Americans could achieve success if they tried.[34]

"There is no Lon Chaney," the reclusive actor once said to the world via his press agent. "I am the character I am creating. That is all."

Perhaps something of the protean power of capitalism did reside in this appeal. But such an interpretation ignores the grotesque transformations with which Chaney shocked his audiences. After all, he transformed himself into aberrations of the human body and psyche rather than into expectant capitalists. These are stories of American nightmares rather than American dreams.

Lon Chaney's most famous role—that of the Phantom, Erik, in Universal Pictures' 1925 silent film *The Phantom of the Opera*—best illustrates how he tapped into the world's terrors in the postwar period. (The studio would release a "talkie" version in 1930, which, however, did not use Chaney's voice.) Like the 1923 *Hunchback of Notre Dame*, the 1925 *Phantom* removed Chaney from his usual American milieu. It brought him worldwide acclaim to a degree that none of his other roles achieved.

The most well-known moment in the film, when Christine (played by Mary Philbin) rips the mask from the Phantom, makes it easy to see why. The horribly disfigured Erik appears to have no nose (an effect achieved by Chaney using hooks to pull back his nose at an angle that, according to the film's cinematographer, made him "bleed like hell") and a mouth smashed in by some traumatic event. His nearly hairless head appears irremediably scarred. Notably, unlike Gaston Leroux's 1909 novel, or the many other adaptations and reimaginings since, the 1925 film provides no explanation for Erik's monstrous appearance. In the aftermath of the Great War, the film allowed audiences to imagine why the Phantom's face had been disassembled and reconstructed wrongly.

Chaney had replicated, as film after film in this era did, the disfigured faces of veterans, exploded by shrapnel and Maxim guns. No one in the Western world could have looked at the visage of Lon Chaney and not thought of what the French called the *gueules cassées* (broken faces) who hid their injuries with marionette-like facsimiles just as the Phantom did.

Perhaps the American fascination with the film grew out of its seeming violation of the temper of the times. If they had not served in the armed forces, had no family members on the western front, and had not been jailed under the Espionage Act for dissent, Americans suffered few ill effects from the war. But wounded American veterans suffered no less than their European counterparts.

The ruined face of the Phantom brooded over America and Europe, reminding viewers of the horror of the trenches and the dark dreams that followed veterans the rest of their lives. No longer could the gore of battle be unseen. The broken faces appeared everywhere on the streets, and sometimes beside the hearth, in England, Germany, France, and indeed the world over. Collections showing the extremity of wounds, sometimes in wax and sometimes in casts previously used by casualties, became tourist attractions in Berlin, Paris, and London. In nearly ritualistic fashion, according to army surgeon Jacques W. Maliniak, "thousands" used their holidays to see "an authentic reproduction of the suffering and mutilation of the war."[35]

Purveyors of culture in the United States worked incessantly to help the public forget this aspect of the war. They covered the American landscape, for example, with statues of soldiers standing or marching bravely. Lon Chaney himself would depart from his usual horror-film formula in 1926 with *Tell It to the Marines*, a romantic comedy that increased the Marines' pride in their wartime service. (Marines had allegedly been called "devil dogs" by exhausted German troops at the Battle of Belleau Wood in 1918;

U.S. newspapers actually used this term, and claimed the Germans did the same, two months before the battle took place.)[36]

The veterans themselves, however, could not hide from the horror. Nor could they ignore the willingness of the nation to turn them quickly into stone monuments. Over 200,000 had returned home wounded. They became corpses at the feast of the Roaring Twenties while, in the words of historian Peter Kuznick, large corporations and banks had "thrived during the war with munitions makers leading the pack."[37]

Lovecraftian Apocalypse

H. P. Lovecraft delighted in his encounter with *The Phantom of the Opera*, Chaney's masterpiece, writing to a friend:

> What a spectacle it was! . . . Horror lifted its grisly visage . . . Ugh, that face that was revealed when the mask was pulled off . . . & the nameless legion of things that cloudily appeared beside and behind the owner of that face when the mob chased him into the river at last.[38]

The writer who enjoyed complaining about almost every aspect of modernity enjoyed movies, or at least this particular horror film. He groused that he had not been able to see *Caligari*, and even when he complained about a production, like James Whale's *Frankenstein*, he often gave a backhanded compliment or two. He thrilled to *Phantom* and the monster Chaney had made at a particularly significant moment in Lovecraft's career, in which he was beginning to think more and more about the revelatory nature of horror.

Lovecraft's failure to make it to the front, or even into the Rhode Island Guard, did nothing to dampen his fascination with the Great War. More significantly for the war's legacy of horror, the abattoir of the trenches contributed to what later cinematic iterations would make into one of the most famous of his tales. While German horror films examined the meaning of death and the very notion of what it meant to be human, and Chaney and Browning focused on body horror, Lovecraft's fiction after 1919 engaged both topics directly.

In the midst of the conflict, Lovecraft had written in his amateur, self-published journal *The Conservative* that condemnations of the war came primarily from "the effeminate idealist" who "shrieks at the mutual slaughter of his fellow-man." Lovecraft, at home in Providence, obviously could have no concept of what that "mutual slaughter" actually looked or felt like. Indeed, his deep and inveterate racism led him to criticize the war only because what he called the "unnatural racial alignments of the various warring powers" signaled danger for "Teutonic stock." In other words, the British should not be fighting their racial brothers in Germany.[39]

Lovecraft's obscene observations about the "mutual slaughter" of the trenches didn't keep him from turning to the Great War in fiction, at first simply signaling his growing interest after America joined the Allies in April 1917. Later, his fiction focused more on the apocalyptic implications of the war. When his best work began to appear, in the late 1920s, he thought through the same themes of global catastrophe and utter alienation from the romanticism of the nineteenth century that other writers and artists began to obsess over during the conflict itself.

"Dagon," written in the summer of 1917 but not coming into print until 1923, raises questions about the possibility of a human future. The narrator tells us that when events recorded occurred, "the great war was then at its very beginning." A German sea raider takes over a cargo ship and takes the crew captive. The narrator escapes only to find himself on an island that turns out not to be an island at all. There he finds a strange monolith and a creature whose amphibian appearance and sloppy, ugly movements defies his abilities to describe.

As in so many of his tales, Lovecraft ends "Dagon" with his narrator losing his sanity. He is haunted by one thought, and it's not even of the thing on the island itself. Instead, he takes morphine to keep at bay his visions of "the nameless things that may at this very moment be crawling and floundering," and he dreams of "a day when they may rise above the billows to drag down . . . the remnants of puny, war-exhausted mankind."[40]

Lovecraft's "Nyarlathotep" represents another reflection on "war-exhausted mankind," as does his story of the fate of a German U-boat in "The Temple." But nowhere does he get closer to the real horrors of war than some tales he suggested he wrote on something of a lark. "Herbert

West—Reanimator" was a serial publication for an amateur magazine called *Home Brew* that specialized in lowbrow humor. Although Lovecraft's own literary pretentions made him grumble about this, he complained a bit too enthusiastically. The prospect of actually being paid for his fiction delighted him. He took the opportunity to tell a mad-scientist tale in which his character Herbert West, a student at Lovecraft's fictional Miskatonic University, develops a serum for raising the dead.

Lovecraft admitted he had written a "gruesome" narrative. The story did, in fact, include much of the biological horror the postwar world obsessed over. In some ways, he joined Abel Gance in producing the first modern zombie tale: West tears bodies out of their own deaths into "the supernal terror and unnatural despair of animate nature." Kicked out of Miskatonic for his forbidden experiments, West turns his former dean into "a voiceless, sadistic monster" that in one night maims its victims and rips them to shreds.[41]

Lovecraft reveals his lingering interest in the Great War by having West take his serum to "the gigantic struggle" before the U.S. enters the war, enlisting in a Canadian regiment in 1915. Here Lovecraft, more than in his ridiculously inhumane essays, displays some limited sense that the world's real horror took place in the trenches: he has West's assistant speak of "hideous things, not mentioned in print, which happened on the battlefields of the Great War." In pulpy style, however, this description takes a backseat to "the shocking, the unnatural, the unbelievable horror from the shadows."

The mad scientist had taken his experiments to the war in search of "freshly killed men in every stage of dismemberment," again showing Lovecraft's awareness of what the war had become since his prattle in 1915 about the conflict's true tragedy residing in "unnatural racial alignments." Still, the pulp formula constrained him again and again in these tales. One minute, there's a reflection on the war's "prodigious supply of freshly slaughtered human flesh" and the next we are hearing of reanimated limbs and the use of a new formula created from "reptilian cell-matter" to rejuvenate the dead.[42]

Lovecraft could never quite break through to a full rendition of the war's horrors. This failure had nothing to do with his lack of direct experience with the combat. Many artists who spent no time in the trenches managed to capture their personal fears and the collective horror. But, unlike *Nos-*

feratu, which compels us to see the specter of death shadowing the world without ever mentioning the war, Lovecraft's use of war as a backdrop diverts our eyes away toward the fantastic horrors of reanimation. "Herbert West—Reanimator" works wondrously as a horror story, and made for a terrific adaptation from Lovecraft fan and filmmaker Stuart Gordon in 1985. But Lovecraft, like many other Americans of his generation, blinked and looked away at those moments in the narrative when the war drew too close.

"Nyarlathotep" and "Dagon" had shown that Lovecraft could use supernatural fiction to entwine global catastrophe with tales of the fantastic. But his output varied widely. When he began publishing in *Weird Tales* after its founding in 1923, he often used what even his most fervent admirer, S. T. Joshi, has called "a hackneyed" set of formulas that appealed to the magazine's readership. Worse, his stories could combine his rancid racism with occultism, as in "The Horror at Red Hook," or tell a simple tale of an evil monster destroyed by a good wizard (specifically a mystically inclined Miskatonic U Professor), as in "The Dunwich Horror."[43]

A change came over Lovecraft's work by the mid-1920s, however, and his supernatural fiction became much more relevant to the larger world, something other than, as Victoria Nelson puts it, "squishy monster stories for boys."[44]

He raised great Cthulhu, a monster that has haunted the century, a new death's head spreading wide his black wings of apocalypse, which was clearly recognizable as the Great War and its meaning continued to menace the world.

Ghosts of No-Man's-Land

Arthur Machen disdained his employment with the London *Evening News*, thinking of it primarily as hackwork to keep his family afloat financially. The daily grind of the newspaper business kept him in the doldrums, lightened by his mystical interests and devotion to his family. He did, however, receive a jolt of inspiration from the strange mixture of war fever and patriotic fervor that seized so many in the first days of the Great War. Machen penned his short story "The Bowmen" first as a supplement for the September 29, 1914, edition of his employer's newspaper. Undoubtedly it pleased him to put his interest in the supernatural to some use at his hated day job.

Reading "The Bowmen" today disappoints if you've had the chance to submerge yourself in the malign and unforgettable tales of horror that Machen produced in the 1890s. The tale recounts one of the early calamitous battles of the war and adds a British officer who, having once seen a Latin prayer to St. George rendered on the plates "in a queer vegetarian restaurant in London," utters the invocation during the heat of battle. Suddenly, in a long line, appear "shapes, with a shining about them," who rain arrows down on the Germans, killing them by the thousands and ending their seemingly unstoppable march on Paris. The story ends with a note that the German general staff, with their "scientific principles" of war, believed the English had used a deadly form of poison gas. But, Machen writes, "the man . . . knew . . . that St. George had brought his Agincourt Bowmen to help the English."

"The Bowmen" became, during his lifetime, Machen's most popular story, in large part because many readers thought it much more than fiction. The particular edition of the *Evening News* in which it appeared, for reasons that have never become known, published another tale entitled "Our Short Story" while simply printing Machen's work under its own title. This made it seem like another edition of Machen's regular column. Perhaps because it was written from a narrator's perspective, readers seized on it as a first-person account of a strange but true occurrence on the other side of the Channel.

A number of parish priests delighted in the story for its pious and patriotic effect and passed it along to their flocks in sermon and anecdote. In fact, one such clergyman contacted Machen to ask if the author would grant permission for the parish to print it in pamphlet form, complete with the sources he used to write the story. Machen replied that he had no sources to provide since the tale had come completely from his imagination. The enthusiastic priest insisted heatedly that Machen had this wrong, that the story had been absolutely true. In 1915, when the story appeared in a collection titled *The Bowmen and Other Legends of the War*, Machen wrote with some frustration that he had failed in the writing of a good story but succeeded in fomenting a myth.[45]

Apparently, he had helped create one of the more persistent fairy tales of the war. On August 23, 1914, British troops had experienced their first major battle with German forces. Fighting with tenacity, the British suffered heavy causalities in what later in the war would count as a mere skirmish but at the time represented one of the greatest clashes of arms ever seen on the continent.

A story circulated that soldiers had seen an angel riding a white horse and carrying a flaming sword that held back the German foe. The story grew in scale until it became many horses bearing up many shining figures. It's worth noting that it took several weeks after the battle ended for the legend of these apparitions to begin making the rounds, about the time Machen's story appeared. As is often true with rumor legends, the story took on a simple, easily retold, form: some soldiers and lots of civilians who had not been present spoke of angels, not of Agincourt bowmen. The "Angel of Mons," as the divine intervention became known, failed rather spectacularly, as the large German contingent did force the British to give ground. Still, the truth has not outlived its romance, and even to this day the legend often gets sentimental mention in the odd brand of nationalism and nostalgia that clusters around British commemoration of the war.

A German soldier, Walter Bloem, saw no flaming swords from heaven helping out either side in those first weeks of war. He remembered only "dead and wounded, quivering in convulsions, groaning terribly, blood oozing from fresh wounds." Phantasmagoria haunted most soldiers, not a world where angels chose sides and saved the day.[46]

Jingoism and its legends aside, Machen managed to convey something of the horror of the times in his short story: "The hearts of men failed within them and grew faint; as if the agony of the army in the battlefield had entered into their souls." And while he portrays the British "Tommy" (the term for the common soldier) facing constant shelling with lighthearted bravery, he forces his audience to remember that bursting shells "tore good Englishmen limb from limb" just across the Channel.

Machen never thought the story really worked and became a bit ashamed of it. He wondered aloud how a "nation sunk in materialism of the grossest kind [had] accepted idle rumors and gossip of the supernatural as truth." Soon Machen found a way to write about the war that went beyond the simplistic nationalism of "The Bowmen." He would return to his roots in cosmic horror and find in the Great War an iconography of the true terror that makes of our world a haunted wood.[47]

A Dance with Death

Berlin, halt ein! Besinne Dich. Dein Tänzer ist der Tod. (Berlin, stop! Come to your senses. You're dancing with death.) Thus read graffiti scrawled all over the walls of the city in the early 1920s.

The far left in German politics struggled to regroup in the years after the failure of the Spartacist uprising and the violent repression that followed. It largely succeeded in this, for a time providing a formidable opponent for the increasingly militant right, of which the Nazi Party represented only one element. But in the earliest years the left largely had to make do with various kinds of agitprop, including the graffiti that suggested Berlin's death mask. "You're dancing with death!" touched a chord in German society beyond the world of disappointed revolutionaries, however, encapsulating the fears of the war years and the privation, widespread disease, and indeed starvation that followed. The graffiti used a line snatched from a poem by the controversial poet Walter Mehring. The surreal sentiment became so well-known that it appeared on a popular German poster by the mid-1920s. It seemed to describe the interest in the macabre displayed by German artists and film directors, their desire to put numerous iterations of rotting corpses and dead-eyed comrades on canvas and screen.

Fritz Lang, home from the war but most certainly bringing the war home with him, had long been fascinated with the macabre, the nature of evil, and the relationship of both to the social order. His work, like that of Murnau, Gance, and Leni, shows us more than how the Great War inspired a generation to embrace a death obsession. We see how such a fascination, in some sense the beginnings of the horror tradition itself, both critiqued and called into being societies in the thrall of dread.

The Great War ended Lang's time as an art student. There are differing accounts of his flight from Paris as the global conflagration began, as there are details left in shadow in much of his biography. Whether he returned to Austria-Hungary to join the imperial armies or became one of the Hapsburgs' many conscripts has little relevance to his bitter experience of combat or how it shaped his art.

Lang's war did become a particularly brutal one, known to us largely through official records and the medals the Hapsburg army awarded him. He himself spoke very little about his experiences. He received his first citation for bravery during a reconnaissance mission in March 1916, during which he had been sketching out a line of Russian fortifications. In June of the same year, he received two wounds in a matter of days, the second leaving him temporarily blind and causing a permanent eye injury that, he later alleged, required him to wear his infamous monocle, which he replaced with an equally well-known eye patch in his last years. During his ten-month recovery, he wrote some of his first film treatments, many of which signal his interest in horror and crime. He scripted at least one werewolf tale and another about a son who inherits his father's "criminal genes," becoming the dead man's evil double.

Lang returned to war as a lieutenant in the early fall of 1917, this time serving in Romania and then on the Italian front. He received some other injury during the final year of the war (although it's unclear that it was another wound). The hospitalization record listed a "nervous disorder" as part of his disability; his symptoms and some aspects of his behavior following the war suggest strongly that he suffered "war neurosis."

Lang found success in the German film industry after the war, with help from producer Erich Pommer, who also worked with Murnau. Lang's already imperious nature took on a sharp and dangerous edge. His outbursts of anger at his first wife, Lisa Rosenthal, reportedly included the unsettling habit of waving around a Browning service revolver he'd brought home from the trenches. This would lead to notorious speculation after Rosenthal used this weapon to commit suicide in 1920 after catching Lang and his lover, screenwriter Thea von Harbou (who later married Lang), in bed together.[48]

Fritz Lang's Great War, and what it did to his psyche, helped him produce some of the most memorable monsters of the era. Indeed, a decade later he and actor Peter Lorre created a corrupted evil that rivaled the vampire born from the imagination of Albin Grau and "Mr. Murnau" (as Lang always respectfully called him).

But first, Lang created one of the most famous automata of the 1920s.

She would voice to German audiences, and the world, her own version of the warning "You're dancing with death."

Burrower in the Wasteland

In August 1917, Franz Kafka began coughing up blood. He had never previously trusted doctors but now found himself forced to do so after they diagnosed him with pulmonary tuberculosis. As the disease racked his lungs he surely thought of his most memorable tragic character, Gregor Samsa in *The Metamorphosis*. His illness, however, did not keep him from writing his unclassifiable tales that dug deep into Europe's worm-rotted battlescape.

Kafka's incomplete story "The Burrow" captured several of the most inhuman aspects of life during the conflict, including the mud and blood of trench warfare itself. It's a rush of images involving digging, burrowing into the earth for survival, and the attendant dark irony of digging one's own grave. The story speaks, as does much of Kafka's other work, of the cruelty that buried the hopes of the twentieth century. The mole-like creature in "The Burrow" has human imagination and a human desire for freedom, light, and even love. But it has alternate and competing motives, a desire to descend into the loneliness of its burrow, to defend it against any who might threaten its security.[49]

Interpreters of the unfinished tale have seen it, as Victoria Nelson writes, as a parable of the divided mind of the artist or a Freudian "burrowing" into the unconscious. She points out that thinking of the story this way makes it too easy to forget that this thing is an animal, in essence a monster that dreams of tearing apart anyone who enters its hidden abyss.[50]

Kafka worked on "The Burrow" in 1923 as death slowly closed in on him. It's difficult not to see the chaos and monstrosity of the trenches in the role that incessant noise and burrowing into the earth play in the making of the monster. Kafka knew that human beings could become, had become, like this creature, which declares that, if someone threatened it, "I might . . . maul him, tear the flesh from his bones, destroy him, drink his blood, and fling his corpse among the rest of my spoil." The monster is Gren-

del and the Maxim gun, the stuff of primal horror myth joined to the history
of the early twentieth century.

Kafka showed some interest in the culture of postwar horror, even
though the genre had only begun to emerge at the time of his death. Gustav Meyrink's 1915 novel, *The Golem*, the book that had become so intensely
popular in central Europe during the war that a soldier's edition had been
released, seems to have impressed Kafka. An account related by Max Brod,
the author's closest friend and later the publisher of his work, tells us that
Kafka not only read and appreciated *The Golem* but also connected it to the
changes wrought by war and history, especially in his native Prague.

"The atmosphere of the old Jewish quarter was wonderfully reproduced,"
Kafka said of Meyrink's work. He would have had no way of knowing anything about that atmosphere of course, at least outside of distant family memories, by the time of the novel's publication. The Kafkas had long moved out
of the quarter.[51] Indeed, a large number of Jewish families, perhaps a fourth
of the population of Jewish Prague, left the quarter in the 1850s. The vast
majority moved to other parts of the city in the next half century. The old
ghetto, known as Josefstadt or Josefov after Emperor Joseph II, who desired
the reputation as protector of the Jews of the Austrian Empire, had become
a decrepit haunt of thieves. Much of it had been demolished and rebuilt by
the beginning of the Great War. "In us it still lives," Kafka said, "the dark
corners, the secret alleys, shuttered windows, squalid courtyards, and sinister inns. . . . With our eyes open we walk through a dream; ourselves only a
ghost of a vanished age." This haunting elegy seems born of a nearly occult
vision of the old city. It captures much of what makes Kafka, in my reading,
a writer of horror—certainly not a genre writer or bound to the formulas that
often limited even the best of Lovecraft's work, but one who nevertheless
found in brutality, alienation, supernatural transformation, and torture the
terrible truths of his age.

Max Brod's anecdote, and Kafka's comment about the ghostly Prague
that had disappeared, could have come directly from Meyrink's novel or
the intertitles of Wegener's 1920 film. Unfortunately, it's probably untrue or at least only partially true. Brod did not publish his biography of
Kafka until 1937. He had luckily escaped Prague after the Nazi seizure of
Czechoslovakia, and memories had likely grown a bit dim in the interim.[52]

Even if Kafka never said these things, in exactly this way, about *The Go-lem*, the anecdote probably has a kernel of truth. He did see in Prague a ruin that represented modernity. His stories often had an essential placelessness about them: the terrible things that occur in them could be happening any-where. But he knew Prague like a lover, indeed better than he knew any of his actual lovers, and his best tales and novels capture the secrets, the traps, the essential irrationalism of the ancient city.

They also, like so much of the horror film and fiction of the era, seemed to call into question the stability of the human body. The war shattered the nineteenth-century consensus about death. The double became an image of mortality that could be tortured and mangled. The terror would become fully incarnated in Dr. Frankenstein's stitched-together horror. Chucky the nightmare doll (*Child's Play*, 1988) and the creepy Annabelle (*Annabelle*, 2014 with a 2017 sequel, part of the hugely popular series *The Conjuring*) have terrified us with the death doll, the waxwork come to life. Extreme horror such as the original French *Martyrs* (2008) or *Dead Girl* (2008), unwatchable by a mainstream audience, takes the pop terror of Hollywood's nightmare dolls to their logical conclusion. Zombies are themselves the ultimate empty corpses, as Abel Gance showed while the Great War still waged, husks wait-ing to be filled with social commentary but also deeply nihilistic reminders of our mortality.

Kafka's Prague, long obsessed with golems, puppets, and automata, joined Paris and Berlin as one of the capitals of an aesthetic of horror. Mean-while, artists joined writers and movie moguls in telling the story of the monsters that came from the trenches. The Great War would give the world a new art of the nightmare.

Chapter Three

Nightmare Bodies

Today I found in Mametz Wood
A certain cure for lust of blood:

. . . a dead Boche; he scowled and stunk
With clothes and face a sodden green,
Big-bellied, spectacled, crop-haired,
Dribbling black blood from nose and beard.
—ROBERT GRAVES, "A Dead Boche" (1916)

Trauma and the Uncanny

Sigmund Freud sat at his desk at Berggasse 19 in Vienna in late 1918 thinking about the chilling nature of dolls, the inanimate that threaten to animate. He held one of his omnipresent cigars while he pondered horror.

He could barely keep his hands warm. The war meant that scarcity of all kinds affected Vienna, and the room chilled for lack of coal. Freud wrote letters around the same time that began with complaints about the cold. In fact, he and his family may have even suffered from hunger without the aid of the occasional packages from friends in Budapest and the Netherlands.[1]

A lack of basic necessities had caused Freud to cut back his twenty-cigar-a-day habit. (Oral cancer forced the physician into sixteen surgeries over the next twenty years, yet he refused to give up tobacco.) On this day, while Freud worried and chewed at his cigar, the ancient dynasty of the Hapsburgs collapsed with shocking suddenness, the end of almost half a millennia of imperial rule. While Austria-Hungary entered its death throes, Freud waited for word of his two sons serving in the final march of the Hapsburg armies. His family, it would turn out, had been lucky. One son suffered a slight wound, and the other, though missing at the end of the war, was soon repatriated from an Italian prison camp.

At the beginning of 1915, just six months into the conflict, Freud had written an odd essay titled "Thoughts for the Times on War and Death" (often translated as "Reflections on War and Death"). It includes some analysis of the psychology of war but primarily contains a set of despairing reflections on the course the world had taken. It's obviously influenced by the possible fate of his own family and Vienna itself, the city of the baroque and bohemian whose coffeehouses had buzzed with caffeine highs and intellectual ferment for decades. Freud believed, even before the war entered its most terrible phase, that life as he had known it had come to an end. "We cannot but feel that no event has ever destroyed so much that is precious in the common possession of humanity," he writes.[2]

Freud had the intellectual's tendency to fail at separating personal problems from conceptual conundrums. His sons' army service on the eastern front, and his wider circle of students and colleagues serving in the medical corps all over Europe, interested him in what many physicians called "war neurosis," known more popularly as shell shock. In response, Freud wrote "Mourning and Melancholia," a work that still shapes our understanding of post-traumatic stress disorder (PTSD). He began the essay in 1915 though he did not published it. In it, he undertook the problem of what happened to human beings subjected to the kind of war Europe was waging on itself. Freud raised the possibility, soon proved by the terrors that an entire generation had to confront, that a specific kind of sadness could possess brain and bones: a phantasm that never died.

Trauma, Freud recognized, settled like a hard frost into a mind grieving itself to death. "Melancholia," the term Freud chose to describe this state, in contrast to a healthy processing of loss, constitutes a kind of mourning without end, a repetition of the original trauma in night terrors, nervousness, anger, and even waking nightmares. Men at the front suffered all these things, along with unexplained blindness (called "hysterical blindness" by doctors in the war), muteness with no organic cause, or sustained crying.

Seeing oneself as a corpse waiting to happen became a legacy of the war. Freud sees in this vast capacity for traumatic sorrow a solution to the riddle of suicide. Why would the human being, whose very existence was predicated on narcissistic self-love, consent to its own destruction? Such a reversal of the deepest instinctual drives of the species becomes possible once the subject sees himself as an object. Trauma turned a human being's "murderous impulses" against himself.[3]

Now, as the war came to a close, Freud thought about the fiction of E. T. A. Hoffmann, the same writer of dark fairy tales whose work Ernst Lubitsch had drawn on for *The Doll*. Why did Hoffmann's subtle short story "The Sandman"—with its two monstrosities: a mechanical doll that becomes an object of desire and a creature that takes the eyes of children in the night—frighten people so badly? The final convulsions of the war caused Freud to wonder about the nature of fear and, in an almost direct meditation on his experience waiting for news of his son, the fear invoked by the return of the dead. His 1919 essay on the art of supernatural terror, "The Uncanny," became his answer.

Freud traced the root of the word *unheimlich* (literally "un-home-like," but translated into English as "uncanny") to the idea of being "un-homed," being in unfamiliar territory but still remembering the familiar. The chill of the uncanny settles on us when we confront strangeness and experience a shock in the midst of the everyday. We look at something that is utterly different from us yet behaves like us. The dread can work in the obverse fashion as well, when the familiar becomes strange, when our expectations of the world are not only proved wrong but twisted into unrecognizable geometries.

We have minor experiences with Freud's uncanny all the time. They range from "things feeling off" to things that are truly chilling. We've all had the experience of mild peculiarity that accompanies seeing an acquaintance out of their normal context. At the other end of the spectrum, learning a terrible secret or confronting a personal catastrophe that makes the normal and familiar utterly disorienting chills us to the bone. (The slang term "the new normal" contains or at least explains this dread.) We try to ward against the uncanny by insisting, gruesomely and probably falsely, that we are "comfortable in our own skin." What other skin would make you comfortable? If you spent much time thinking about being a bundle of nerves and muscle wrapped in skin, would you remain comfortable in it?

Freud's reflections on the nature of horror make only one definitive allusion to the war, but its presence hovered behind him as he wrote. He chooses to illustrate the idea of the uncanny, this sense of existential homelessness, by reflecting on the ideas of the doll and the doppelgänger (the ghostly double), both terrors reflecting a world filled with corpses and the most shudder-inducing possibilities of the uncanny manifested on a global scale.[4]

The doppelgänger has long haunted tales of morbidity. It's not clear whether Freud ever read Edgar Allan Poe's tale "William Wilson" (1839), but had he done so it would have confirmed his idea that the existence of a double can only create terror, coming at us like the incarnation of the sadistic punisher of the ego that haunts the halls of the mind. Although he only broaches the idea that Poe fully explores in his tale, Freud conceptualizes the double as the representative of our own death. It is an agent of terror—found in a doll, a puppet, a mirror, or an automaton—a reminder that we are bodies destined to become corpses.

In fact, Freud writes that for most people the uncanny "is represented by anything to do with death, dead bodies." One of the many peculiar aspects of the essay is that it digresses and repeats itself, with Freud sometimes undermining his earlier claims. It's as if he doesn't want to talk about what he's actually talking about. We get to the end of the essay before he admits that he's really writing about the dead. He doesn't fully explore the possibility, but our fascination with—or, alternatively, revulsion to—mirrors may come precisely from the fear of the double, our fear of death.[5]

The brief mention of the significance of mirrors represents one of the more interesting of Freud's meanderings. It's true that some people can stare at an image of themselves for long periods, attempting to meet unrealistic expectations of beauty. But we have myths, tales, and urban legends reaching back to the classical story of Narcissus that warn about the dangers of gorging on the image of the self. One example that centers on the danger that lies in the mirror is the performance ritual of "Bloody Mary," first recorded by folklorists in great detail at midcentury. To perform the ritual, you stand in front of a mirror in a darkened room and repeatedly invoke a name, most often Bloody Mary but sometimes Mary Worth, sometimes Mary Weather. After a certain number of repetitions (some accounts say three times, others thirteen, still others some other number), you will see the monster—Mary's spirit—in the mirror. Variations of the ritual involve lighting a candle and turning around three times. Whatever the details, the monster accompanies the reflection, hugs itself to the reflection of the self, another kind of repetition. It becomes a vertiginous hymn to our own death, sung as a duet.[6]

Like the doppelgänger, the doll can cause "intellectual uncertainty," a concept that doesn't capture the truly dizzying effect of such an encounter. But Freud used this phrase to evoke a disturbing sense of the unknown that produces the sense of being "un-homed." When this occurs, not only are we having an unpleasant experience, but we are asking a question: Will it become alive? Freud realized that we are also asking the obverse: Are we really just like it?

Sitting at his desk, shivering in the cold, he wrote that the doll, the automaton, the waxwork, "arouse in the onlooker vague notions of automatic-mechanical processes that may lie hidden behind the familiar image of the living person." Then, perhaps after looking around the office at his collection of Greek and Egyptian artifacts and wondering if his sons had died, he changed the subject. He didn't really want to talk about it.[7]

Closer to our own time, discussions of artificial intelligence have broached elements of Freud's thesis. Masahiro Mori, a robotics expert at Tokyo's Mukta Research Institute, first used the term "uncanny valley" in 1970. Mori's original idea suggested that once we began to build more and more lifelike computers, we will at first look at them with empathy, but, as time goes by, they will become eerie to the point of revulsion. This observation led him to conclude that engineers should refrain from constructing robots that are too lifelike, a suggestion most of his influential students have ignored. They have instead assured themselves that they can navigate the uncanny valley if they successfully humanize artificial intelligence.

Why does this happen? Why would an atmosphere of the weird rather than a sense of interest and curiosity accompany a machine that appears "too human"? Theorists use a technical term that, like many technical terms, seems specifically crafted to avoid a hard truth: a mechanical double of ourselves, like the eerie feeling that automata of any kind produce, creates what robotics experts call "mortality salience." They are mechanisms that look and act like us, and when we interact with them the possibility arises that we, too, are soulless automata. They can be disassembled into parts, and so can we. Mortality salience transforms them from objects of interest into memento mori, reminders that our death approaches and that we will likely not extrude a shining soul, acquire wings, and float to the sky.[8]

Freud might have liked the notion of mortality salience, since he also saw the grim phantasm of our own corpse in the doll and the double. Then again, perhaps he would have dismissed the idea, given how he seemed to be reaching toward it in 1918 and kept getting himself lost. Freud scholars have in fact noted that there's something uncanny about "The Uncanny," as if Freud had penned a gothic novel rather than a highfalutin academic essay.[9]

For example, in another head fake, Freud claimed that he personally had almost no experience of the uncanny—a strange assertion for someone who seemed to suggest that the shudder-inducing experience can, indeed, must, appear before all of us like the cold shadow of a vampire. Speaking of himself in the third person, he insisted that it had been "a long time since he experienced or became acquainted with anything that conveyed the impression of the Uncanny." The entire first section that follows, before he settles into writing about dolls and doubles, contains an exhaustive (and, honestly, for most readers exhausting) linguistic survey of the possible meanings of *unheimlich*.[10]

When he finally makes his point in language that needs no interpretation, it comes toward us like the final jump scare in a horror flick that makes the theater scream: "Severed limbs, a severed head, a hand detached from the arm . . . all these have something highly uncanny about them." Indeed they do, but why after so much theoretical discussion of the terror of the unfamiliar in the midst of the familiar are we suddenly in a pile of mutilated bodies?[11]

These final observations come within a page of Freud's most direct allusion to the Great War. The severed body parts lying half buried in collapsed trenchworks on the western front, and on battlefields from the Balkans to South Africa, startled the very beginning of the twentieth century into an uncanny fever dream. The war had made an entire generation confront the idea of the human body as an object, eyes lightless in death, disassembled into separate pieces.

Paul Fussell, a combat veteran of World War II as well as a scholar of the literature of the Great War, observed, "In a war, as in air accidents, 'insides' are much more visible than it is normally well to imagine." A corpse surrounded by funereal ritual might help us sentimentalize death. Living through—barely—four years of a war in which human beings are transmuted into corpses by industrial processes removes the possibility of sentiment. The world willingly watched films about death dolls like Caligari's Cesare or Paul Leni's carnival horrors come to life. Suicide, Freud's "murderous impulses" against the self, took on new meaning. Suicide had a simplicity in its method of making a corpse.[12]

The many suicides among those traumatized by the Great War confirm this. In 1919, veterans accounted for 40 percent of all the suicides in Canada. In New Zealand, whose troops had seen some of the most horrific fighting on the western front and at Gallipoli, suicide rates among veterans ran as high as four times those of nonveterans in the same age cohort.[13]

Shell-Shocked

The encounter with the uncanny in the trenches could portend a meeting with a new monster born of modern warfare. Early in the war, the last week of August 1914, military authorities sent home a small number of British soldiers described as "broken" by their first experience of battle at the Belgian city of Mons. A British physician in September described the hospitals filling with "frequent examples of gross hysterical conditions" associated with what the doctors considered trivial bullet and shrapnel wounds. War neurosis, or shell shock, had first appeared, though few understood the reasons why in those first months.[14]

A report on shell shock produced by the British War Office in 1922 sought to investigate the phenomenon, apparently not to reconsider the inhuman decisions made in the war, but instead to help military personnel and medical professionals contend with the problem adequately in future conflicts. The committee appointed by the War Office spent a rather significant amount of time discussing how the term "shell shock" had come into use to describe the effect of concussive shelling on the human psyche but also represented a more generalized description of the emotional effects of the trenches themselves.[15]

This discussion seems somewhat moot, given that the vast majority of soldiers experienced both. They endured the continuous shelling, worsening at times of major offensives. Their defensive fortifications became death traps. Corpses piled up unburied, sanitary water became scarce, and increasingly aggressive rats emerged to feed on the dead. The absurdities of nighttime patrols led by officers into no-man's-land provoked tormenting anxiety.

Even four years after the end of the conflict, many of the witnesses for the committee—a group that included as many recruiting agents, high-ranking officers, and men charged with the training of troops as physicians—raised the possibility of malingering and wondered about how class and social status affected the high incidence of shell shock. Some assured their readers that the condition could be prevented if future soldiers received better training. The savage lack of empathy aside, none of the committee's witnesses denied its reality. Something terrible had been awakened in the human psyche by this new kind of war.

Unsurprisingly, physicians who had actually treated the condition provided the most detailed and empathetic accounts. J. I. C. Dunn, who served as a medical officer beginning in 1915, doubted that shell shock accounted for much of the war trauma of the men he treated. Moreover, while concussive shelling played its deadly role in creating unbearable anxiety, Dunn also noted the conditions of the trenches he personally experienced at the Ypres salient in 1915. Worry over the use of mustard and chlorine gas became chronic. Melting snow in the spring forced men to stand and crouch in trenches that had become little more than giant shell holes and filled with water (creating the condition of "trench foot" to further their misery). Moreover, despite official insistence that soldiers regularly rotated off the front lines, Dunn noted that his own division had been in the salient for fourteen months.[16]

These psychological conditions made the uncanny an almost daily reality for many veterans of the trenches. Their minds had been permanently "un-homed." Martin Gilbert, one of the foremost historians of the Great

War, remembered that he'd been warned by family members never to speak of the war to his uncle Irvine, who had fought at the Somme. This ban continued until his uncle's death at the age of ninety-three. One of Gilbert's first history teachers spoke frequently of the war to his young charges and would march in front of the classroom, broom over his shoulder, singing military airs. When the teacher published his memoir, Gilbert discovered that such seeming buffoonery hid the enormous suffering the man had endured and that he wrote about it with "great sensitivity."[17]

Horror films, fiction, and art—creating for oneself the experience of the uncanny—offered one way to express, without overtly identifying with, the "war neuroses" that left a generation psychologically devastated. Certain aspects of shell shock seem closely followed by the art of horror across several media in the war's aftermath. Soldiers' experiences mirrored the feeling of the uncanny described by Freud and darkly illuminated in film and fiction.[18]

Soldiers testified to a mental state they experienced during the war that left them feeling like zombies, somewhere at an intersection point of nightmare, dream, and their own death. The 1922 War Office committee's further investigation of so-called commotional shock, involving a shell exploding near you or a sap mine underneath you, proposed that such incidents could lead "to delirium or stupor; in some cases by automatism or fugue." Physicians suggested, though much disagreement existed on this, that such an experience often created a "mental wound" that endured long after the experience, even after the end of the war. One French physician described his patients experiencing "mental confusion," a term he preferred to what the soldiers themselves called "battle hypnosis."[19]

The horror tradition replicated this fugue state over and over again. Cesare and Frankenstein both seem shell-shocked, as do their victims and creators. Freud, in "The Uncanny," described the "uncanny effect of observing epileptic fits and manifestations of insanity." He seems to have detected here, though he takes the idea no further, that the empty eyes of the shell-shocked man weren't so empty after all; they reflected one's own death.[20]

We can understand this through the uncanny effect of some Japanese horror films, often themselves drawing on the trauma of a later war. Samara in *Ringu* (remade in America as *The Ring*, 2002) or the enraged dead in *Ju-on* (remade as *The Grudge*, 2004) depend on the unsettling movements of the starving ghosts who haunt their victims. Their limbs move in a way we don't think limbs should. They crawl but also slither. Sometimes they skitter toward us, insectoid and reptilian. We shudder and wince because such images call into question the stability of our own bodies and their boundaries.[21]

The soldiers themselves told of experiences with phantasms that assaulted them on the battlefield and then came looking for them long after the war had ended. Ernst Jünger wrote in his diary, later to become the renowned German war memoir *Storm of Steel*, of leading his troops while in a detached, dreamlike state induced by shelling. He described his mind refusing to tell his body of "the curious fluttering and whooshing sounds over our heads." This sense of chilling unreality increased at the sight of stretcher-bearers on a village street. Jünger described them as "groups of dark figures" carrying "a blood-spattered form with a strangely contorted leg." The scene increased his sense of delirium, "a queasy feeling of unreality . . . like a ghostly manifestation in broad daylight."[22]

The eerie nature of these visions point forward to the culture of horror born in film and fiction and backward to the Gothic tradition. British private Frank Richards remembered that some soldiers fell into a semiconscious state. In one instance from the early days of the war, a fellow infantryman pointed out "a fine castle" on the side of a French hillock, but Richards saw no castle. He wrote of the sightings of the Angel of Mons that certainly soldiers marching for hours into the night saw all sort of oddities: "Very nearly everyone was seeing things, we were all so dead beat."[23]

"You must become Caligari!" threatened the advertisements five years later, but it had already happened for many soldiers in the early months of the war. Looming castles haunted combatants before they reared against iron-gray skies in *Nosferatu*. They called to mind the haunted castles that many veterans had been raised on in fairy tales and Gothic novels, places of death and carnage that wrecked the illusion of immortality that the young always embrace.[24]

Numerous reports of soldiers finding themselves in a hypnotic, and highly suggestible, state became common on the battlefield. Soldiers have, of course, feared combat since the beginnings of organized armies. But the

Great War unleashed several kinds of new technology that collapsed the human psyche as well as sundered the body, technology perfectly inflected by the art of the uncanny.

The constant barrage of shelling, the steel patter of the Maxim guns, and the threat of gas choking and blinding soldiers made for the hypnotic, even mystical, state sometimes described. Walter Flex entitled his autobiographical work written in the trenches *Der Wanderer zwischen beiden Welten* (*The Wanderer between the Two Worlds*) to suggest how the experience of war made porous the boundary lines between reality and the world of dreams, the living and the dead. The book became a bestseller. Flex himself died on the eastern front in 1917.[25]

In a letter to his wife written during the first weeks of the war, the German expressionist painter Franz Marc noted the strange feeling of unreality, as if he had already died. He described this experience in supernatural terms as "a spirit that hovers behind the battles, behind each bullet." The result, he admitted, transformed "battles, wounds, movements" into a "mystical, unreal effect." He knew already that this war had been like no other and as a painter noted that "it is unbelievable there were times in which war was represented by painting campfires, burning villages, galloping horsemen, . . . patrol riders and the like." He would die a year and a half later at Verdun.[26]

World War I shattered psyches and turned the landscape into what Murnau and Grau in *Nosferatu*, drawing on their own experiences, called "the land of phantoms." The effect of shell shock and life in the trenches more generally has attracted much attention from historians, so much so that often the most obvious and terrifying effect of their experiences has gone unremarked. As Denis Winter writes in his history of British troops in the Great War, many soldiers described their encounter with corpses as the most horrifying aspect of their lives. He quotes one Tommy who spoke in tones that suggest the soldiers had come to regard the omnipresent corpses as holding no real meaning other than death itself:

Death lies about in all its forms. A limbless body here, the tunic fitting the swollen body like a glove. He may have wanted a tunic to fit him like that

all his life—he gets it in death. A boy without a head like a rumjar without
a label. A form fast turning green lying in a pool of grey-green gas vomit.
Death in a thousand different masks.[27]

No sentimentality and no words about love for the fatherland, the empire, the monarch, or the value of sacrifice. The dead mark nothing and, in
this first war that followed the second industrial revolution, the headless
body makes the young soldier think of an empty bottle missing its label,
nameless and meaningless.

The soldier confronted Freud's uncanny in its most blood-drenched
form—the death doll and, perhaps most significantly, the double. Writing
more than a decade after the war, another soldier remembered looking at
corpses half buried by the muddy trenches and thinking that they seemed
"emptied of life." He then added, "A man dies and stiffens into something
like a wooden dummy. . . . One forgets quickly. The mind is averted as well
as the eyes. It reassures itself after the first cry: 'It is I. No, it is not I. I shall
not be like that.'"[28]

The sense of a world filled with corpses, and all the nightmare images
that attend such a sensibility, followed soldiers from the battlefield. The
English poet and novelist Siegfried Sassoon found that the dead came for
him even after he'd been sent to a London hospital to recuperate from a
wound. In April 1917, he wrote of how he would spend the day talking to
his compatriots about the war in catchphrases and clichés, conversations
that seemed as irrelevant as speculations about the weather. But then,
when night fell "and the ward is half shadow," the reality of the war came
back to him:

> The horrors come creeping across the floor; the floor is littered with parcels
> of dead flesh and bones, faces glaring at the ceiling, faces turned to the floor,
> hands clutching neck or belly; a livid grinning face with bristly moustache
> peers at me over the edge of my bed, the hands clutching my sheets.[29]

Sassoon's experience of watching a horror film unfold before his eyes
lasted much longer than the war itself for most veterans and indeed for their
families. In "For the Duration," the poet Ted Hughes wrote, years after his

veteran father's death, about the night terrors that threatened to destroy his childhood home:

> I could hear you from my bedroom—
> The whole hopelessness still going on,
> No man's land still crying and burning.

William Hughes had been part of the disastrous landing at Gallipoli, where his regiment spent months pinned down on the beach under Ottoman guns and, according to a medic who served there, "men had lost arms and legs, brains oozed out of shattered skulls, and lungs protruded out of riven chests; many had lost their faces and were, I think, unrecognizable to their friends."[30]

The terrors of the psyche broken by such conditions cannot be fully hidden. The trauma of the body certainly cannot. Historians Stéphane Audoin-Rouzeau and Annette Becker point to specific medical advances—including better evacuation techniques, the use of anesthesia on the battlefield, X-rays, techniques that prevented gangrene and reduced the necessity of amputation—that appeared during the Great War. But, they note, the brutality of combat "counterbalanced" all these techniques. The effects of shrapnel, large-caliber shells, the steel spray of Maxim bullets, and poison gas combined to create a generation of disabled people.[31]

Catastrophic physical trauma conjoined with psychological trauma in the war's aftermath. The war left over 20 million men wounded. Some of them, like Freud's son, recovered quickly. Millions suffered for the rest of their lives. In France, where the toll of the wounded has been estimated at 1.1 million, the sheer number of the disabled forced the public to give special attention to men permanently disfigured by the war.

The first Armistice Day celebration in 1919 placed amputees, men with catastrophic facio-dental injuries, and those blinded by gas and shell fragments at the front of the parade. This induced a haunting for those in the crowd who found the display out of touch with a victory celebration. It's well to recall that many who cheered the men bore their own psychic and physical wounds from the war. The scene seemed a strange enactment of the return of the dead in *J'accuse*.

The number of facial injuries in France led to the creation of a veterans' organization in the 1920s called the Union des Gueules Cassées (Union of Broken Faces or, more literally, Union of Broken Mugs). Five thousand strong, the group received significant coverage by the French press, including photographs of some of the membership appearing in the popular magazine *L'illustration*.

The description of the men, however, reads as less than empathetic, suggesting only the horror they invoked. The article calls them "a hideous sight" and invites us to consider faces that have undergone "sinister hollowing from bullets, the pulverizing from grenades, the stabbing from bayonets or daggers." The piece concludes by capturing the spirit of the uncanny the wounded veteran inspired, calling them "the monsters whose lot is worse than death."[32]

In Germany, men physically scarred by the war made the streets of Berlin seem a haunted place to the Soviet diplomat Ilya Ehrenburg in the fall of 1921. He saw the evidence of the recent "catastrophe" everywhere but also noted that the war had become the ghost at the feast, visible and yet purposefully hidden. The "artificial limbs of war-cripples did not creak, empty sleeves were pinned up with safety-pins. Men whose faces had been scorched by flame-throwers wore large black spectacles. The lost war took care to camouflage itself as it roamed the streets."[33]

Massacres

Soldiers did not suffer alone, and to understand the popularity of horror in the years following the war, it's essential to grasp the evils wrought on noncombatants. The war inflicted the same psychological and physical wounds on civilian populations. Nurses, ambulance drivers, and battlefield physicians experienced shell shock, as did millions of civilians caught near, or almost literally in the middle of, the war in Europe, Africa, and western Asia.

In many dark corners of the war, the fate of civilians proved worse than that of the combatants. Although cloaked in the language of propaganda, especially the British use of the "German atrocities" in Belgium as a reason to enter the war, investigations by medical and legal authorities during the conflict and historians' subsequent research show that war crimes did occur on a mind-numbing scale between 1914 and 1918. Unfortunately, soldiers from both the Allied forces and the Central Powers targeted civilians, even if more evidence exists for the inhuman acts of the latter. We can account for this fact in part due to the Central Powers successfully invading and occupying Allied territory (at least in Europe) such that civilians became targets of opportunity.[34]

Rape, an act of extreme violence generally ignored when calculating the human cost of war, occurred on a massive scale in the global conflict. A German-Swiss criminology professor, Rodolphe Archibald Reiss, visited Serbia in the fall of 1914 to carry out an intensive investigation of battlefield atrocities. The politics of the moment certainly shaped his findings, but it's worth noting that Reiss went beyond eyewitness accounts, investigating sites of atrocities and even determining the expenditure of bullets. He gathered and compared both Austro-Hungarian and Serbian reports. He found a living horror.[35]

Even in these early months, as Hapsburg armies began their advance into Serbia, gang rapes that included other forms of torture and often ended in disembowelment became common practices among invading troops. At least one young Serbian woman, Reiss discovered, had been raped by as many as forty soldiers, who then cut out her genitals. Many of the women not murdered had been otherwise tortured and then blinded. In a grisly irony, the Balkan conflict of 1991–1999 saw a virulently nationalistic and embittered Serbia use its armed forces to carry out precisely the same kind of terror inflicted in the Great War against ethnic minorities inside the nation's allegedly historic borders.

The aftermath of war often finds traditional military historians, and the nation-states whose nostalgic interests they serve, using something along the lines of the argument "a few bad apples" in discussing such atrocities. Consider the more recent case of U.S. reaction to the 1968 Mỹ Lai massacre in Vietnam, in which close to five hundred civilians died at the hands of American soldiers, many of the women raped, in an all-day slaughter that troops had to take a lunch break to finish. Though the antiwar movement pointed to the massacre as one more reason to get out of Vietnam, polls found a frightening number of Americans who "were not bothered" by the story.

Nixon's decision to unilaterally change platoon commander Lieutenant William Calley Jr.'s twenty-two-year sentence to a three-year sentence under house arrest caused a ripple of disapproval but not the kind of public outcry that might be expected.[36]

We now know that American war crimes in Vietnam and the rest of Southeast Asia occurred on a massive and systemic scale. Nick Turse's examination of American policy in Vietnam, *Kill Anything That Moves*, reveals that the American military adopted a "managerial approach" to warfare that produced an entire "system of suffering." The very conception of "free fire zones" was intended to maximize a body count that by definition included noncombatants.[37]

Reiss concluded that something similarly diabolical had been at work in Serbia. These acts of evil did not simply occur, Reiss suggested, in some explosive fit of combat-induced savagery by a few bad sorts among the conscripts. He believed they had been "governed by a system." This "collective sadism" constituted not simply a psychological phenomenon but a state policy of "extermination."[38]

German forces repeated similar crimes in Belgium. The occupation itself transformed one-fourth of the tiny nation's population into refugees. A less well-known fact concerns the use of Belgian and French civilians in labor camps, many of them taken as prisoners to Germany itself as slaves to the war effort. German soldiers massacred hundreds of civilians, including the elderly and the very young, in the Belgian towns of Dinant and Leuven in 1914 because they believed (wrongly) that they had been fired upon by *francs-tireurs* (free shooters, or partisans).[39]

Although Allied forces never occupied Germany during the Great War, civilians still experienced enormous suffering due to specific Allied policy in the months following the 1918 armistice. British naval supremacy, and Germany's global isolation, ensured that a blockade in the North Sea cut the empire off from essential foodstuffs. The blockade continued after the armistice in order to wring more and increasingly humiliating concessions out of the defeated Central Powers. A famine ensued that caused the deaths of three-quarters of a million German civilians.[40]

A naval blockade may seem far removed from the slicing of bayonets and the mutilation carried out in the other torture chambers of the war. But the cold, bureaucratic decision men made to allow widespread starvation in order to humiliate the foe and ensure the expansion of empire represents the savagery of the state and the people who make its machinery run, what Hannah Arendt later called "the banality of evil" that became a feature of the inhumanity of the twentieth century.

Death and Sentimentality

The atmosphere of horror became palpable, and the Western world increasingly became drenched in the atmosphere of the uncanny. The beginnings of both modern art and the modern horror film are inexplicable without the experience of trenches and trauma. Both sought not psychological catharsis, but something much more pointed and political. *J'accuse* became a paradigm of the need to produce horror, the need to scream a demand that the memory of the war's horror not disappear.

Artists allied with filmmakers, and increasingly they actually became filmmakers, in order to shatter the illusions of the audience, to make them see the horror of millions of deaths. The audience for these new kinds of works often immersed themselves in the shadows that lurked on canvas and screen. The suffering of tens of millions made the new culture of horror intensely recognizable.

The desire seems to have been to rip off the veil of sentimentality. Given what both soldiers and civilians experienced in the war's combat zones, the need to destroy sentiment seems at odds with what had to have been the already prevailing mood of cynicism. How could anyone hang on to any of the values of the world before 1914?

We can perhaps better grasp the need to produce horror if we consider how even current attitudes about the Great War reveal a need to forget that accompanies the need to commemorate. Or, perhaps more pungently, how the passage of time quickly allows sentiment to cloud the memory of the war. The symbol of the poppy—beauty growing on the graves, a short-lived bloom that represented the war generation—had been suggested by Canadian physician John McCrae's essentially martial 1915 poem "In Flanders Fields." The poem speaks in the voice of the dead, but rather than calling

into question the meaning of their own deaths, the poet evokes death to demand more sacrifice: "To you from failing hands we throw / The torch." Paul
Fussell described the poem as both "vicious" and "stupid."[41]

Fussell's informed opinion aside, the symbol of the poppy appeared in
most of the Great War's centennial celebrations in 2014. Now it dominates
British memory of the war, an often weepy mixture of nostalgia and cultural conservatism not so different from the cauldron of conflicted emotion that led to Brexit and that, in relation to the Great War, shades into
a kind of poppy-porn version of the conflict. A visit to contemporary Ieper
(Ypres) confirms this: the Belgian town, part of the ghastly Ypres salient,
has acquired a theme-park atmosphere, an annexed outpost of the British
tourism industry on the continent. Not only do souvenir shops hawking
poppy-themed shirts, coffee mugs, and shot glasses line the street leading to
Menin Gate—the "east gate" through which tens of thousands of English
and Indian troops passed to their deaths—but you can purchase chocolate
Tommy helmets and wolf them down, presumably not thinking too much
about what an empty helmet means. The town has become crowded with
faux British pubs serving toasties and shepherd's pie while making the town
one of the few places in Belgium where it's hard to find decent beer.

It was not surprising to discover that Flanders and Ypres itself had long
been critiqued for commercializing the war. However, I did not expect to
learn that the effort to commodify the conflict had occurred so quickly and
had affected veterans and their families who returned to the deadly salient.
A German veteran, Gerhard Schinke, found himself nearly assaulted in 1927
by locals trying to sell him rusted helmets and rifles. Christopher Isherwood, whose father had died at the salient in 1915, looked bitterly on what he
found there in 1935. In his diary, Isherwood wrote that the town had indeed,
in the words of a poem, become "'forever England' . . . the England of sordid
little tea shops, souvenirs, and touts."[42]

Perhaps the feeling that by "touring" you can find some kind of authentic experience of the past may be the false premise at work, even for
those of us who think we are not part of the commemoration industry. The
notion that a contemporary visitor, including a historian, can bicycle the
paths around Ypres, view the region's graveyards and collapsed trenches, and
reflect on the appalling crime against human beings that occurred there it-

self reeks of war tourism. Still, one encounters museums and restaurants that remain shocking in their insouciant vulgarity. A "British pub" attached to the Hooge Crater Museum (one of the many points in the trenches both sides sap-mined) serves a beer called "The Wipers Times," a tribute that's really the commodification of the British soldiers' experience. The name references the satirical title of newspapers produced by the soldiers themselves, men who had begun calling Ypres "Wipers" out of sheer confusion over the pronunciation until it became a much-used joke about one of the most terrible places in the world between 1914 and 1918.[43]

Horror as representation of the world threw down a gauntlet to efforts to remember the war sentimentally, to apply outworn conceptions of patriotism to the ugliness of what had happened. Art critic Maurice Nadeau described the surrealist movement as an effort to crack apart "the thick carapace of centuries of culture—life pure, naked, raw, lacerated," art that sought to undermine any kind of war commemoration that forgot the pile of corpses. Surrealism forced the viewer to connect, even if by an indirect route, the horror of the trenches with the horror of their own deaths and of the world.[44]

Perhaps the surrealists failed in the long run. But there's unquestionably something deeply significant about how quickly authors, poets, and even composers joined painters on the world's dark carnival ride. American composer Aaron Copland, somewhat surprisingly given his reputation for soaring orchestral suites like *Appalachian Spring*, produced a one-act ballet, *Grohg* (1922–25), born out of his obsession with *Nosferatu*. It's only loosely based on the film and, rather than using vampire mythology, concerns a necromancer with the power to reanimate corpses. Copland drew his inspiration not only from Murnau but also from his reading of Freud and what he called the era's "taste for the bizarre."[45]

"Dada Means Nothing"

The taste for the bizarre had begun as an antiwar protest before disillusion and suffering turned men and women who experienced the war toward the borderlands of nightmare. A group of painters, poets, photographers, collage artists, and sculptors congregated in Zurich in 1914 as the Dada movement, the art of anti-art. Dadaists sought to unsettle the viewer, give them a vertiginous sense of their world. In this way, they reproduced the borders of the wasteland where the constant din and danger of war made the world unreal. They reimagined the soldiers' hypnotic state of horror, their "battle hypnosis," in the trenches and put it on canvas.

Artists who allied themselves with Dada consciously chose the confusing name. Some authorities claim it's a reference to the French word for "hobbyhorse," suggestive of the playfulness of the enterprise. More likely, it calls to mind a kind of nonsense babbling, da-da-da-de-de-da. A typical Dadaist project might involve a collage that included newsprint, a photo of soldiers marching off to war, and a painting of a tricycle. None of it made sense because the world had ceased making sense.

German author Hugo Ball became the titular leader of the movement, but, like most artistic enterprises academics label a "movement," Dadaism remained loosely organized at best. Ball moved to Zurich, in neutral Switzerland, at the beginning of World War I with the singer and performance artist Emmy Hennings. Together they shocked the city's deeply embedded bourgeois conceptions with both their art and the unconventionality of their relationship.

Both Hennings and Ball had their sensibilities shattered by the slaughter of the Great War. The latter wrote in 1915:

I had no love for the death's-head hussars
Nor for the mortars with girl's names on them,
And when at last the glorious days arrived
I unobtrusively went on my way.

In February of that year, Ball gathered together a group of artists in a cabaret he and Hennings had purchased in a seedy part of town and renamed the Cabaret Voltaire. At the first meeting, Ball read a manifesto, a favorite pastime among intellectuals of the day. The group agreed on its basic principles even though they soon would split into factions and argue endlessly, and rather paradoxically, about the meaning of Dada.

All agreed that they cared little for the public's need to understand their work. They consciously sought to short-circuit rationality in the belief that this forced their audience to see the world differently. Europeans, especially the principal combatants in the current conflict, believed themselves heirs of the Enlightenment tradition of reason and bearers of civilization. Perhaps reason itself, or at least the presumption of rationality, had been at fault?

Hans Arp (also known as Jean Arp), one of the first of the group that huddled with Hennings and Ball at Cabaret Voltaire, later told the German painter Hans Richter that the group had been "revolted by the butchery of the 1914 World War." This sense of revulsion had an oddly optimistic side in its perhaps naïve belief that art could "cure the madness of the age."[46] We know, with the benefit of unfortunate experience, that it did not.

By the end of the war, the Romanian-born author Tristan Tzara—who in his 1918 "manifesto" wrote "Dada Means Nothing"—emerged as probably the most well-known of the Dadaists because of his popular plays, poems, and essays. It's a sign of the fluidity of the movement, and the necessity of fluidity of nomenclature when talking about art in this era, that when one of the first of the major Dada exhibitions appeared in 1920, it included work by the German veteran Otto Dix, often classed by art historians as an expressionist or a surrealist.

Dix actually did represent something very different from the original intent of Dada, in part because he wanted his meaning made clear—horribly and irredeemably clear. His images became inhuman and monstrous. Christopher Bram's novel *Gods and Monsters* (originally published in 1995 as *Father of Frankenstein*) features James Whale, the director of the 1931 film *Frankenstein*, sexually fetishizing the idea of the gas mask. The "inhuman" look of the mask enthralls Whale and, it's suggested, provides the inspiration for his design of his Monster, an image much more industrial than the description Mary Shelley gives of her creature.

Consciously or not, Bram's description resonates perfectly with a new artistic vision that emerged from World War I of the inhuman combined with the human, or perhaps the human being dissolved in the savagery of nature. In fact, the gas mask as symbol of death became a kind of totem for artist-veterans such as Dix. Georges Limbour, a French poet who counted himself one of the Paris surrealists in the 1920s, described the gas mask as "the only authentic modern mask." Its image had taken the place of ritual uses of the mask in earlier civilizations. A mass-produced image of death rather than a sacred object, the gas mask made the wearer appear to have a mutilated human face with insect-like eyes suggestive of the animal world.[47]

Otto Dix produced this effect in his first major work after having the experience of surviving almost every major action on the western front. In a cycle of prints and etchings published in 1924 as *Der Krieg* (*The War*), human beings are hidden by gas masks or ripped apart to lie in a pile of corpses. His etching "Storm Troops Advancing under Gas Attack" presents figures hidden behind their gas masks, each looking like a Halloween pumpkin carved with sinister features. It's almost as if the human beings inside them have *become* these masks, another kind of death doll. Rather than rendering them as heroes of imperial Germany under attack, Dix gives the storm troopers (and, as a veteran, by extension himself) a monstrous aspect, hands curled like talons around rifles and hand grenades.

Dix created images in which the battlefield itself became a Gothic, haunted castle. His "Collapsed Trench" features a soldier who perhaps crouches for safety or perhaps has become a corpse. Over him hang what a quick glance suggests are pieces of cloth but on closer inspection appear as a vulture and a skeleton, perhaps even the Reaper himself. Another print, "Crater Field Near Dontrien Lit by Flares," shows no-man's-land as literally a place where no human being could imagine being, a wasteland and perhaps a postapocalyptic one.

Dix often turned the human form into a kind of monstrosity even when it did not wear a mask or wield weapons. In "Front Line Soldier in Brussels," he has a soldier on leave standing in a demonic gloom while around him parade sex workers who, the etching suggests, are charging more than he can afford. The women are voluptuous and dressed in expensive clothes, drawn in purposeful contrast to the soldier's own garb.

Dix here showed a tendency, also found in Gance's *J'accuse*, to forget the immense suffering of civilians. Prostitution became as significant a venture as it always does in wartime, though the sex workers themselves saw little of the profits. Most, along with frequently becoming the victims of homicidal violence from men recently in combat, lived in extreme poverty. Importantly, in Dix's etching the soldier appears as no simple victim: he strikes the viewer as looking predatory, his ratlike face leering out of the shadows while the women pass, a down-at-the-heels Nosferatu robbed of his victims.

The German, and soon international, public who viewed Dix's sketches in 1924 may have been most struck by the simply titled "Skull." The fleshless human skull crawls with worms and, in context, alludes to the numerous skeletal body parts discovered in the trenches beginning in 1919. It obviously symbolized death, but in the cycle *Der Krieg* it brought together grotesqueries that had never precisely intersected before.

Skulls frequently appeared in Renaissance and baroque religious paintings as memento mori, reminding viewers that they were mortal and, in the context of Christian theology, that death gave their temporal choices an eternal meaning. Ossuaries across Europe displayed skulls in this context, one famous Austrian example featuring skulls painted in festive colors suggestive of the hope of resurrection.

However, the growth of religious skepticism made the skull and the skeleton an image of death outside of the Christian worldview, perhaps most famously in Van Gogh's *Head of a Skeleton with a Burning Cigarette* (1886). The world of entertainment used the macabre in the magic lantern show and the phantasmagoria, frequently featuring dancing skeletons along with coffins and bloody daggers in the night.

Otto Dix's "Skull" offered the world something much more disturbing. His verminous skull looks like the skulls associated with Gothic horror while at the same time reminding viewers of the elements of trench life that few wanted to speak of and most sought to forget. Corpses had gone unburied in piles, sometimes gnawed to the bone by rats grown fat on the true spoils of war. Corpses attracted so many vermin of all kinds that, at least after gas masks had been widely issued, soldiers wrote of occasionally hoping the enemy might lob a few chlorine shells their way and exterminate the rats and lice. Thus, "Skull" captures this world of horror and intersects with *Nosferatu*'s land of phantoms, the trudging corpses of *J'accuse* whose flesh hangs on their bones, and, in less than a decade, the comedies of death his fellow veteran James Whale produced. Whale's *Bride of Frankenstein* (1935) would build one of its most horrific, yet oddly comic, moments around just such a skull.

All of these different images of the war ripped the body from the world of immortality, denying the possibility of resurrection held by the religious worldview, whether specifically Christian or spiritualist. The body became the corpse. Abel Gance's shambling horrors and Frankenstein's Monster, blasphemies of both nature and theology, offered the only return from the land of the dead. Distortions of the body, monstrous hybrids of human and animal, mocked the resurrection of the body. Meditation on trauma, mutilation, and death had quickly become an essential part of entertainment and the arts.

Death had a fandom.

Horror for the Moralist

Dix had created an art taken directly from no-man's-land. His paintings and drawings proved controversial even in the early 1920s, and Dix welcomed the controversy. As he continued to experiment with images of death and dismemberment, he described himself as creating "new things" that would "cause nervous shock to the faint of heart; horror for the moralist."[48]

André Breton also took his experience of war, his time among those driven to insanity by the violence, both to make an art of death and to act as an impresario for a generation of artists who, like Dix, had been irrevocably shaken by the war. He called this movement surrealism, and it became the conduit for terrible visions in the 1920s and '30s, often drawing from and contributing directly to the horrific on the movie screen. Their work continues to influence contemporary horrors from the slashers of Wes Craven to the grotesque fictions of Thomas Ligotti and David Lynch.

André Breton set himself up as the leader of the new multimedia movement, later earning the moniker "the Black Pope" of surrealism. Breton sought to define the movement in his *Manifesto* of 1924. The essay praised Freud and described the world of dream as the place of creative fecundity for any artist.

The Black Pope seemed to consider battle hypnosis, the twilight land of the dead, as the well of creativity for the surrealist movement. Breton believed that artists experienced "the waking state" as "a phenomenon of interference." The borderlands of dream and nightmare offered the visionary artist access to the historical moment as much as their own consciousness.[49]

Given the Gothic tenor of so much surrealist work—its morbidity and willingness to wallow in body horror—it's no surprise that Breton illustrates what he means by reference to the most popular terror novel of the eighteenth century, Matthew Lewis's *The Monk*. Sensationalist and bizarre, containing murder, sexual depravity, and pacts with the devil, the book shocked and obsessed readers in 1796. Its ending, in which demons tear apart the lascivious, homicidal monk, earns praise from Breton as "a paragon of precision and innocent grandeur."

What could Breton mean by such a claim? He's trolling his readers a bit while also, like so many impresarios of the art of horror, inviting us into the sideshow, seating us comfortably in the car for the dark carnival ride before he scares us out of our skin. He's also making a point about the 1920s, that time after the Great War when Antonio Gramsci's "morbid symptoms" had begun to appear, and a time that made the marvelous gore of *The Monk* seem a fantasia while also giving its supernatural horrors a special status in registering the moment's real-world brutalities.[50]

Surrealism and its wide popularity represented more than a mood in the world of aesthetics, separated from daily life and experienced only in the cool quiet of museums or in "manifestos" debated among intellectuals. Breton himself became something of a continent-wide celebrity, having an incredibly successful tour with his collaborator Paul Éluard in 1935. In Prague, capital of a newly established and democratic Czechoslovakia since 1918, crowds received the pair like rock stars. Flyers plastered the city screaming "Breton in Prague!" For two nights in a row, he lectured to a crowd of seven hundred people who came to listen to a rather obscure talk on aesthetic theory.[51]

People across the social and cultural spectrum saw in the surrealist movement something very different from what we conceive of today as the parochial world of "the arts." The new movement voiced a collective cry of pain in the war's aftermath, an attempt, interwoven into the fabric of the first horror films, to deal with monstrous impossibilities suddenly become real. Surrealist artworks, like film and literature, registered the horror of the times by breaking down the walls between waking life and nightmare. Like Lon Chaney, they distorted and mutilated the body.

The connection between the horror film, war neurosis, and the art of nightmare appeared in more than a similarity of themes. Surrealism embraced film, particularly horror film, as offering a form of art that in some respects recalled the dream state. *Nosferatu* became a special favorite among surrealists and their followers, both for its willingness to play with the line between dream and waking, what Breton called the "surreality" that collapses the dream into waking life. More important, the film's absurdist construction of the body of the monster—an animalistic face and talons atop a grossly distended body—proved irresistible to surrealist artists and their legions of young followers. They disrupted screenings by yelling lines they had memorized from the intertitles, not unlike, David J. Skal has noted, delirious fans who "decades later would attend *The Rocky Horror Picture Show*."[32]

The body of the vampire and his victims seemed to many of the first generation of surrealists every body left on the Great War's meaningless battlefield or physically traumatized by combat. German painter Max Ernst best defines the exploration of the body tormented by war, his canvases exploding in all the bright, harsh colors of rage and pain. He, like so many of those who created the new vision of horror, had direct experience of the slaughter.

Ernst, like Breton, began his career studying to join the psychiatric profession and engaging with the emerging movement of psychoanalysis. Although he studied both art history and philosophy at university, he read much of Freud's prewar work and returned to him after 1918. While he studied medicine, Ernst visited psychiatric hospitals as an observer.[33]

Raised in a strict Catholic household, Ernst spent much of his life provoking outrage among people with a bourgeois sensibility. His numerous affairs and marriages seem a kind of performance art of a piece with his frequent artistic sallies against middle-class virtue. (It would likely delight him to learn that some of the more experimental, occasionally inaccessible indie rock bands of the twentieth and twenty-first centuries such as the Mars Volta and Mission of Burma have paid homage to his work.) The relationship of his painting to the macabre might have pleased him even more, given his interests in the themes of distorted bodies, human savagery, death, and horrific manifestations of the dead.

Thin and handsome, with incredibly piercing eyes, Ernst made friends, and lovers, rather easily. He managed this despite a temperament that ran to the morbid even before his experiences in the Great War. One of the most influential and enduring of these friendships began in 1914 when he met Hans Arp, one of the founders of Dada. A friendship with German expressionist painter August Macke made it possible for Ernst to have his first gallery show in Berlin immediately before the outbreak of the war.

Ernst later became very close to the surrealist poet Paul Éluard in the 1920s and began an affair with the poet's wife that eventually so depressed Éluard that he left the pair to themselves and moved for a time to Vietnam. Éluard remained friends with Ernst despite this romantic drama, the unconventionality of which had at first made the situation acceptable to him. In 1939, Éluard used his influence to get Ernst out of a French detainee camp for "undesirable foreigners."

No other experience of his strange and adventurous life, however, compared to what happened to Ernst in the Great War. "On the first of August 1914, M[ax] E[rnst] died," he later wrote. "He was resurrected on the eleventh of November 1918." The theme of death and reanimation came to him early, fascinating him around the time that H. P. Lovecraft acquired a similar obsession that resulted in tales like "The Tomb," "Herbert West—Reanimator," and "Cool Air," as well as the short novel *The Case of Charles Dexter Ward*.

Ernst once tried to explain his own interest in the return of the dead and his obsession with terrifying avian imagery by connecting them with an odd childhood experience in which he discovered his pet bird, Loplop, dead and, at precisely the same moment, his father burst into the room to announce the birth of his baby sister. Perhaps of more importance, however, Ernst's own biography became a peculiar series of metaphorical deaths, each followed by a Freudian resurrection. Time and again he found himself faced with near-certain extermination, then rescued, and then once more threatened with death, only to have his circumstances dramatically change and grant him yet another resurrection.

His first death and reanimation began with his early days on the western front. He spent much of the opening months of the war with an artillery unit, but, through extraordinary luck, his commanding officer had studied art history and recognized Ernst's name from a Paris exhibition. Ernst left the trenches and joined the officer's staff, drafting maps.

In yet another turn of fortune, this one for the ill, another officer saw some of the paintings Ernst had prepared for an upcoming antiwar exhibition and ordered him back to the front as punishment. Ernst managed to survive the 1918 spring offensives, injured not by the enemy but by a mule kick and the recoil of a gun.

The end of the war found Ernst not only deeply traumatized by what he had seen but also isolated by the war's outcome. In 1922, virtually trapped in Cologne, he falsified papers so that he could repair to Paris. He abandoned his first wife and child in the process.

Almost immediately after the war, Ernst began to depict monstrosity in his work. Many of his post-1918 paintings combine human, animal, and machine in novel ways. (These paintings influenced a number of later artists, such as H. R. Giger, the Swiss painter whose "biomechanical" visions inspired the set and creature design for Ridley Scott's 1979 horror film, *Alien*.)

Painted while Ernst was attempting to find a way out of Germany (and his first marriage), *Celebes* (1921) illustrates how his vision of horror had been shaped on the western front. A giant mechanical beast, elephantine but without any features recognizably organic, moves ponderously across a dead landscape while a leaden sky hangs heavy on the horizon. More disturbing than the creature that seems a living machine, the headless body of a woman flails in the foreground. The thing sliding across that empty no-man's-land has apparently decapitated her.

Viewers who first saw *Celebes* found themselves deeply disturbed by the image, reportedly often gasping outright. The painting invoked the industrial nature of combat on a landscape destroyed by constant, unending shelling. But the violated headless body may have caused the most disquiet, another one of the postwar period's death dolls, Benjamin's image of the fragile human body, alone on a landscape of death.

Bodies shorn of their heads represented nothing particularly new on canvas. Painters had been using headless bodies in devotional art, or simply paintings that made use of a religious subject, since the Middle Ages. Saints martyred by beheading often carried their heads about in these images, on canvases, in frescoes, and in stained-glass windows. Artists had repeatedly depicted the head of John the Baptist on a silver charger since the medieval period.

However, Ernst had done something much more uncanny in painting simply a headless body. This was no saint in glory but rather a victim of the modern world, mutilated and helpless. Ruthlessly ripped out of the context of religious faith, the body became an empty husk, soulless in a fashion that would have troubled the cheerful rationalism that people brought with them from the nineteenth century as much as it offended the most devoutly religious.

Ernst remained in Paris throughout much of the 1920s, developing a technique he called *frottage*, in which etchings are made from rubbing the canvas with objects of varied textures. This achieved a rough but mechanistic look that Ernst used for his series *Natural History*, a set of paintings that create a decidedly unnatural history. His 1927 "Forest and Dove" contains an almost childish-looking drawing of a bird, another incarnation of Loplop perhaps, against a dark forest. Ernst admitted that the image recalled his own early fear of the woods and notions of the "haunted forest." This imagery, important for fairy tales and horror films, takes on an even more disturbing tenor in "Forest and Dove," as the trees have the look of gears, perhaps drill bits, penetrating the sky. His youthful fears are with us, but they have passed through the fire of war. We are back with him on the mechanized battlefield.

Ernst's interest in the macabre even appears in what many art historians refer to as his "collage novels" but that are perhaps best understood as some of the first graphic novels. Ernst attempted this form in 1929, but it did not come to fruition until 1934 with *Une semaine de bonté* (A Week of Kindness).[54]

The collages of *Une semaine* evoke anything but kindness. Ernst grouped the images, with no obvious relationship to one another, dividing them into chapters denominated by a day of the week. The book contains no narrative or explanatory text besides a few quotes from Breton. None of them are especially revealing. There's no meaning other than the effort to conjure terror, itself a meaningful exercise as the 1930s grew ever more menacing.

Monstrous hybrids work black magic against human bodies on every page of *Une semaine*. A lion-headed bureaucrat, officious and angry, chases a young woman. Two beastly faced figures hold a man and a woman captive in a train car. The creatures have strapped the nearly nude woman to a mechanism of torture, a cousin of all the technology of the Great War and of Kafka's infernal engine from "In the Penal Colony."

One image that sums up the terror-driven theme of the work might once again prompt us to think of Giger's designs for *Alien* or the work of H. P. Lovecraft: A vicious avian figure with a human form rips at the head of a classical nude. Beneath them, a creature part bird, part reptile, part something that bundles gibbering insanity with an all-too-disturbing naturalism perches on top of a corpse, the eyes wide with the mad horror of his final moment. A scaly tentacle penetrates the corpse's throat for reasons that are, lucky for us, left unexplained.

The unsettling, undeniably erotic and necrotic aspects of many of the collage prints in *Une semaine* bring a special intensity to the horror, a point that has been the subject of all manner of Freudian and post-Freudian analyses. These academic analyses sometimes miss the simple fact that the fascination with sex and death are two of our great obsessions. Melding together the morbid and the lascivious produces mental frictions of unremitting intensity. Horror auteurs, from Albin Grau to John Carpenter, have understood that coitus and murder are boon companions, their relationship primeval.

Nudes, usually women, fill *Une semaine*. Ernst made sure that he blended any image that might incite desire with the macabre. A woman on a midnight rendezvous with her lover watches somnolently (Is she responsible?) as he contorts into an owl-faced monstrosity from whose visage begins to emerge something that's part erect penis and part cobra. A voluptuous nude woman lies on a tombstone carved with a skull (in case we miss the message), while avian monsters prepare to assault her. Another woman lies trapped beneath a skeletal spine that claps her against a bed turned vertical, her face a mask of terror. Numerous eyes wink at us on the bony appendage.

Ernst had been visiting with friends in fascist Italy when he produced *Une semaine de bonté*. In a flurry of activity, he put the work together in three weeks, each print a collage from popular magazines, advertisements, and various ephemera, the joints of the images made invisible during the process of printing. The nature of the book, indeed the fevered rage in which Ernst produced it, recalled his experience of the reprehensible during his time in the kaiser's army, a period in his life that now seemed darkly illumined by Adolf Hitler's recent appointment as chancellor of Germany and his rapid consolidation of dictatorial powers.

Many of the surrealists, even if they had little or no contact with the Great War, still picked up on the macabre attitude of the times, what Aaron

Copland called a "taste for the bizarre." Surrealist artist Leonora Carrington claimed that "everything happened after I was born."[35] She entered the world in Lancashire, England, on April 6, 1917, the day the United States entered the Great War. The years leading from that conflict to World War II, all the years of violence and death in between and that followed, irrevocably shaped her vision.

Carrington was an accomplished painter, but, like many female artists of the era, she has most often been referenced in relation to the male artist who shared her bed. In her case, she's frequently described simply as Max Ernst's mistress (or one of them). However, her personal and artistic independence is clear to anyone who looks. Although certainly influenced by Ernst, and by surrealism more generally, her paintings portray her own vision of the terrible times and her place in them. The painting *The Meal of Lord Candlestick* (1938), for example, managed not only to mock her father and her Catholic upbringing but also to distort the human form into frightening shapes.

Her painting of Ernst in 1939, simply labeled *Max Ernst*, imagined an elderly, misshapen man in a winterscape. At the time, he was forty-six and she had just turned twenty, but she paints him as much older and more decrepit, another version of Lord Candlestick. In a self-portrait painted in 1937–38, Carrington gives herself wild hair sprouting from her thin form. Her right hand raises itself in a motion that could be writing, painting, or showing us that she's shaking uncontrollably.

After the French released Ernst from his detainment in 1939, he was then captured by the Germans, who considered his art degenerate; he escaped and fled to America, leaving the young Carrington behind. Soon she began to seem unstable to almost everyone who knew her. In fact, her tendency to say off-kilter things, including that only the family fox terrier had been present at her birth since her "mother was away at the time," attracted the wrong kind of attention. Odd and even outlandish behavior, a pattern that brought the Dalís of the world fame and admiration, got Carrington sent to an asylum. Kathryn Davis writes in an introduction to Carrington's short stories that she "lost her mind," but in this period women did not necessarily have to suffer from a major mental illness for family and friends to institutionalize them. In fact, husbands and fathers could lock women away in the "snake pits" (as they became known) for anything from alleged alcohol abuse to "promiscuous" behavior.[56]

Compared with her paintings, which have garnered admittedly limited interest, Carrington's equally interesting short stories—many of them fairy tales in which things go horribly wrong—have been even more obscure. But in fact, her paintings and stories form a cohesive set of personal and collective surrealist myths, reflections of the horrors that followed the Great War. In her tales, women dressed down to their skin and then stripped to their very skeletons. Her story "Pigeon, Fly!" might have been written by Kafka if he'd used fairy-tale imagery. In it, an androgynous figure visits a nameless female protagonist and demands that she entrust all her talents to their emissary. The protagonist is then taken into a dark forest where a sheep-faced creature tells her to paint what she sees. She sees a coffin rise out of the ground, opening to reveal a corpse whose beauty is unspoiled. The woman begins to paint, and as she furiously sketches the face of the lovely dead, she realizes she has made a self-portrait.

Other of Carrington's tales use the era's grotesqueries to a distinctly political end: they are what can only be described as feminist horror fiction. "The Oval Lady," for example, features a teenage girl begging her father not to destroy her beloved Tartar, a painted hobbyhorse that seems, in the logic of a Carrington tale, to somehow be alive. Her father does destroy the magical creature. Lord Candlestick, Carrington's favored image of male violence, poisoned all around him.

Carrington also wrote a novel based on the appalling nature of life in a midcentury asylum. Sometimes described as her "memoir," *Down Below* (1944) represents a kind of fictionalized autobiography. Reading it feels like taking a walk through a hall of funhouse mirrors. It became part of a floodtide of literature that has made the idea of the "haunted asylum" one of the more common tropes in contemporary horror.

During the war, a young girl who eventually went by the name Dora Maar lived in Argentina with her father, Joseph Markovitch, an architect commissioned by the Austro-Hungarian embassy in Buenos Aires. His work gained him a medal from the emperor himself. (It was, though, just one of many handed out by Franz Josef, who, like his predecessors, loved to give medals. Hapsburg army officers walked about weighted down with them during the war.) After the imperial lands fragmented, making the emperor's medal nothing but a relic and hopes for commissions nothing more than ashes, Dora's father wanted to stay in Argentina. Dora, however, longed to live in Paris, and the family moved there in 1926, apparently due in part to her wishes. The young woman, nineteen at the time, took up the study of photography.

Although most frequently described as the "mistress and muse to Pablo Picasso," Dora Maar was herself a photographer, painter, and poet whose work displayed a combination of vitality and morbidity. She once did a shoot for fashion designer and illustrator Christian Beard that portrayed him as a disembodied head, almost as if he had been guillotined but continued to live. One critic wrote of the images that Maar made Beard appear like the head of "John the Baptist on a silver platter." In the early 1930s she shared a studio with Pierre Kefer, the set photographer for Jean Epstein's film *The Fall of the House of Usher* (1928).

Maar's political activities overshadowed her photography when she threw her energies into France's Popular Front in the 1930s, an alliance of the antifascist left. She continued with photography and painting as well. She had a longtime affair with Picasso, who sought to force her to imitate his own cubist style very closely. Her relationship with him had a deleterious effect on her own career and legacy.

Paintings and photographs of Maar are easier to find than her own work. She often inspired artists to take her undeniable beauty combined with what one admirer called "her disturbing stare" and transform her into a death's head, a meditation on morbidity. In Leonor Fini's famous 1936 photograph, she poses like a wide-eyed corpse surrounded by the accoutrements of contemporary fashion that throw disturbing shadows all around her. She would provide both inspiration and some fairly direct instruction to long-time paramour Picasso when he sought to bring the monsters of war to life.

"Nonsense, carnage, wit, and melancholy"

When talking about surrealism as a response to the Great War, intertwined with the horror film, most people recognize only the name of Salvador Dalí.

His fame, and thus the familiarity of his images, has certainly overtaken an earlier reputation he had as master of the grotesque. It has also provided him cover for indefensible political positions, generally unknown to those who decorate their rooms with posters of his painting *Persistence of Memory* (popularly known as "the one with the watches"—a joke H. P. Lovecraft actually made about Dalí's work). His style influenced the pop art movement and, to a certain degree, comic art. Part genius and part con artist, he succeeded at a level of personal showmanship never achieved by André Breton, who is little known today.

Born in Spain in 1904, Dalí began painting at age six. Spain remained neutral during the Great War and, in any case, Dalí would have been too young to fight had the troubled country entered the conflict. At university, he engaged in radical left-wing politics, authorities briefly imprisoning him for taking part in a student riot. He would be kicked out of school for refusing to take final examinations. He thought the "incompetency" of the faculty made them superfluous.

This youthful radicalism attracted him to Paris, where he fell under Breton and Éluard's influence. Wastelands, art historian Sidra Stich points out, played a defining role in Dalí's earliest popular works. She finds in them the "the sense of the hauntingly empty no-man's-land and the covert, putrefied conditions of the trenches."

Perhaps. Dalí's wastelands are enigmatic, but they are hardly empty. Floating images and impossible elevations give the viewer a vertiginous experience. His human figures, though not always distorted, are tiny in comparison to the sometimes monstrous objects that live in his worlds. In a 1933 painting, the ominously titled *The Dream Approaches*, the only trace of humanity appears in a minuscule figure on a dead if brightly colored landscape. The androgynous figure faces a wasted and glaringly illuminated landscape partially covered in a death shroud. A tower rears in the distance, seamless and smooth save for one portal set too high for human entrance. We are back again at Nosferatu's tower in the land of phantoms, with Walter Benjamin's fragile human figure in the wasteland.

Dalí attained his popularity for images that are intriguing and perhaps less overtly grotesque than those of some of his colleagues. However, a viewing of *Un chien andalou* (*An Andalusian Dog*), a film project that emerged from a collaboration with the then unknown Luis Buñuel, transforms any viewer's understanding of Dalí's work.

"Seventeen minutes of nonsense, carnage, wit, and melancholy" is how film scholar Rob Stone has described the project. The unsettling images, coming one right after another and refusing to establish a narrative, are a nightmare landscape offering the viewer a new, explicit version of the wasteland.[57]

The film sought to accomplish the defined task of surrealism and the task the horror film had set for itself: that of forcing audiences into a confrontation with reality by an uncathartic encounter with fantasy. The film's images of bodily mutilation, the infamous slicing of the woman's eye being the most frequently and viscerally remembered, are unwelcome reminders that mutilated bodies are buried under the subflooring of the twentieth century.

Buñuel claimed, with much hyperbole, that at the 1929 Paris premiere of *Un chien andalou* he stood at the back of the theater with rocks in his pockets, planning to defend himself. He fully expected that the audience might violently reject the film's gruesome imagery and fundamental irrationality. He needn't have worried. The audience greeted the end of the film with applause, and Buñuel and Dalí found themselves admitted into the surrealist Montparnasse café culture at the behest of André Breton himself.

Here surrealism and horror meet their paradox. The attempt to explode the expectations of the audience has often been met with cheers, with the enthusiasm of the crowd that the practitioner of the grotesque seeks in some fashion to alienate.

Buñuel continued to produce films, many of them classifiable as absurdist horror, particularly *The Exterminating Angel* (1962). He remained little known until the 1950s. Meanwhile, Dalí's absurd mustache, clownish personality, and ability to monetize his work effectively in America go far in explaining his continued popularity. Ironically, Dalí's career and worldview took him to places much darker than those where many of his colleagues went.

Surrealism sought to become an art of the people rather than the preserve of elites. However, cinema quickly became the most patronized entertainment in the world and, over the next several decades, even the most popular of the arts, popular in every sense of the word, soon became relegated to museum spaces.

Indeed, by midcentury "modern art," a catchall term that took in everything from expressionism to surrealism to cubism, had become the very definition of highbrow and aspiring middlebrow taste. Many readers likely imagine academics, precocious students, and the wealthy as the primary patrons of art in the twenty-first century. However, Jay Winter, the historian of World War I in popular memory, has pointed out that surrealist themes would not have seemed especially esoteric to early audiences. Indeed, Winter writes, "images of shattered forms and landscapes were all too mundane for millions of ex-soldiers."[58]

In fact, even art that stuck with realist conventions began to look like visits to hell. Great Britain's Imperial War Museum holds a set of etchings by Percy Delf Smith that used medieval themes to portray what he experienced as a gunner with the Royal Marines on the Somme. His *Dance of Death* series shows, among other representations of corpses in barren wastes, a striking image titled "Death Awed." In it, a traditional representation of the Reaper stands humbled before the myriad butcheries of the war. British painter Paul Nash, no surrealist, created image after image of the Ypres salient as a blasted moonscape, empty but more undead than dead, a landscape of dismembered trees consuming and digesting itself in shadow.

These are representations that, like so much of surrealism, most everyone who lived through the Great War could grasp without an art history degree. They embodied their fears and experiences. Heavily influenced by French communism, Breton would have been horrified that the oft-repeated cliché "I don't get modern art" has become more a statement of taste registering class status than confusion about form and meaning.

Surrealist artists loved film, another form they rightly saw as appealing to the masses, since for them cinema essentially re-created the dream life of human beings. Over and again film, and specifically the much-derided horror film, created nightmare worlds in conjunction with the new aesthetic movements of the postwar era. The earliest surrealists likely would have been pleased that their outré experiments continue to have a profound influence on how millions see the world through the "disreputable" horror genre.

The first horror films depended on surrealism and related movements. Albin Grau had been a painter and architect before he became a cinematographer. Hans Janowitz's vision for *The Cabinet of Dr. Caligari* borrowed from early surrealist efforts of his fellow Czech Alfred Kubin. Paul Leni's work as an expressionist painter shaped the contorted visions in *Waxworks* and the two horror films he produced for Universal. James Whale had been influenced by the German expressionist painters and later used his skills to expand his role from director to designer of sets and, in partnership with Jack Pierce, makeup. Looking back forty years after the first release of *J'accuse*, Abel Gance put his work alongside surrealist art that, to his mind, "sought to liberate the ordinary from its servitude."[59]

Body horror on canvas had transferred definitively to film stock. The surrealist nightmare of wastelands and tortured bodies became part of the imagination of people who would never consider visiting a museum.

Metropolis

"Death to the machines!"

Fritz Lang's *Metropolis* (1927) features the female android Maria shouting this line in front of the oppressed workers soon after a titillating sequence in a nightclub where the elite ("the upper ten thousand") have gathered even as the nightmare city moves irrevocably toward violent revolution. The android dances seductively and the men turn wolfish; indeed in a dreamlike collage the crowd lusting hungrily for the mechanical puppet become mirrored reflections of countless, covetous eyes. Their desire for her becomes so violent they do violence to one another, dueling and murdering in her name and for her attention.

The android then speaks to the workers, calling for death and chaos. Death to the machines! Her cries echo the scrawl of street graffiti that fascinated Lang: "Berlin, stop! Come to your senses. You're dancing with death."

Lang's film remains a cryptic mishmash of European politics and anxiety in the Great War's shadow. In some respects, it's the first example in cinematic history of the city of horror that has become standard in dystopian or postapocalyptic films. Not unlike *Frankenstein* in the 1930s, *Metropolis* became one of the most censored, and thus recut and heavily edited, films of the era. This made a story that already seemed to some audiences a fascist fairy tale and to others a parable of Marxist revolution even more confusing.

As censors chopped up Lang's movie with real fervor, it became simply a perplexing science fiction yarn.

Based on a novel by Lang's wife, Thea von Harbou, *Metropolis* tells of a city of the future whose technological marvels and comforts rest on the back of an army of laborers "in the depths." These men, numbers instead of names, very literally turn the gigantic wheels of industry for the elite who live in the towering complexes aboveground.

A female prophet named Maria preaches to the workers a message of human brotherhood in one of the film's many nods to religious symbolism. This idea, though containing the seeds of religious feeling, actually has nothing whatsoever to do with economic equality in the story Lang and Harbou tell. Maria is no Marx, but rather a new Francis of Assisi for the industrial age, calling for the sentiment of fraternal feeling rather than for class struggle.

Unwittingly, the prophet becomes the dark inspiration for the inventor Rotwang, the twentieth century's original mad scientist. His laboratory, an absurdly shaped premodern cottage set inexplicably in the midst of the gleaming city of the future, features a pentagram on the door. The scene in the laboratory, particularly the operating table and what appears to be electricity (but may actually represent a more occult energy), decisively influenced James Whale four years later when he designed Dr. Frankenstein's workshop.

Rotwang appears in *Metropolis* to have even darker motives than Dr. Frankenstein's obsession with finding the boundaries of life and death. He builds a robot version of Maria and hopes it will bring chaos to the city. The false Maria, the android, sows discord everywhere, leading the workers to smash the machines that keep the city running. Here the plot becomes increasingly hard to follow, even in the version Lang wanted the world to see. Does Rotwang simply want to bring chaos? Is it an opportunity to prevent reform by forcing a violent revolution with false, mechanical Maria, a revolution the ruling class will have to destroy? Here, as in much of Lang's film, viewers will find themselves baffled in the attempt to tease out a single political message.

Presented as the embodiment of Rotwang's own diseased mind, the mechanical Maria carries out a program of utter chaos. It's very possible that "the false Maria" may have been modeled on Rosa Luxemburg, the Communist theoretician who had worked for revolution in Germany (though certainly not with a Luddite "Kill the machines" agenda) and been murdered by the *Freikorps*. Whatever her origin in Harbou and Lang's imagination, she, like her inventor, represents monstrosity, and the film concludes with a confusing message in which capitalist and worker (called, respectively, "the brain" and "the hand") agree that they need "the heart" to mediate between them. Sentimentalism—indeed emotion of a kitschy variety, according to the film's critics in the 1920s and since—brings an end to class conflict.[60]

A combination of political and commercial concerns led to the infamous cuts in the film. Many of the epics of the 1920s and '30s (there are, of course, important exceptions) had a running time of seventy to eighty minutes, and so distributors worried whether or not an audience would sit through two and a half hours. More important, the growing power of various nationalist movements in Germany, including the Nazi Party, made the production company, UFA, anxious that it might be accused of helping create Communist propaganda simply by presenting a film that took the plight of the worker seriously. This worry remained even if the ending suggested that workers would find the solution simply in feeling better about things. The United States had begun to leave behind the Red Scare and moved culturally, and soon politically, to the left. In that climate, the explicit rebuke of class struggle in the film made it seem like propaganda for the right. Thea von Harbou, later to have a minor role in the Nazi regime's film industry, probably intended just such a message. So the American cut, an expansive one that took out at least an hour of running time, made it a fairly simply story of workers in revolt against the bosses.[61]

For our purposes in exploring horror, the politics of Lang's film matter much less than how he successfully used the era's nightmares, making the film into what can only be described as Gothic science fiction. *Metropolis*, in whatever version an audience saw it in the late 1920s, resonated primarily for its use of one of the period's most memorable death dolls, the false Maria, the human being imagined as machine in much the same way the art of the era worried over how the Great War had created a giant technological horror. If the film has a heart, it's not the cloying ending. Instead, it's the hallucinatory moment when Freders, the son of the robber baron who rules the city, sees the great machine that runs Metropolis as Moloch, a deity from the Hebrew Bible that demanded the sacrifice of children. In *Metropolis*, the monstrous god swallows whole generations of workers, a reminder of how the war had been itself an industrial process that consumed and demanded more. Moloch the machine tortures a entire class, just as the device in Kafka's story "In the Penal Colony" makes an individual body writhe in pain and despair. Moloch is Golem and Frankenstein's Monster on a rampage; it is also the machine gun, the tank, poison gas, the biplane, the U-boat, and the enormous artillery gun hurling shell after shell after shell into the trenches.

Freders himself embodies some aspects of Lang's own experience of the consuming horror of the war. Clearly Lang had come back wrong from the front, his tendency to interpersonal cruelty best symbolized by the pistol-waving that led to rumors after his first wife's suicide. In *Metropolis*, seeing the android Maria creates a series of "phantom dreams" for the young man: he relives his encounter with the mechanical creature in a moment that shows us the inside of his tortured mind as a landscape of shells exploding. Like Hutter in *Nosferatu*, he becomes passive and takes to his bed. Prostrated by the experience of meeting the empty death doll, he hallucinates images of the Reaper swinging his scythe with abandon.

This, more than the confusing mélange of political ideas the film introduces in its original two-and-a-half-hour running time, remained with audiences. Throughout his life, Lang remained infuriated at how the film had been cut, expressing bitter anger about it even in interviews in the early 1970s.

Joseph Goebbels quite enjoyed the version screened in Berlin.

"The Hollow Men"

T. S. Eliot, poet of nightmare cities like Lang's, watched from the sidelines as the disaster of the postwar years unfolded. A bitter conservatism took hold of him, a philosophical despair evident in *The Waste Land* further soured by both his gloomy personal life and his reactionary political influences.

Eliot's marriage continued to degenerate. He and Vivienne Haigh-

Wood simply had not known each other very well, and it's actually difficult to imagine a pair more fundamentally unsuited. Eliot, even at age twenty-six, had the demeanor of a stuffy old man with a fairly severe case of sexual repression thrown in for good measure. Eliot told his friend Conrad Aiken that he had gotten married to lose his virginity. He apparently lacked the imagination to find another way to accomplish the task.

Haigh-Wood fully embraced the liberated spirit and attitudes of the age. She smoked in public and danced to jazz, activities Eliot seems to have sniffed at uncomfortably. Surprisingly, some of the more disorienting moments in *The Waste Land* employed jazz-like rhythms that caused a distinct split over the poem's value when it first appeared. The weird syncopations seemed out of step with the classical allusions, and this in some ways may have been part of Eliot's point. He wanted to express disdain for the modern age, to describe the cacophony he thought he saw across the tea table when he looked at his own wife.

Her influence, possibly negative, on his poetry aside, few of Eliot's friends and admirers cared for her. Virginia Woolf called her "a bag of ferrets" around Eliot's neck. If it's a canard that Haigh-Wood slept with Russell during her own honeymoon, she certainly began an affair with the famous mathematician and essayist soon thereafter. Eliot remained unhappy and, we must remember, so did she.[62]

Eliot suffered from more than the unhappiness of a bad match. His 1925 poem "The Hollow Men," while brief in comparison to *The Waste Land*, has at least as many ghosts of the Great War shambling about in it. The dead inhabit it as spirits that still roam the empty places, "the dead land . . . cactus land." Corpses shuffle about in echo chambers of memory that are themselves filled with death dolls, the empty husks that so many feared the war had revealed as the true story of the human experience.

The poem opens with snatches of speech heard in crowded streets that chills the reader to the bone. "Mistah Kurtz—he dead / A penny for the Old Guy." Eliot evokes Kurtz from Joseph Conrad's *Heart of Darkness*, the man who saw mass slaughter and became the living, or rather the dying, embodiment of Europe in its grave. Kurtz had looked into the heart of things and seen only horror.

"A penny for the Old Guy" echoes the traditional cry of British children on Guy Fawkes Day. In American culture it reads a bit like "Trick or treat?" its implicit threat defanged by time and frequent use. In the case of Guy Fawkes Day, it accompanies the burning of a stuffed effigy, a true hollow man set on fire.

Eliot has also taken us among the dead immediately with a reference to the bribe for the ferryman, Charon's obol it had been called in classical sources, the coin placed on the eyes or in the mouth of the corpse so it could cross to the land of the dead. Classic horror fans are likely to think of that strange, allusive moment in *The Exorcist* over a half century later when a homeless man whose demeanor suggests death and decay startles Father Karras on a lonely subway platform with the sudden croaking plea, "Could you help an old altar boy, Father? I'm Cat'lick." The demon later utters the same phrase in the claustrophobia of the possessed girl's bedroom. A penny for the Old Guy, a coin for the dead.

Eliot steers much more quickly away from the street vernacular that took up much of *The Waste Land* and becomes the oracular witness to the twentieth century. He summons up the voices of those not lucky enough to have died but instead live in the purgatory of "the hollow men" and "the stuffed men" whose very emptiness prevents them from passing to "death's other kingdom." Eliot suggests with this phrase that the 1920s had been a kingdom of the dead, the terror of the underworld made fully manifest in the Great War's aftermath.

Eliot's despairing poem, the famous last lines predicting that the end of the world would come as a kind of anticlimax to the torment that had already occurred ("Not with a bang but a whimper"), offers the war as evidence of a much greater horror. The dry and crackling voices that ask not to be remembered as "lost violent souls" but as "hollow men" sound like they cry out from the trenches, creatures that have become something more terrible than ghosts. They are ghouls caught in the half-light between this world of death and death's true kingdom.

Eliot hints at something even more obscene. What if the hollow corpse is, like the effigy of "the Old Guy," nothing more than the thing about to burn to ash? In Part III of the poem, hands reach out in a plea for help from "the dead land" but are only "The supplication of a dead man's hand / Under the twinkle of a fading star." Parched, cracked lips can try to kiss or attempt to pray, but in both cases they find only "broken stone" and not lovers or gods. We are in Lovecraft's "Nyarlathotep," the void of the crawling chaos with "charnel winds" blowing chill across dead skies.

Cthulhu Rises

In "The Call of Cthulhu" (1926), the minds of artists and those of people the tale's author regarded as racially inferior are especially susceptible to the vision and intimations of the rise of Cthulhu, a gigantic Great Old One that sleeps in a city of the dead sunken beneath the waves that may, if the stars are right, emerge from the depths to destroy the human future.

Lovecraft divided his tale into four sections, each involving the examination of mounting evidence of a worldwide "cult of Cthulhu." In the story's opening section, "The Horror in Clay," an artist described as "a thin, dark young man of neurotic and excited aspect" pays a visit to Professor Angell, an authority on ancient languages. The aesthete had begun dreaming of "great Cyclopean cities of titan blocks and sky-flung monoliths," and from his dreams he'd sculpted a bas-relief inscribed with glyphs he cannot himself understand. He begins to visit the professor regularly to tell him more of his dreams of dead cities where the chant to Cthulhu and his sunken city endlessly drones.

We learn from Lovecraft's tale that "artists and poets" the world over had experienced hallucinatory night terrors in which the dead city makes an appearance. These terrible visions would lead an artist named Ardois-Bonnot, whom Lovecraft describes as "a fantastic painter" (which in context meant a painter of the weird, rather than a very good one), to create "a blasphemous dream landscape" that frightened all who saw it.

"Ardois-Bonnot" may have been a scrambled allusion to "André Breton." How did the isolated writer keep up with such edgy developments? Never fulfilling his dream of traveling to Europe, Lovecraft became one of the twentieth century's greatest autodidacts and most prolific correspondents. He used both talents to soak up knowledge about everything from physics to modern poetry to world politics. Modern art interested him deeply—as "The Call of Cthulhu," "Pickman's Model," and other works show—perhaps because he saw it as a symptom of "the decline of the West." It's also easy to see some of the indescribable monstrosities of Lovecraft's fiction in the impossible hybrid horrors of surrealism.

Lovecraft certainly knew the surrealists' work, specifically writing now and again to correspondents about Dalí. His persistent conservatism made him cautious of what he saw as "the practitioners of that school [giving] their subconscious expressions too much automatic leeway." However, he also saw the relationship of what he called the surrealists' "nightmare landscapes" to his own work. He wrote to his friend James Morton of a correspondence he found between the work of surrealism and horror, both interested in "mad or daemon-haunted artists."[63]

"The Call of Cthulhu" features not only "daemon-haunted" artists but also a vision of monstrosity that owed much to the apocalyptic feeling of the times in which he wrote. The planet had seemingly lurched off its axis during the Great War, and Lovecraft's vision of a world hastening toward its destruction made the changes the war had wrought all the more disturbing to him.

Lovecraft's imagined past reflects the need of most varieties of conservatism for a golden age, something worth conserving. T. S. Eliot took a seemingly more sophisticated but equally blinkered view of history. He valorized a period of uncertain time in the "high medieval" era when Christian civilization allegedly subsumed and transmuted the best of the classical age. Lovecraft's golden age constituted the era of British Empire before about 1783. He always saw the American Revolution as a gigantic blunder.

Unlike many conservatives, however, Lovecraft had the intellectual perspicuity to see the illusory nature of his worldview; he understood that he had lashed himself to the mast of a belief amid howling chaos. In an argument via correspondence, Lovecraft admitted to his socially progressive friend James Morton, "The eighteenth century is my illusion, as all mankind is yours—but I don't believe in mine any more than I do in yours!"[64]

Lovecraft's idea that human beings create traditions for themselves in order to make the world livable echoes throughout his fiction but perhaps nowhere more than in "The Call of Cthulhu." The opening passage does not evoke the eponymous tentacled terror, but instead achieves what can only be described as philosophical terror. What Lovecraft saw as the modern world's "attitude of alarm, pain, disgust, retreat" caused him to seek to incite the cosmic horror his best tales achieved. "The most merciful thing in the world, I think, is the inability of the human mind to correlate all its contents," the story begins, suggesting that we are lucky in what we do not know. "We live on a placid island of ignorance in the midst of black seas of infinity, and it was not meant that we should voyage far."[65]

When we finally meet the tale's titular monster, it's truthfully a bit underwhelming—a giant octopoid dragon, Godzilla with tentacles. And yet he's a monster raised from the depths in the aftermath of the Great War, and he has become part of the iconography of popular culture. The bas-relief from the tale has been endlessly reproduced; Cthulhu himself has inspired a proliferation of tentacles among artists; and versions of the monster decorate hundreds of T-shirts and coffee mugs, even inspiring thousands of tattoos.

The meaning of the monster doesn't inhere in the creature itself. Although the slow unraveling of the tale leads us to expect something truly obscene, when Lovecraft finally allows his most famous horror to rise, it almost immediately sinks back down into a watery sleep after a rather minor human intervention, a clumsy element in Lovecraft's otherwise brilliant tale. The real fright comes when the narrator of the story tells us, "I have looked upon all that the universe has to hold of horror, and even the skies of spring and the flowers of summer must ever afterward be poison to me." The despair in the tale does not come from the character seeing a large amphibious dragon. The terrible secret of Cthulhu, the secret of universal death that haunted most minds in some way after 1918, represents the true chilling nature of the story's appeal.

What had survived in the aftermath of the Great War seemed to Lovecraft a kind of epilogue to human experience. He, unlike his nemesis T. S. Eliot, had significant admiration for Oswald Spengler's two-volume *Decline of the West* (1918, 1922). He accepted the notion that every civilization dies in a cyclical fashion but that the possibility of a final apocalypse set in motion by the Great War threatened to bring an end to this cycle and close off the possibility of a human future.

"Who knows the end?" says Lovecraft's nearly suicidal narrator at the end of "The Call of Cthulhu." "Loathsomeness waits and dreams in the deep, and decay spreads over the tottering cities of men."

"Cthulhu" calls to mind the tale "Dagon," written in 1917, in which Lovecraft spoke of "nameless things" that may "rise above the billows" to destroy "puny, war-exhausted mankind." We sense with Lovecraft, and the entire generation that followed the Great War, that a war-exhausted humanity had decided, through the structures it created and the political apathy that reigned, to relinquish its claim to existence. When we consider the decisions made in the last century, the stars have been right for Cthulhu's "deadly light" to reveal a truly post-human future.

The Castle

Franz Kafka died in 1924, his breath gone, his lungs rotted to incapacity, and blood spewing out of every cough. Pulmonary tuberculosis in the early 1920s essentially meant a slow suffocation. He drowned by degrees.

The final two years of his life had, in many respects, been the most eventful. He met a woman named Dora Diamant, who became the last dim flame of his rather anguished love life. This last connection had not been his most important. Five years before, in 1919, he first corresponded with Milena Jesenská-Pollak. She became his editor and also his infatuation, her own writing, politics, and apparently deeply inciting personality making her a much greater force in his life, as his *Diaries* seem to suggest, than longtime lovers such as his fiancée Felice Bauer.

Jesenská fell in love, at first, with Kafka's writing. They met after she wrote to him from her home in Vienna, asking permission to translate Kafka's published work into Czech. Her admiration for his writing and the romantic feelings she developed are obvious, but it's unknown whether she returned his ardor at the same fever pitch. In any case, a rather serious barrier to Kafka's hopes presented itself in the form of Jesenská's husband, a minor Vienna literary critic.

After it became clear in 1920 that Jesenská would not leave her husband for him, Kafka apparently took the initiative in ending their relationship. They had a desultory correspondence in 1922–23. He last saw her in May of the same year. However, he had given all his past diaries to Jesenská, which for the very private Kafka was a rather extreme act that underscores his feelings for her.

Six months later, Kafka met Dora Diamant. Although theirs was certainly a romantic entanglement, she primarily played the role of Kafka's caretaker when he made the enormous step of leaving Prague to live with her in Berlin during the autumn of 1923.

While his health worsened, his writing reached fever pitch in its oddity and terror. Following his death, his friend Max Brod called the final years perhaps his most productive and creative period. Kafka wrote *The Castle* between January and September 1922. We know from his diary (which he had resumed in 1920) that he experienced "something like a breakdown" during a month he'd spent in a hotel in a Czech mountain town—the shadows of the world, the loss of Jesenská, and his own health trapping him in bleak isolation. Writing, however, offered him "a leap out of murderer's row; it is a seeing of what is really taking place."[66]

His work provided him with a way of looking at history from the outside, not only his dreadful personal history, which he knew would soon come to a close, but also that of the early twentieth century. While other artists and intellectuals threw up their hands or raged in various ways against the new mechanized order of things, Kafka showed more concern for what becomes of the human being, the plight of victims of the new kinds of societies being built and indeed of the universe itself. His work exhibits the reverse of Lovecraft's concerns; his places are abstract, but his characters are memorable in their confusion and pain. The cosmic order may be uncaring, and human beings' systematic efforts to control it futile, but Kafka asked for compassion rather than bitterness in the face of all that outraged the human body and mind.

The Castle completed Kafka's work, providing the reader a summation of horror and alienation. He gave us a protagonist with whom we cannot help but identify: K., the land surveyor, who, in simply trying to complete his work, finds himself in a maze of contradiction and marginalization. He waits to receive an audience in the castle while insistently being reminded by a series of puppet-like personages, "You are not of the village, you are not of the castle."

Worse, the castle, often "oddly dark" at the wrong time of day, summons for the reader simultaneous images of Gothic terror and the irrational malevolence of modernity's maze. K. must contend with forces called simply "control agencies" that are described to him but that he cannot contact, in order to make his way to the unreachable castle. Indeed, in an often unremarked supernatural element in the novella, he struggles to walk toward the physical spot of the castle, to regain reality while it shifts around and underneath him, and the physical structure itself becomes a phantasmagoria, receding into the distance every time he appears to have reached it.[67]

Meanwhile, in a horror that seems prescient given our age of data mining, "outer offices" and "inner offices" of an undescribed nature are employing numerous functionaries to work toward the compilation of files on him, all for undisclosed purposes. In such descriptions, he presages the zany horrors of Terry Gilliam's *Brazil* or the intensely morbid oddities of David Lynch's *Eraserhead*. Terrible forces grind away in silence and secrecy, calling into question the very substance of the human being.

A warm distance exists between Kafka and the nihilist horror that emerged on canvas, screen, and page after 1918. He might have agreed with Lovecraft's estimation of the indifference of the cosmos to human experience. Unlike Lovecraft, however, Kafka did not place himself on the side of the universe. "In the Penal Colony" and *The Trial* tell tales of torturous destruction of the human psyche and the human body, but we are never allowed to forget that it's human beings who are destroyed. At the same time, nearly impossibly, Kafka forces on us a paradox of feeling both empathy and disgust for the soulless bureaucrat obsessed with the machinery he's charged with maintaining—so utterly obsessed, in fact, that he makes a decision revolting in its insane logic, a horrific choice that could only have been made in our era, the era that opened with the guns in 1914.

Jesenská wrote Kafka's obituary in June 1924, almost immediately upon hearing of his death. She called him "a recluse, a wise man who recoiled from life." But, she claimed, even as he drew back from the world, he acted as "an artist possessed of such a scrupulous conscience that he remained vigilant even when others, the deaf, felt themselves secure."[68]

Kafka's great love could have been writing about herself. Her own vigilance led Jesenská, an active Communist, to write against the rise of fascism and then take a role in the resistance against the Nazis. The Gestapo arrested and imprisoned her in 1939, first in Prague and later in Ravensbrück, where she died from kidney failure exacerbated by torture. The Nazis also murdered Kafka's three sisters. They killed Ottla, certainly one of the three most important people in his mental geography, in Auschwitz in 1942. The writer had written his last words almost two decades before.

The dark shape at the heart of history that made Kafka, as Jesenská put it, recoil from life, even as he remained its vigilant witness, bloomed bloody into the modern world.

Chapter Four

Fascism and Horror

Those people told us the war was over. That was a laugh.
We ourselves are the war. . . . It envelops our whole being
and fascinates us with an urge to destroy.

—FRIEDRICH WILHELM HEINZ, member of Hitler's SA

Murderers among Us

Fritz Lang, internationally known following the success of *Metropolis*, premiered his shadow-drenched serial killer film *M* in 1931. The previous year had seen the Nazi Party begin to build a power base in the weakening parliament of the Weimar Republic. A second wave of economic depression had recently battered the country and in the September election the Nazis won 18 percent of the vote. This meant that, among the numerous and often divided political entities of Weimar, the Nazis became the second most powerful party in the Reichstag.[1]

M—Eine Stadt sucht einen Mördor (*M—A City Looks for a Murderer*) had not been Lang's original title. He at first used the more evocative *Murderer among Us*. The slight title change came after Lang received a number of threatening letters and the head of the studio, Staaken, refused to allow the director to use the set for filming. Taken aback by public reaction and the manager's vehement rejection of the production of the film, Lang at first thought that the dark subject matter, the reign of terror of a child murderer (played by Peter Lorre) with a somewhat ambiguous moral conclusion, caused the troubling response.

But the manager of Staaken knew only the title and not the plot. When Lang explained the story to him, the studio manager simply smiled and said, "Ah, I see." A flash of black, white, and red on the man's lapel revealed a swastika, marking him a member of the swelling Nazi ranks. The studio manager assumed that only a blatantly political film would take the title *Murderer among Us* at this moment in German history—thinking it referenced his very own party's penchant for street violence and intimidation by the movement's paramilitary arm, the Sturmabteilung (SA), or "Stormtroopers" (in reference to the assault troops of the trenches). Lang later frequently claimed that his political education began at this moment.[2]

Horror films after the Great War never strayed far from the terrors engendered by the conflict. But the philosophical and psychological chaos created by the conflict took many forms, some so powerful that the filmmakers themselves could not fully harness their effect and meaning. *Nosferatu*, in ways that went beyond the intentions of both Grau and Murnau, prepared the way for the tale of creatures from the outside who threatened, disturbed, and mauled—monsters that threatened the safe spaces Germany tried to create after 1918.

The shock of how the Great War had seemingly burst from nowhere to change the lives of millions forever can be seen in how the sinister invasion of the profane and deadly became the monster du jour between the wars. *M* appeared in the same year that, across the Atlantic, Universal Studios released both James Whale's *Frankenstein* and Tod Browning's *Dracula*. All three films told stories of white women, either as children or in the first bloom of youth, endangered by a monster from outside what the audience imagined as their secure world. *Frankenstein* and *Dracula* embodied, respectively, the horrors of the post-human monster and the threat from the supernatural. *M* prepared the way for the murderous maniac that became the horror film's obsession in the 1970s.

Both *Frankenstein* and *M* feature the death of a small child as a central plot point. *Dracula*, like Lang's masterpiece, featured a killer of innocents driven by inhuman urges. However, it's impossible to imagine all these themes combined in a popular American horror film of the 1930s, particularly one that featured a fully human monster. British and American cinema did not explore this subject for another three decades. Even then, the themes of *Peeping Tom* (1960) and *Psycho* (1960) proved so controversial that it's open for debate whether we can describe their first audiences as being ready for them.

Lang's *M*, with its stark violence, certainly shocked Weimar moviegoers. Still, the postwar generation, soon to surrender itself to a criminal regime, seemed ready for the film's bleak examination of their society even as they ignored its conclusions. Peter Lorre's Hans Beckert, a role that made him an international star, is the ancestor to Norman Bates in *Psycho* and "Buffalo Bill" in *Silence of the Lambs*. The film opens with children at play and a mother setting a table while she waits for the family to return. We first learn of Beckert through a wanted poster's warning of a child murderer who remains at large. The killer's features are unknown, so the placard represents him as a single grasping hand, talon-like and frighteningly skeletal, the claw of Nosferatu once again.

Beckert rises menacingly over the first victim, not unlike Nosferatu's shadow of death, illness, and plague. His murderous shade appears as he whistles Edvard Grieg's "In the Hall of the Mountain King," an eerie tune drifting out of the most threatening dimensions of the land of faerie. The diegetic sound interweaves with the quiet film's minimalist score and warns us of the maniac's presence. This technique, conveying threat and an atmosphere of evil, has become a common motif in modern horror, employed frequently by Hitchcock while also used to great effect in classics such as *Jaws* (1975), John Carpenter's *Halloween* (1978), and the original *Friday the 13th* (1980).

The shadow of death menaces little Elsie Beckmann, whose mother we have seen waiting for her return from school. As Elsie playfully bounces a ball, Hans Beckert's shadow speaks and asks if she would like a balloon. In a series of grim, spare shots, *M* conveys more horror than the most lurid violence could achieve. We see Elsie's rubber ball abandoned in the grass. The balloon Beckert purchased twists on an electrical wire. The woman seen in previous frames setting the table continues to wait, increasingly anxious. She will wait forever.

A significant portion of the film's second act becomes something along the lines of a strange police procedural, a genre that film critics have credited

Lang with inventing. The police begin a massive search of the city of Berlin. They seek to discover Beckert's identity using, for the first time onscreen, fingerprinting and handwriting analysis.

The criminal underworld joins the hunt for the murderer, giving *M* layers of meaning it would not have contained otherwise. Crime lords fear that the police dragnet will haul in some of their own operatives during the search, but they also find it pleasing to imagine that they act according to their own code of thieves. Child killing marks a moral boundary even for them, or at least this is what they tell themselves. They hire beggars, whom they apparently exploit regularly, to keep an eye on the children and on the lookout for Beckert.

The gangs of Berlin, not the police, are the first to catch the killer. After sadistically torturing night watchmen in office buildings where the killer might be hiding, they seize Beckert and hold a mock trial in a distillery. Lorre as Beckert gives a mad, impassioned speech that raises a number of troubling questions about the nature of law and morality. How can a mob lynch a child-killer without becoming like him, especially when his fictitious judge is already wanted for several counts of manslaughter? If it's true that Lorre's character suffers from insanity and cannot control his urges, how are the assassins, pimps, and safecrackers who actually revel in their crimes able to pass morally sound judgment? The police arrive and arrest both Beckert and the outlaw who captured him.

The intervention of regular law enforcement does not signal the reaffirmation of a simple moral order. The final scenes features the allegedly real trial of Beckert by the German judicial system that, Lang suggests, may have the same flaws as the kangaroo court of crime bosses. We do not hear the verdict leveled against Beckert. Instead, the film closes with Elsie Beckmann's mother, the woman who prepared dinner while a maniac did unspeakable things to her child, rising to say that no penalty will bring back her daughter, or any of the other dead children. "One must watch the children," she says as the screen fades to black. Out of the dark we hear her voice whisper an accusatory warning: "All of you."

Nosferatu and Hans Beckert, their stories told almost a decade apart, are the two great monsters of postwar German horror. Both are seducers and murderers of innocence. Both films show us, if not sympathetic monsters, then monsters driven by urges they are unable to control. Both asked German audiences questions about their culture and the world the Great War had made. Murnau and Grau's personal losses asked why a plague-bringer had been invited to a peaceful Germany, why greed and gain had raised the "cosmic vampire" to "suck the blood of millions."

Lang's encounter with violence led him to raise questions about the legitimacy of a murderous state. He took an extraordinary chance with his portrayal of Beckert. Phantom-like vampires are one thing, but the idea of the child killer, given clear pedophilic overtones in the film, represented the epitome of moral degeneracy in Weimar Germany. Moreover, fascist propaganda that urged Germans to question the moral state of their country had begun to seep into the culture at an alarming rate in 1931. Nazism has often been imagined as primarily a political movement that used defeat in the Great War to rally Germans to their cause. This is true. But Nazism also represented a *Kulturkampf* (culture war) in the early 1930s that warned how art itself, and particularly what one might find in either the cabaret or the *Kino*, could become a medium of moral disease, the weakening of true German virtue. *M* represented exactly the kind of film that enraged them—a film that asked questions about evil and forced the viewer to examine the mentality of the populist mob.

The transformation of the vampire's victims into mesmerized death dolls and the recurrent motif in *M* of the killer doubled in the mirror's reflection underscores the death obsessions at horror's roots in the Great War. In the decades to come, Romero's zombies moved dead-eyed and empty across the American landscape. The nearly interchangeable young victims in American slasher films exude a palpable emptiness. The void behind their beautiful young faces robs their bloody deaths of the kind of meaning we would normally attribute even to cinematic mortality. Even in the classic slasher films, the killer himself—Michael Myers or Jason Voorhees—seems a kind of waxen image, a walking void. If we learned that *Halloween*'s Michael contained nothing more than a mechanism of sand and clockwork, the logic of his drives, movements, and near invulnerability would actually make a terrifying logic.

Both *Nosferatu* and *M* reminded cinemagoers of *das grosse Sterben* of the Great War. But these terror tales also demanded that audiences think about how entire systems of death formed interlocking gears, a vast mechanism that hummed ominously beneath the more obvious stresses and strains of Germany's cultural life like Moloch in the depths of Lang's *Metropolis*. Nosferatu, like so many other vampires of both popular culture and folklore, awaited an invitation to come to Germany. The film shows some, like Knock, willing to welcome the great plague—until the climax of the film, when innocent Ellen offers herself as a feast, an invitation to death.

M made it appear as if Beckert's mad perversions grew naturally from the unnatural social relations of a Germany on the brink. Lang's numerous close-ups of Beckert (made more frightening by Peter Lorre's signature pop-eyed expressions of insanity) show us a mind twisted by desires unfathomable even to the killer himself. Throughout the film, the camera zooms uncomfortably close to numerous tortured faces: police, parents, criminals, beggars, and even judges. Horror at the monster prowling the streets of Berlin touches on a deeper disgust, something so rotten that they, and the audience, have to focus it fully on Hans Beckert.

The whole country smelled of death.

A Fierce Joy

The failed Austrian artist who became the dictator of a new German Reich. Benito Mussolini, chest absurdly puffed out, looking cartoonish as he stands on a tank amid cheering crowds. Leni Riefenstahl's *Triumph of the Will*, its title misappropriated from Friedrich Nietzsche, showing the lockstep, jack-booted march of tens of thousands at the Führer's command. Allied film footage of the liberation of the death camps showing starved survivors and corpses in mounds being buried by tractors, shoveling them into oblivion. Margaret Bourke-White's photographs of Buchenwald, the most terrible of them unseen until 1960 because editors believed them too graphic for readers, but a few published in *Life* magazine in April 1945, with the people in them appearing "like living corpses."[3]

All these images come to mind when we think of "fascism" or "the Nazis." Nazis in particular have been the ultimate bad guys in our popular culture. They appear in undead form in a subgenre of films and video games.

Their historical crimes have come to seem less real or perhaps examples of hyperrealism.

An enormous literature attempting to capture the reality of the fascist worldview that emerged after the Great War proves daunting to every scholar who encounters it. In contemporary America, we rightly ponder if we are slipping into the same temptations of that dark period of the twentieth century, given the rise of a fervid right-wing movement. We have to wonder if the presentation of Nazis as Disneyesque villains, the nemesis of *Indiana Jones*, the model for the Empire and the First Order in *Star Wars*, blunted our ability to recognize them in the "alt-right" or in the rhetoric that elected a president.

There exists a welter of arcane arguments about the definition of fascism. It's no exaggeration to say that tens of thousands of books, articles, and papers have been dedicated to the subject. Scholars have actually argued over whether or not we can define a movement as fascist if it does not use armbands. Although it's essential to speak precisely about history, and to worry over the definitions we employ, historians may have obscured the most obvious characteristic of these movements that found large, enthusiastic audiences within months of the end of the Great War.

"Fascism resembles pornography," the cultural historian Walter Laqueur writes, "in that it is difficult—perhaps impossible—to define it in an operational, legally valid way, but those with experience know it when they see it." This is not a throwaway definition, a surrender to subjective feeling. Laqueur instead makes the point that fascism has a recognizable style, an actual aesthetic that especially "those with experience" can recognize. The damning of enemies as subhuman and monstrous, the theatrical violence (operatic even in the very real violence of the Italian Blackshirts or Hitler's SA and later SS), in fact even the chosen uniforms and symbolism are meant to induce terror. Fascism fed on the loathsome carnage of the Great War for its meat and demanded that its adherents wallow in the same bloody offal.[4]

A different vision of horror than first proposed by Murnau, Gance, and Leni coagulates in the black beating heart of fascism. Movements emerged after the Great War that used the terrors associated with that war to find reasons for the immense suffering, to locate those reasons above all in a monstrous enemy. The style, a faddish, cool style at the time, adopted by these movements served as theater and indoctrination to stir mass public support for campaigns of unthinkable violence. People in the grip of fascism approved and applauded what they believed to be a campaign to destroy monsters.

Politics became horror in a way that contemporary critics of the dangerous new political movements of the 1920s and '30s noticed. Walter Benjamin worried that fascism had become politics as art, or in his more difficult description "efforts to render politics aesthetic." This means in essence that politics became for fascism a style and horror. Their own fears and the need to prompt others to become afraid constituted that style. Fascism did not give the workers or the landless rights. It did not change the economic power structure as communism aspired to do. It left, Benjamin pointed out, the workers and the lower middle class in exactly the position they had always been but now with a "chance to express themselves." Fascism gave the average German permission to vent rage and pain onto marginalized groups, justified its adherents' worst fears and most bitter hatreds, and urged them to act on them. The offer to let this political horror film play out became a poison running like mercury in much of Europe.[5]

The scars of the war midwifed the fascist impulse. These scars ran even deeper than shell shock, loss, and the terror suffered by civilians. The Great War marked the end of a mental world, an apocalypse of the paradigm of the proper workings of both life and death. Italy's Partito Nazionale Fascista (PNF), the first successful fascist party in Europe, reveled in this destruction and asserted that the wasteland gave them a place to build their iron fortress of fear. Europe's "land of phantoms" offered a dead world where Nosferatu's tower could rise. The despair of the world after the Great War allowed fascist theorists to claim they could create a new future on the bones of the past.

The murder dolls of the horror film are the totems of this emptiness. Peter Lorre's Hans Beckert spends much of his screen time in *M* looking into the silent pools of mirrors, staring at himself in shop windows as if peering into his own emptiness to find what he calls toward the end of the film "the fire, the voices, the torment" that drive him.

The right-wing movements that emerged in Europe after the Great War harnessed this torrent of fear. Many of them had their beginnings in an angry bitterness among veterans, a scouring terror they felt toward the world after 1918. The violence unleashed by the *Freikorps* against the Spartacist uprising continued after 1918. Some became mercenaries for right-wing nationalist causes in the bloody wars that erupted in eastern Europe after 1918. Many more found their way, like World War I veteran Adolf Hitler, into the National Socialist movement. Mussolini's PNF had at its heart rural Italians who worried over the influence of socialism in the labor unions of the cities and Great War veterans unwilling to lay down their arms, organizing themselves into battalions and marching in what contemporaries described as "squadrons" of armed Blackshirts, beating up labor leaders, burning socialist presses to the ground, and bringing the war home with them like some curse they could not break.

The case of Italy, which fought alongside the Allied powers, reveals that you did not have to find yourself among the defeated to drink from fascism's poisoned well. Italy had "won" its war but had also endured a disastrous and humiliating defeat in the Battle of Caporetto at the hands of Austro-Hungarian forces, backed by German stormtroopers that included a young Erwin Rommel. This defeat, which included a mass surrender of Italian troops, so haunted the country that the word "Caporetto" entered fascist vocabulary as a symbol of the decadence Italy must overcome.[6]

The immense suffering of civilians and soldiers, the way physical and psychological mutilation called into question conceptions of masculinity, and the burst of nationalist fervor that accompanied the 1914 declarations of war combined in making the conflict the diabolical cauldron for Europe's political derangement. In describing the Italian situation, the historian and philosopher Benedetto Croce wrote in 1918, "Italy comes out of this war with a serious and deadly disease, with open sores." The same could have been said of much of the continent.[7]

France, which suffered more casualties during the conflict than any nation other than Germany and the Russian Empire, also had fervent postwar fascist movements. The right-wing Action Française dated back to the turn of the century but had received special impetus after the beginning of the Great War. The Croix-de-Feu (Cross of Fire), active from 1927 to 1936, formed from groups of dispirited veterans. While they displayed certain aspects of a kind of textbook fascism (their paramilitary aesthetic above all), historians argue about whether or not they truly fit the mold, given the socialist tinge of some of their priorities. Still, a number of the country's leaders of far right organizations ultimately collaborated with the Nazis in 1940 and readily took posts in the German puppet government known as Vichy France.[8]

Relatively small, though very influential groups appeared in Britain as well after Mussolini's successful march on Rome. Until the late 1920s, the National Fascists in England had a fair number of aristocrats supporting them as either members or declared sympathizers. Many of the original founders looked to the ideals of the early-twentieth-century Boy Scout movement, of which they had been a part.[9]

Oswald Mosley's New Party, formed in 1931, proved far more politically savvy. Heavily funded by old money, Mosley favored stripping Parliament of its prerogatives and centralizing the government into a "war cabinet" not dissimilar from the emergency powers a similar body exercised during the Great War. He began publishing the journal *Action*, which wrote admiringly of continental fascism. In 1932, with electoral success appearing unlikely, he united a number of far right groups called the British Union of Fascists (BUF). The group reached a membership of twenty thousand by 1939. Even beyond their numbers, the BUF had wide support until their proscription after the beginning of World War II.

The influence of British fascism appears in the silent sympathy King Edward VIII expressed toward Mosley's efforts. He famously abdicated in 1936 under pressure from the royal family and Parliament following his marriage to American Wallis Simpson, herself a Nazi sympathizer. Thereafter, he became openly friendly to Hitler's regime. The couple met with Hitler in 1937 and gave him the Nazi salute. Joining the British army as his social position required in 1939, Edward essentially abandoned his post in France in 1940 and gave interviews that, by any definition, offered "aid and comfort to the enemy" by arguing for peace with Germany. Winston Churchill gave the former king the governorship of the Bahamas in hopes he'd remain quiet. He did not; in fact, he spoke favorably of the Nazi regime into the 1950s.[10]

The United States proved far from immune from fascism's promise. A number of far right organizations emerged during the interwar years, many of them born out of the postwar "Red Scare." The Ku Klux Klan, revived in 1915 after its death during Reconstruction, grew two million strong, according to the most conservative estimates, with middle-class white men making up the majority of its membership. The governors of Indiana and Georgia joined, as did senators from Texas and Colorado.[11]

The Klan declined in the late 1920s (due in part to internal squabbles), but rightist sympathies held a powerful place in American life. After Mussolini seized power in 1922, Alvin Owsley, the national commander of the veterans' organization the American Legion, praised the Italian dictator and urged Great War vets "to take things into their own hands—to fight the reds as the fascisti of Italy have fought them." Leaders of American business and culture, including Henry Ford and Walt Disney, played footsie with fascist ideas and political organizations in this same era.[12]

All of these diverse movements across two continents are united in their use of horror as a lens through which to see the world. Fascism has often been described as an extreme form of nationalism, one in which devotion to the state intrudes into spheres of life once considered private and becomes, to use the word popularized by Hannah Arendt, "totalitarian." This definition owes more to the nightmarish warnings of Orwell's *1984* than to how fascism ever worked in practice. The movements that seized power in Germany and Italy, and that had wide influence in France, Britain, and even in the United States, proved much more seductive.

Nationalism calls forth armies. But the extreme nationalism of the kaiser's Germany, or of Edwardian Britain, did not develop into a fascist state in the time of the Great War. Something more than a sense of national superiority and a centralized government labored in the shadowy rise of Mussolini and Hitler. Fascism needed horror in order for its leaders to bring these movements to unnatural life and take the reins of power.

The importance of terror to these new movements can be seen in how they often disdained the old idea of the nation-state. Fascism did not see the state as an end in itself and at times regarded it as antithetical to its own goals. Mussolini claimed that the state suffered from decay. He, or more correctly the speechwriters and philosophers he kept on the government dole, believed that democracy itself contained an essential weakness in the face of Bolshevism. The philosopher Giovanni Gentile, who lent intellectual respectability to Mussolini and the PNF, clearly delineated the ideas of "the state" and "the people." He worried, in language that became mimetic in right-wing circles, over the "mechanical" nature of the liberal state (remember that Lovecraft frequently used such language). The nation-state represented a danger in that, since the French Revolution, it had been seen as a repository for what Gentile called "supposed rights." Communism represented the monstrous state; fascism offered a "spiritual" alternative to the nation-state's limitation, a spirituality of horror that embraced war as the natural urge of "the people." Mussolini summed up this idea when he said that the state should act as nothing more than "the people on the march."[13]

Mussolini seized power in 1922 when conservative elements in Italian society saw him as a bludgeon to use against the Communist and Socialist Democratic Party delegates, who held nearly half the seats in parliament, all selected in free elections. Gioacchino Volpe, a medieval historian, Great War veteran, and a fascist delegate in Italy's parliament, wrote approvingly of how Mussolini had mocked the socialists as "failing at both collaboration and at revolution" while the fascists promised action . . . and demanded sacrifice.[14]

Mussolini promoted a cult of violence fully grounded in his own and his generation's experience of combat. The horror of the Great War did not exist in his rhetoric, except in the form of Italy's enemies. He described as "sublime" any violence visited on these monstrous threats. Against what he insistently saw as the febrile response of democracy to the danger of communism, Mussolini claimed the PNF sought "to infuse the liberal state with all the vitality [*forza*] of the new generation that had emerged victorious from the war."[15]

Before the October 1922 march on Rome, the aspiring dictator proclaimed the violence of his infamous Blackshirts as "not the petty violence of individuals, occasional and often fruitless, but the grand, the beautiful, the inexorable violence of decisive moments." For him, "the democratic habits of mind" meant only the "drab" and "gray," while the fascists, in their worship of violence, would root out the corruption and transform the people into "warriors." On October 31, Mussolini watched 100,000 Blackshirts march past him across the Villa Borghese.[16]

Hitler did much the same in Germany, claiming that the Weimar Republic had been so deeply implicated in Germany's allegedly needless surrender in the Great War that it had always been weak, ineffective, and, in one of the Führer's favorite metaphors, a monster. In fact, he said, the republic's founding in Weimar in 1918 represented a "monstrous event" that gave birth to "a monster child." Social democracy itself, reached toward tentatively by the new German constitution, appeared in Hitler's malefic vision as "misbegotten" and a "a monstrosity of excrement and fire."[17]

This talk of monstrous births, deadly effusions of fire and waste, and the horror of decay appeared in fascist rhetoric as a defense not of the state, but of "the people." In Germany, Nazism used the specific term *Volk* (folk) to suggest the true Germany, "real Germans" (not so different from the phrase "real Americans" employed in contemporary rightist discourse). In one of the paradoxical claims of the fascist worldview, the folk are seen as racially and culturally superior to all outsiders and yet imagined, almost defined, as facing a deadly threat from these supposed inferiors.

Hitler claimed that the state found its purpose only in acting as "the living organism of nationality." In other words, Nazism saw the state as the organic protector of the true German and a weaponized system for the destruction of racial enemies. The German government, in a metaphor that would have appealed to the Nazis who drew inspiration from composer Richard Wagner's operatic celebration of Nordic warriors, became a sword in the hand of the monster slayers.

These monster killers had a significant difference from the warriors of epic and fairy tale. What's most striking, when examining the writings of fascist thinkers and the speeches of fascist leaders, is the degree to which sheer terror shaped their view of the world. Adolf Hitler himself admitted this on the eve of World War II when he asserted, "The people need wholesome fear. . . . They want someone to frighten them. The masses want that. They need something that will give them the thrill of horror." The Nazi Party repeatedly used this language, and the people of Germany, along with fascist movements around the globe, felt they had grasped the secret of the world. The world held horror at its heart.[18]

This horror found expression in the monstrosity of the people's enemies. In an article about fascism's frequent use of Gothic themes, philosopher and historian Mark Neocleous notes that "one notices something rather odd" when reading *Mein Kampf*: "Hitler is really quite scared. In the opening chapters, Hitler is simply terrified." Neocleous cites a number of examples of this, noting that Hitler found in social democracy an "infamous spiritual terror," that trade unions represented for him "instruments of terror," that Marxism moved against Hitler's imagined Aryan superiority "in terrifying numbers," and that he remembers his time as a day laborer in Vienna as a time of "terror at the place of employment," as his allegedly degenerate fellow workers failed to take seriously the glory of the fatherland but instead drew German ideals "through the mud of a terrifying depth."[19]

A historical cottage industry understandably exists to try to explain Hitler. There are even a gaggle of books and essays dedicated to the idea that one cannot, or even should not, analyze what the Jewish theologian Emil Fackenheim saw as his "demonic" eruption into history. If we are to discuss the meaning of Hitler, and I think we must, we have to consider how the dictator's horror at the world, and his ability to communicate that horror, helps explain the rise of his regime. Friedrich Meinecke, a German historian who was an acquaintance of some of the German army officers who attempted to kill Hitler in the 1944 "July plot," recalls an anecdote about Hitler being shown a pamphlet written for soldiers that encouraged them to put their confidence in both God and the Reich. "God?" Hitler reportedly said. "Terror is the best God."[20]

Both Mussolini and Hitler successfully made a politics of horror out of both their own terror and the terror of their generation. The philosophical sources of Italian fascism decried peaceful existence between peoples as a meaningful goal, making war without limits or foreseeable end central to their creed. "War alone keys up all human energies to their maximum tension," wrote the fascist philosopher Giovanni Gentile (in an essay credited to Mussolini himself), "and impresses the seal of nobility upon the people who have the courage to embrace it." The terror of the enemy—the monster Bolshevism in fascist Italy—encouraged "self-sacrifice." Fascism encouraged the embrace of death, for its adherents to see horror as sublime. German and Italian fascism had looked on the trauma of war and declared it a fierce joy.[21]

Monsters

Julius Streicher occupies an odd place in the world of Nazi propaganda. He actually managed to shock some of the most committed Nazis with his anti-Semitic claims and cartoons. Some of his colleagues in the Third Reich believed him mentally ill. A few in Hitler's inner circle actually criticized some of his extreme portrayals of the Jews in the 1930s by suggesting they bordered on the pornographic, even as the same men laid the groundwork for the Holocaust.

Streicher seems to have been nothing more than a somewhat popular Bavarian elementary school teacher before 1914. He had grown up in a large Catholic family and married the local baker's daughter. He later claimed that in childhood he had discovered that "the nature of the Jew was peculiar" when his parish priest terrified him with tales of the Jews plotting and carrying out the crucifixion of Jesus, a particular obsession of Christian anti-Semitism through the centuries (and not officially denied by the Catholic Church until the Second Vatican Council of 1962–65).[22]

The Great War completed Streicher's journey into horror, though he clearly shared the folkloric anti-Semitism common in central Europe for centuries. Streicher won the Iron Cross, received a battlefield promotion to lieutenant, and went to fight on the eastern front. Following the armistice, he seems to have been one of the many veterans who bought into the notion of *Dolchstoss* (stab in the back), which asserted that the Jews and Marxists who allegedly controlled German finance and media had ensured the German defeat. Generals of the German High Command, Paul von Hindenburg and Erich Ludendorff, helped spread this idea with their attacks on "the Jewish press," a notion that would obsess Streicher in the years to come. Streicher founded a right-wing paramilitary group after the Spartacist uprising and merged it with the Nazi Party in 1921.

Streicher began to publish *Der Stürmer* (*The Stormtrooper*), a Nazi propaganda paper, in 1923. His efforts also included the writing of children's books that warned of Jewish influence. One, *The Poison Mushroom*, circulated widely in the 1930s after Hitler came to power. By 1940, Streicher had largely fallen from favor within the party hierarchy, yet his anti-Semitic propaganda continued to be read widely and encouraged the German people to actively participate in, or willfully turn a blind eye to, the death camps.

The title of the publication, *Der Stürmer*, echoed Streicher's time in the trenches while also serving as a symbol of the violence fascism sought to inaugurate in a new German Reich. The images of Jews presented in the paper, published until the collapse of the Nazi regime, encouraged the German people to view them through the lens of monstrosity. Frequently, Streicher used images from horror fiction to make his point. Although the U.S. Holocaust Museum is technically correct in saying that *Der Stürmer* portrayed Jews and other ethnic groups as subhuman, it's more accurate to see the paper as presenting those outside the mythic circle of Aryanism as inhuman, perhaps superhuman, monsters.

Images of Jews as demons, vampires, witches, serial murderers, and sometimes an amalgam of all of these nightmares became common in *Der Stürmer*'s propaganda cartoons. A 1930 image portrayed Judaism itself as a giant spider. Simply titled "Sucked Dry," it claimed that Germany's economic woes resulted from Jews feeding off the very vitals of the German self. An image in the July 1932 edition caricatured the Jew as Satan, ladling the German people fake news from a bubbling cauldron that read "the Jewish Press."[23]

Monsters are often hybrid creatures. The vampire has a demonic soul joined to a human form or, in the case of Germany's most well-known vampire, a dark emptiness embodied in a shell that barely passes for human. The monster proves all the more terrifying, induces the uncanny, when it combines some elements of the familiar with the utterly inhuman.

The Nazi propaganda machine created just such a hybrid monster for the German people to fear. Hitler described Jews, Slavs, and Communists as "the anti-man, the creature of another god . . . a creature outside of nature and alien to nature." The Jews, he said, are the "amorphous monster" that hides in plain sight, appearing with a human face but waiting to pounce on the German soul and eviscerate it.

The political and ethnic horrors in the fascist imagination may seem to contradict one another, but they are precisely the hybrid horrors that the Nazis feared, and wished all Germans to fear. The Jews are not simply individuals; they are conglomerated into a monstrous "Jewish-Bolshevik World Conspiracy." Sometimes the Nazis created even more baroque explosions of hyphenated terrors such as "Marxian-demoralizing-Liberal-Capitalistic" or a ridiculous portmanteau like "Jewish Financebolshevism."[24] The monster contained multitudes, and the confusing conflation of ideas, people, and systems that have nothing to do with one another was entirely purposeful.

The Nazis did not use such language for analytical precision. They made monsters out of this mayhem of adjectives searching for frightening nouns.

This tendency has frequently appeared in right-wing discourse, including in recent American politics. The use of the nonsense term "Islamo-fascism" seeks to create a hybrid monster, not to explain the origins of terrorism. Barack Obama, during his eight years as president, found himself accused by the far right of being a secret Muslim, an atheist, and a socialist all at once—with the term "fascist" occasionally thrown in for good measure. Such accusations made no sense, since one cannot adhere to all these clashing worldviews at the same time. But the vocabulary of fascism does not seek to make sense. It expresses fear and seeks to induce terror in others while, above all, demanding people take action or simply agree that those in authority take action.

In Nazi Germany, the apogee of the use of horrors born of the Great War for propaganda appeared in the 1940 film *The Eternal Jew*. Produced even as the Schutzstaffel (SS) death squads began machine-gunning entire villages of Jews in eastern Europe and experimenting with "mobile killing units," *The Eternal Jew* represented a declarative announcement to the German *Volk* of the need to fight the monstrous menace, to destroy the entire Jewish race. The film borrowed, or rather simply stole, elements of Germany's haunted screen, drawing implicitly on the image of *Nosferatu* and explicitly from other films, to make its case for genocide.

Joseph Goebbels, the Nazi propaganda minister, called German cinema "the vanguard of the military," and in the case of *The Eternal Jew* he may have been correct. Much of the footage used in the film came from documentary material of the Nazi invasion of Poland, which began in September 1939, using the catastrophic conditions Polish Jews found themselves in as proof of their "unsanitary" nature. Thus, in a dark irony, a film that portrayed the Jews as monstrous invaders of the German fatherland took footage from the German blitzkrieg against Poland.

The use of footage from Poland allowed the film to claim that the unbathed, half-starved human beings who had been herded into the Warsaw ghetto represented the Jews in "their natural state," warning the viewer that the "civilized Jews" they knew in Berlin offered a deceptive picture of their "oriental barbarism." Like Nosferatu, the film implied, the monsters that invaded the German homeland came from the East, semihuman and lethal.[25]

The film claimed that the Jews brought plague, exactly like Murnau's vampire. In perhaps the most notorious sequence of the film, the camera shows hordes of rats writhing over one another, swarming out of a sewer, while the narrator reminds the audience that rats carry disease. They are, he intones, "an insidious underground destruction—just like the Jews." But, like the "amorphous monster" that Hitler always conjured, the Jews who, in the words of the film, "leave their nests" and come to Germany, "change their appearance." Too many Germans, the film insists, have been fooled by the "parasites" that are draining the lifeblood of the German economy.[26]

A study of the film reveals how fascist imagery sought to create a pastiche monster, one that contained all possible expressions of horror and malice. In one shot the film claims that the Jews created pornography and spread it to the pure German young even as it rushes on to show an image of Albert Einstein, whom the film calls "the relativity Jew" who practiced "obscure pseudo-sciences." This phrase perhaps evoked the Jewish alchemical tradition and the more generalized imagery of "the dark arts" that Paul Wegener's *Golem* films had associated with Judaism. (The elderly Wegener aided this notion by taking part in Nazi propaganda films.) The film leaves Einstein and begins to offer a generalized condemnation of the "degeneracy of art," condemning, among others, Charlie Chaplin, by incorrectly identifying him as Jewish.

Peter Lorre's most famous scene from *M* appears in *The Eternal Jew*, his plea before the kangaroo court of Berlin's crime lords in which he screams that he has no control over the impulse that burns within him. Lorre, who fled Nazi Germany in 1933 to a long career in Hollywood, symbolizes the Jews as inherently depraved monsters. Like all the film footage lifted for *The Eternal Jew*, the Reich Ministry of Propaganda simply ignored copyright laws. Lang, after a time in Paris, had also emigrated to the United States.

The use of Lang's work without his permission shouldn't surprise us. The idea of the Nazi propaganda machine giving thought to "fair use" seems more than ridiculous. On the other hand, using Lorre's image to advertise the film to the German public does seem odd. The Jewish actor, having clearly seen the direction his country had taken, escaped Germany in 1933, two years before the Nuremberg Laws—excluding Jews from citizenship and prohibiting them from marrying or having sexual relationships with "citizens of German or kindred blood"—took effect. Yet, in 1940, his image appeared prominently in at least one of the publicity posters for *The Eternal Jew*, almost as if he were a recognizable "star" associated with the film. His scenes from *M* are cut for maximum effect, portraying him as monstrous and insane and leaving out how the film indicts society more generally. Lorre the actor blends with Lorre the degenerate character, who in turn blends with Lorre the actual Jewish man forced to leave Germany for his safety. Yet he's also a celebrity in the film the Propaganda Ministry sought to promote to the German people using the wattage of his star power.

A speech by Hitler and a march by the SS conclude the film, the Führer promising "the annihilation of the Jewish race in Europe." Heinrich Himmler, the head of the SS and one of the principal architects of the Holocaust, had his units watch the film as they headed east to carry out mass murder. Nazi youth organizations screened *The Eternal Jew*, and it appeared at local *Kinos*, where it had a poor box office performance, although word-of-mouth tales of the film made many Germans feel as though they had seen it and led them to speak of it in such terms.

Did the horror tradition born out of the Great War make such propaganda, and the atrocities it symbolized, possible? Siegfried Kracauer's gloomy interpretation had been that film aggravated something in the very nature of the German people, making them predisposed to Nazism. The films that had appeared since the Great War, he claimed in *From Caligari to Hitler*, reflected these dark proclivities.

Is there anything to this claim? Kracauer, much like other German intellectuals in exile such as Theodor Adorno and Max Horkheimer, had been commissioned during wartime to write a book that would help U.S. leaders better understand their enemy. Most of his comrades were associated with an intellectual movement called the Frankfurt School, named because their privately funded research institute had been in the city of Frankfurt (before they had been forced to flee the Nazis). Many of them wrote academic studies during the war years for the Office of Strategic Services, the forerunner of the Central Intelligence Agency. In the history of strange bedfellows, communist intellectuals writing analyses for the very agencies that would soon hunt them must take pride of place.

The *New York Times* claimed that Kracauer's *From Caligari to Hitler* represented "a refugee's revenge." This goes too far, but the book certainly had a polemical purpose. When Kracauer concludes that the emergence of Hitler's regime represented Germany playing out "what had been anticipated by her cinema from the very beginning," we're witnessing a keen mind writing war propaganda rather than thinking about the different meanings that audiences gave to the films they watched or, certainly, what the films' directors, set designers, script writers, and actors may have intended.[27]

The horror film, at least, might seem to some readers to have fed the dark impulses of Nazism just as Kracauer claimed. Doesn't the Nazi use of images of horror suggest that there's something protofascist about the horror film itself? *Nosferatu* has been arraigned by some contemporary film historians as anti-Semitic, even though there's no evidence that Murnau and Grau intended it as a comment on racial purity or that the first audiences received it in this way. The film might seem the ultimate tale of the foreign invader or a threat within the social body. However, it's tendentious to claim that Grau, Murnau, or Galeen wanted to signal audiences, even by inference, that the vampire represented the Jewish people. Grau spoke frequently and often about the meaning of the film and never made reference to anything but the war providing the dread that shadowed the film, the "cosmic vampire" that murdered millions. Murnau had died in the United States before Hitler's rise. The Third Reich forced both Galeen and Grau into exile; Grau fled to Switzerland after the Nazi Party proscribed his occult interests. Anti-Semitism acted only as a deeply buried subtext that could be read into, not out of, the film. No one tried to do so until the Nazi mythos successfully harnessed central Europe's centuries-old traditions of pogroms and blood libels against the Jewish people.[28]

Kracauer himself wrote only briefly about *Nosferatu* and did not focus specifically on indicting it for anti-Semitism. Instead, he described the character of Nosferatu as a tyrant and wrote, "The German imagination . . . always gravitated toward such figures in this period." Otherwise thoughtful online articles about the history of horror still make use of Kracauer's simplistic reading of such films.[29]

The determined scholar even found a way to blame films banned by the Nazis for the catastrophe of the 1930s. Regarding Lang's film *The Testament of Dr. Mabuse* (discussed later in this chapter), Kracauer claimed that even if it had been released in Germany, the character of Mabuse only served to show the Nazis' "demonic irresistibility." In contradiction with himself, Kracauer insisted that the German people were too insensitive to pick up on Lang's social commentary anyway. Kracauer tied himself in knots in order to maintain the appearance of consistency. "This anti-Nazi film betrays the power of the Nazi spirit over minds insufficiently equipped to counter its peculiar fascination," he irascibly insisted.[30]

Fascism did borrow fragmentary images from the tradition of horror born of the Great War. The haunted screen rising from the trenches introduced images that, when removed from their context, gave a very public face to the Nazi obsession with monsters. This comes as no surprise since, in Germany, the Nazis used popular styles ranging from children's books to radio shows to catchy jingles to inculcate the German people with their message. This provided left-wing thinkers with plenty of reason to ponder the menace of kitsch, what its silly sentimentality and sensationalism might mask. Kracauer and his colleagues worried not only about the horror film but also about all of what they called "mass culture." In fact, after the war they wondered aloud if the vapidity of their adopted home's pop culture also lent itself to fascism. Max Horkheimer and Theodor Adorno wrote of the "culture industry" of American capitalism in which "automobiles, bombs, and films" all served the same purpose.[31]

It's easy to understand how these scholar-émigrés came to feel as they did. By the time Kracauer wrote *From Caligari to Hitler*, he vehemently believed that German popular culture had enabled the country to goose-step into its doom. In his eyes, all film, all mass entertainment, represented a playground for fascism. But given his and his colleagues' experience, the terror that drove them to flee, who can blame them if in their minds it was always about to become January 1933 again? Since those dark times, hasn't it become every human being's responsibility to see the world in this way?

I think so, while also being certain that Kracauer was often just wrong. Didn't the Nazis' decision to show fragments, clips, stolen bits and pieces of the haunted screen betray the fact that the horror film had an uneasy relationship to their worldview? They could show only a moment from Lang's *M*, and only then if *The Eternal Jew*'s authoritative narrator interpreted it for the audience. The same can be said for the rats that look very much like the vermin that rush into Wisborg along with Murnau's vampire. It's an image the Nazis had to plunder from a larger story, one terrifying moment from Weimar's "kingdom of shadows" that would have made, in 1922, millions think of the trenches, the rats, dysentery, and the dead. Great War veterans like Murnau and Grau had looked at their life in the trenches as being not unlike the lives of vermin and held on to the desire that human beings never again face such horror. *Nosferatu* stood as a terrible monument exactly as Grau said he hoped it would, a reminder that the war had been a "cosmic vampire" and that millions had died of this monstrous plague.

The Nazi propaganda machine needed the people of Germany to feel a horror of the outsider, the monster. But the very ambiguity of monsters frightened the propagandists themselves. Nazi efforts to control the haunted screen, and limit its political possibilities, are the best argument that horror held contradictory impulses, that it made an eerie static noise out of which whispered voices saying all manner of sinister things—some true, some not—all of them warnings and portents. Monsters.

The Invitation

Not long before he fled Germany, Fritz Lang found himself invited to the office of Joseph Goebbels, head of the Reich Ministry of Enlightenment and Propaganda, which oversaw the effort to reshape politics by changing culture. The new department had seized control of the film industry within weeks of Hitler's assuming power. In the early spring of 1933, Lang had produced *The Testament of Dr. Mabuse* and, for good reason, assumed he might be in significant trouble.[32]

Testament represented a follow-up to Lang's 1922 film, *Dr. Mabuse the Gambler*. The earlier film strongly resembled *The Cabinet of Dr. Caligari* but pushed further into the realms of horror and social satire than *Caligari* had been willing to go. Mabuse is a crime lord who rules a secret empire of depravity, and, unlike Caligari, he's no delusion. In Lang's original conception,

Mabuse heads a hierarchy of thieves and counterfeiters and has the ability to mesmerize the public prosecutor with unexplained mental powers.

The world of *Dr. Mabuse the Gambler* seems much like the dark fairy-tale Germany in which Cesare walks. The film ends with Mabuse descending into madness while hiding in a cellar from the police, who have finally cornered him. He experiences the waking nightmare frequently described by veterans, a kind of shell shock in which angry ghosts huddle around him, threatening and accusing.

Lang believed the film had been so successful because it captured Germany in the early 1920s, the Great War having left the nation in a state that combined sorrow and chaos. Publicity material for *Dr. Mabuse the Gambler* portrayed the story of the criminal underworld in apocalyptic terms: "Mankind, swept about and trampled down in the wake of war and revolutions, takes revenge for years of anguish by indulging in lusts . . . and by passively or actively surrendering to crime."[33]

The Nazis would have had little problem with the picture of society presented in *Mabuse the Gambler*, at least on a simplistic level. Thea von Harbou had scripted the film, as she had done with most of Lang's work. As with his masterpiece, *Metropolis* (1927), some elements of at least protofascist thinking made their way into the final production.

However, Lang constructed in *Testament*, as with *M*, a particularly complex horror tale involving madness, mesmerism, and, in a Lovecraftian turn, a powerful, forbidden text that both drove the reader mad and unleashed supernatural powers of evil on the world. Picking up with Mabuse ten years after his capture, the criminal mastermind scribbles away at a manifesto of crime in his asylum. Like the dread *Necronomicon* of Lovecraft's tales or the cursed videotape of *The Ring*, anyone who hears the words and images contained in the book goes mad and enters a world of death and horror.

Outside the asylum, the followers of "the Leader" are making use of his book to build "the empire of crime" that Mabuse's writings describe. Portrayed as a vast network of terrorists, they act as a kind of bureaucracy of evil. Mabuse's cultists receive orders like those that come from Kafka's "control agencies" with their "inner and outer offices." They work on their sinister projects as "Division 5" or "Division 9." Most terrible of all, feared even by the rest of Mabuse's small army, is "Section 2-B," whose members act as enforcers. Contemporary Germans, had they been able to see the film, would have almost certainly connected "Section 2-B" with the Nazis' SA, the feared predecessor of the SS.

After his alleged death (it's not entirely clear that Mabuse does or even can die), Mabuse possesses his psychoanalyst, Dr. Baum, in a ghostly sequence in which an extreme close-up reveals the madness and the power in the gaze of Mabuse. Baum raves about the need to "extinguish humanity" through "terror and horror" so that a new world can emerge, a criminal *Reich*.

Mabuse uses his possession of Baum (*Twin Peaks* fans watching *Mabuse* will automatically think of the terrifying powers of BOB) to circulate his ideas beyond death, along with the new technologies of voice recording. Mabuse gives specific, practical instructions about how to undermine the social order. But, at its heart, his manifesto proclaims a philosophy of terror. Human beings must be made to feel horror until their minds are shivered to bits. The empire of crime, a phrase that the specter of Mabuse repeats like a fetish, will emerge from the chaos. In perhaps the most famous passage of the madman's proclamation, Mabuse exclaims:

> When humanity, subjugated by the terror of crime, has been driven insane
> by fear and horror and when chaos has become supreme law, then the time
> will have come for the empire of crime.

Lang had gone even further and made some fairly specific allusions to Hitler. Mabuse writing his manifesto in the asylum seemed to parody Hitler working on *Mein Kampf* during his short prison term in 1924. More important, the slogans and the ideas behind it seemed borrowed from the Nazi conception of the world. Hitler asserted that the people want to know the "thrill of horror," and Mabuse offers them precisely this sumptuous madness, the delights of anarchic savagery. On a landscape of horror, not unlike the nightmare world of Lovecraft's "Nyarlathotep" or Eliot's *Waste Land*, the "empire of crime" had its nativity.

Goebbels would have none of it. He banned *The Testament of Dr. Mabuse* before it could even be released.

In an interview for the German talk show *Zum Beispiel* in the 1960s, Lang related the story of attending a dinner at Berlin's Hotel Kaiserhof soon after completing the film. Goebbels praised Lang's early work, and then, glass raised to the assembled guests, the slightly tipsy propaganda chief announced, "But today I had to ban a film in Germany. *The Testament of Dr. Mabuse.*" He let the announcement hang in the air, a chilly threat. Lang knew he was in deep trouble, and an invitation to the propaganda minister's office shortly after the awkward dinner seemingly confirmed it.[34]

Goebbels's purpose for summoning Lang, despite what the director might have reasonably feared, was not to berate, threaten, or perhaps even arrest him. Instead, the invitation had a sinister, indeed a Mabuse-like, intent behind it.

Lang's account of his visit to Goebbels's office sounds like the experience of Kafka's K. in *The Castle.* Speaking in 1974 with William Friedkin (who had just released *The Exorcist*), Lang remembered appearing at the ministry and being roughly greeted by Nazi guards who told him to walk down a long corridor and turn left down another corridor to find the propaganda minister's office. Lang followed their instructions only to find himself at another desk manned by yet more armed and uniformed Nazi loyalists who for their part instructed him to walk down a series of long corridors. Lang remembered this happened three times before he arrived at a large doorway, where a polite figure asked him to wait a moment.[35]

Ushered into a cavernous office, Lang saw that Goebbels sat at an enormous desk at the very end of the long room. It was "disagreeable," he told Friedkin. But to his surprise the *Reichsminister* greeted him effusively. In one version of the story Lang told, Goebbels did not mention the film at all. In another, he simply said that it could not be shown because of the ambiguous ending. Instead, he praised *Metropolis* and claimed that the Führer loved Lang's work. To Lang's shock, Goebbels asked him to become head of the propaganda ministry's film department. Fritz Lang would become censor in chief for the Nazi state.

Lang agreed, he told Friedkin, although he mentioned to Goebbels that his grandparents on his mother's side were Jewish, two years before the Nuremberg Laws would have made such an admission lethal. Goebbels laughed and said, "Mr. Lang, we decide who is Aryan." Perspiring heavily, as he'd been doing throughout the interview, Lang thanked him and spoke of his pleasure at being offered such an honor. Goebbels then spoke at length of how Hitler believed Lang would create the "National Socialist epic," while Lang, watching a clock on a tower visible through the enormous office window, made a plan to leave Germany on the midnight train.

Lang's biographers disagree about when precisely the director fled Germany, but certainly within a matter of months he had left for Paris. Moreover, he had been planning this move for a long time, having sequestered funds in a French bank and smuggled a print of *The Testament of Dr. Mabuse* across the border. His exile marked his final break with his wife, Thea von Harbou. They had fallen out over the political climate after the making of *M*. Harbou worked in the Nazi motion picture industry in the 1930s, though, as we will see, the extent of her collaboration remains a matter of dispute.

Theaters briefly screened *Testament* in Budapest in April 1933, and the New York City premiere occurred in 1943, while American troops engaged German forces in North Africa. At that time, Lang claimed that his tale of possession and horror offered "an allegory to show Hitler's processes of terrorism. Slogans and doctrines of the Third Reich have been put into the mouths of criminals in the film. Thus I hoped to expose the Nazi theory of the necessity to deliberately destroy everything that is precious to a people."[36] The film did not appear in Germany until 1951.

Kracauer, who had befriended Lang after his exile, wrote that such a heroic reading by Lang of his own efforts "smacks of hindsight." Perhaps. But *The Testament of Dr. Mabuse* did become the film that forced Lang to flee his home and Europe itself. If he read too much into his own tale of maniacal horror, it must be said that Nazi Germany's propaganda minister had done the same, had recognized how it successfully mimicked the regime and even told its greatest secret: the Nazis sought to terrify and destroy so that they could fill the vacuum with terror. Lang had made a horror film about politics in response to the Nazi effort to make politics into a horror film.

Lang told Friedkin that he met with Siegfried Kracauer many times after he emigrated to the United States. He expressed shock at what he found when he read Kracauer's book. It was, he said, an "untrue book." People in the German film industry, especially "Mr. Murnau," did not capitulate to the spirit of fascism. Lang insisted that, with the exception of "one or two films" that he did not name, the haunted screen of Weimar sought to show social evils, to portray what the world had become after the Great War.

Friedkin asked during the course of the interview why his films had shown an interest in degradation and the criminal. The true murderers, Lang told Friedkin, always interested him because they looked so normal. He suggested that this is precisely why he chose not to show the violence of the child molester in *M*, the full extent of Peter Lorre's madness. The audience's own imagination could conjure the horrors of the murderer. In this way, he said, viewers became "collaborators" with the horror of *M*. An extremity of violence allowed them to distance themselves, to fail to understand the message of Lorre staring at his double in the mirror. They needed to see that their very normalcy made them very much like the terrors that exuded from Hans Beckert. They needed to see themselves implicated in the crime rather than watch a monster movie.

M's viewers, many of whom would shout "*Sieg Heil!*" at gigantic rallies in the years ahead, would have to collude with the horror if they wanted to truly understand it. When the time came to decide whether to collaborate with true evil or not, the German people faltered. Some refused. Others openly embraced the Third Reich. Almost all, however, actively or passively participated in the maintenance of the Nazi regime.

Arts of Horror

The art of horror immunized many of its practitioners from becoming collaborators with the terror of the real world. Experimental art after the Great War had put the horror of the mangled corpse on full display. The absurdly twisted bodies of Max Ernst and the sinister images of Otto Dix made the corpse ever present. Surrealism had become an art of horror, a meditation on the wounded and ruined human form.

The new world of fascism had no place for art that presented war as horror, the state as terrorist, and killing as inhuman and monstrous. In the fascist worldview, the war could be remembered only as a series of courageous acts, men of steel charging forth into the hard rain of shells and machine gun fire. In their eyes, the sublimity of the war effort had been undercut only by the lurking monsters at home: weak-willed politicians and disloyal civilians, the Jews running the whole show. In Nazi folklore, the iron men of the trenches had been "stabbed in the back" by the degenerate and the malicious, above all by that imagined secret clique of *Juden* who snatched defeat from the jaws of victory.

Otto Dix stubbornly insisted on depicting the malicious cancer the war had been. Immediately after the rise of Nazism, he painted the giant canvas *Flanders*, in some ways his definitive statement on the war, completing the terrifying visions he had etched in his 1924 series, *Der Krieg*. Dix worked on the piece between 1934 and 1936, while the Nazi Party fully consolidated its power, passed the Nuremberg Laws, and began the first steps toward the Holocaust. *Flanders* portrays a blasted and ruined French countryside. Phantom-like figures huddle in quivering lumps behind shattered rock that appears unworldly and impossibly proportioned. The central large figure, a German soldier who may be a corpse, leans against a stark stump of a tree, a figure simultaneously pathetic and monstrous. A dead comrade sinks beside him into the miasma.

The Nazis also wanted the Great War portrayed as a sort of horror story, but not one that indicted the conflict itself, particularly at a moment when Hitler had begun to transform German industry into a vast war-making machine. Dix's bravery went beyond his Bosch-like representation of the war by dedicating the painting to the French socialist Henri Barbusse, who had published the acclaimed antiwar novel *Le feu* (*Under Fire*) in 1916. The book used fragmentary narrative and images of pointless and inhuman suffering to portray the daily horrors of the war in Flanders's fields, not unlike Dix's work making use of a splinter image of the war's reality to communicate the totality of its casual brutality.

The Nazis saw real danger in work like Dix's. Steve Bannon, part of the inner circle of Donald J. Trump during the first year of the administration and an admitted admirer of Italian fascist thinkers, once said, "Politics is downstream from culture." This idea, prominent in Mussolini's Italy, apparently came to Bannon from his reading of fascist philosopher Julius Evola. The fascist societies forged in both Italy and Germany took this idea seriously, believing that culture actually trumped politics in touching the most affective elements of human life. Politics must become art; art must not comment on politics.[37]

Goebbels's concern with establishing firm control over Fritz Lang and the German film industry provides a striking example of this effort to shape political life by reshaping culture. The Nazi Party's attempt to assert control over art offers another example. The death dolls of surrealism, the empty-eyed victims of shell shock, and the blasted landscapes had to be replaced by the kitschy posters of Nazi propaganda, an image of modern war as glorious rather than an engine for the mass production of corpses. The Nazi propaganda machine wanted its people to feel only a specific kind of horror: a terror of the outsider, the labor union, the Slav, the Jew, the Communist, the foreigner, all lurking in the shadows, waiting to pounce on German innocence.

The Reich's Ministry of Propaganda targeted literature and art even as it pursued control over film. Any publications using the imagery or language of horror to portray the Great War went out of print; some copies were publicly burned. The Reich suppressed German author Ernst Johannsen's 1929 novel, *Four Infantrymen*, which portrayed tanks rolling over shattered German dead. The novel had described a young shell-shocked lieutenant who hallucinated images of a "death's head." The Nazis themselves repurposed this image for their own brand of horror, making the death's head the symbol of their most elite SS units. They could not allow the symbol to represent the horror of the war they glorified. Famed German director G. W. Pabst used the novel as the basis of his film *Westfront: 1918*, which the Nazis also banned, Goebbels calling it an exercise in "cowardly defeatism."[38]

Dix, along with other artists who portrayed the haunted landscape of war, had been under attack by local conservative councils since the 1920s. Hitler's new regime increased the pressure as early as 1933, displaying the work of Dix and others as examples of "cultural Bolshevism."[39]

If the Nazi term "cultural Bolshevism" sounds familiar, it's because the American alt-right makes frequent use of a version of it. *Breitbart News* uses the phrase "cultural Marxism" for anything they find objectionable. It's been applied to diverse cultural attitudes and historical movements ranging from vegetarianism to the sexual revolution to challenging theoretical ideas you will meet only if you take an advanced course in literary criticism. But, as in all conspiratorial thinking, all these strands are connected, and if you deny the connection, you are part of the conspiracy. Such thinking has been a component of fascism since the Great War.[40]

In their war on "cultural Bolshevism," Nazi propagandists described the artists who sought to portray the monsters of the Great War as monstrous themselves. The new Reich used metaphors of disease, infection, and abnormality to describe the work of all modernist painters. Alfred Rosenberg, a Nazi art critic in the 1930s, claimed that mestizo (mixed-race) sources polluted the art of Weimar and had produced "bastard excrescences." This bizarre, and bizarrely racist, art criticism used the language of the weird tale, language not out of place in a Lovecraft story, to characterize modernist art.[41]

The Nazis removed Dix from his teaching position in 1933. He had been undermined in part by fellow faculty members who rushed to join the Nazi Party en masse. Richard Müller, the head of the Dresden Art Academy and once Dix's teacher, actually led the charge to have Dix removed from his post. Müller serves as a representative of every crabbed and cringing academician, a combination of arrogance, insecurity, and eagerness to please the powers that be. Müller may or may not have been a committed Nazi, but he certainly despised the international success his former student attained. He even penned an editorial for Dresden's Nazi-controlled paper in September 1933 in which he lamented that Dix had been able to "expose the youth for years and years to his poisonous influence." Worse, Müller joined his Nazi colleagues at the academy in circulating the rumor (possibly true) that many of Dix's students had joined the German Communist Party, leading to their harassment and in some cases arrest. Soon after, Dix found museums unwilling to exhibit his work and agents unwilling to sell it.[42]

Indeed, in Nazi Germany his art continued to appear only in exhibitions meant to show the "degenerate nature" of Weimar modernism in place of what the Nazis called "clean realism." The vicious Müller organized just such an exhibition in Dresden's New Town Hall the year he ensured the end of Dix's teaching career. Nuremberg also held such an exhibit in 1933 called *The Chamber of Art Horrors*, paradoxically speaking a truth about the verity and power of the works on display. The most famous of such exhibitions appeared in Munich in 1937, a hateful repudiation of the work of some of Germany's greatest artists, with particular focus on those who had sought to depict the true horror of the Great War. After this display of "degenerate art," the Nazis destroyed about 260 Dix paintings in museums throughout the country.[43]

Unlike most artists proscribed by the regime, Dix managed to survive in Germany even after losing his academic position. He worked on *Flanders* in secret while creating increasingly allegorical compositions that expressed his disdain for the Third Reich and reminded his fellow Germans of the horror of the Great War, the true meaning of the death's head. For a few years, international acclaim and a group of influential supporters prevented him from being arrested, much to the exasperation of some. In his Gestapo file, the Nazi commandant of Saxony scribbled in frustration, "This swine is still alive?"[44]

Dix could have emigrated to America after his dismissal from the academy in 1933. He had a small network of friends in New York City, where his work had been much admired. Instead, he and his family retreated to the German countryside to live in a ruined castle owned by the cash-poor but property-rich family of Dix's wife. He painted landscapes but also worked on allegorical images containing an inescapable message of confrontational horror. His painting *Seven Deadly Sins* presents yet another nightmare landscape of the trenches, where monstrous figures run riot in a chaos of baroque symbolism. A corpse in a skeleton costume exposes its heart, blackened to a crisp, and, bearing a scythe, forms something like a swastika. In front of him is Envy, a frowning and needy infant who wears the face of Adolf Hitler, complete with inkblot mustache. Gluttony gives the Nazi salute. In the background, the empty dead land has been torn apart with an inscription, a quote from Nietzsche's *Thus Spake Zarathustra*: "The Wasteland grows, woe to him who hides the wasteland within!"

Shockingly, Dix survived the war even though he faced terrifying persecution. After the factory worker and carpenter Georg Elser failed to assassinate Hitler and other Nazi leaders with a homemade bomb in November 1939, Dix became one of the many prominent antifascists arrested. The Gestapo interrogated Dix, held him for two weeks, and then somewhat miraculously released him. In March 1945, the Wehrmacht drafted the fifty-four-year-old artist even though the war was drawing to a close. Dix promptly allowed the Allies to capture him and spent a year in a prisoner-of-war camp, a harrowing experience that resulted in a self-portrait as a prisoner.

In an interview after World War II, Dix was asked why he had not taken the opportunity to go to the United States before the war, a country he had always expressed a fascination with. Dix laughed. "To America!" he exclaimed. "There I already saw the ghost of the Daughters of the American Revolution commanding how art should be made."[45]

Collaborators

French writer Louis-Ferdinand Céline knocked about in his youth working for delivery services and jewelry shops. He hated his middle-class parents and apparently joined the French army in 1912 to spite them. He participated in the first Ypres campaign in 1914, was wounded in the arm (not the head, a lie he later perpetuated), and received a medal for bravery. After the war, he went to what was then British Cameroons (a region of Africa now part of Nigeria), took a job there, and lost it. He returned to France, where he became first a doctor and then for a time France's most celebrated writer.

Eventually, Céline became one of the most hated men in postwar France, now more or less repudiated by the French literary establishment. Sometimes more, sometimes less. Today right-wing nationalists, who have seized real estate in France's public square much like they have in the United States, are predictably attempting to defend and regenerate his reputation.[46]

The Nazis' attempts to silence the output of artists, directors, and writers with a vision of horror born in the Great War proved largely successful between 1933 and 1945. Otto Dix worked bravely but in obscurity. Max Ernst and André Breton faced capture and fled. Leonora Carrington, after her institutionalization, went to live in the States and then in Mexico.

Fascism's tale of history moved by brute force attracted a few of those who saw in the Great War a new kind of horror rising. They cheered from the sidelines on behalf of Mussolini and Hitler, while throwing their support behind homegrown versions of the fascist impulse. When the opportunity presented itself, they threw in their lot with these dictators and their movements.

The case of Céline offers one of the more troubling examples. Céline's masterpiece, *Journey to the End of the Night*, immediately received deserved accolades. Many saw in it the definitive French response to the Great War and its aftermath when it first appeared in 1932. The semiautobiographical novel—whose protagonist, Ferdinand, is an obvious avatar of Céline himself—rejects any sentimental view of the war and confronts its readers with not only the folly of the trenches but also their irremediable horror. Céline understood that the war had ripped open more than human flesh; it had shattered the worldview that made human flesh seem more than itself.

What he called "the monstrous enterprise" that opened in August 1914 had a "nocturnal aspect" that forced every soldier to wonder if he had walked into purgatory, some dark alternate reality where amid shot and shell he now lived between life and death. Death's companionship became constant, "so close to our noses that we couldn't see anything else."[47]

The human body as a corpse waiting to be made, a theme appearing on film and canvas throughout the 1920s and '30s, obsessed Céline. The war created for him a profound distrust of the body's stability, and the novel overflows with viscera, gutted bowels, the stench of death, and the general nastiness of a war being waged by men who had been "duped to the entrails by a gang of vicious lunatics." The lesson that Céline takes from the war is that human beings are bags of meat, their desires not even interesting enough to write tragedies about. They are, in a favorite term of his, "crummy," and deserve their often bloody and ridiculous deaths. Bodies are not only disgusting; they carry within them a stupid consciousness and allow themselves to become something worse than corpses—zombies marching on a journey to nowhere, to the end of night.

The Great War made even sexual pleasure into an exercise in body horror for Céline. The portrayal of sex that made the novel much talked about has a repugnant quality. Lola, who believes deeply in the war and finds herself horrified that Ferdinand understands neither patriotism nor courage, provides him with the same pleasures he could receive from an automaton. She's portrayed not as an object of intense desire but only as a willing body that Ferdinand convinces can lose weight by having more sex. Notably, all conventional descriptions of the beauty of a beloved are ignored, and she becomes another one of the era's death dolls, empty-eyed and spouting patriotic phrases. Ultimately, she's like a corpse dissected for the author's pleasure rather than an object of love, or even particularly avid lust.[48]

There's a sense in which *Journey to the End of the Night* constitutes a sort of comedy about death in the same way that James Whale used the idea for his Hollywood-produced horror films. It's perhaps more accurate to see it as a comedy about the body dying, a comedy of corpses, since nothing could be further from the novel's dark spirit than to think in terms of "death" as a magnificent final act. The mysterious figure of Robinson, who convinces Ferdinand to desert not once but twice, runs from the battlefield only to see his captain dying: "Bleeding all over and rolling his eyes. . . . He was through. . . . 'Mama! Mama!' he was sniveling, all the while dying and pissing blood. . . . 'Shut up!' I tell him. 'Mama! Mama! Fuck your mama!'" The crude heartlessness of Robinson passes for a kind of wisdom in the wasteland of corpses that Céline describes.[49]

Céline's political right turn in the mid-1930s—if the nearly insane hatred he displayed for Jews and Communists falls into the category of the political rather than the psychiatric—has today obscured the terrifying genius of his novel. Perhaps it should. He openly advocated for a French alliance with Nazi Germany against the USSR. He wrote three anti-Semitic screeds, *Trifles for a Massacre* (1937), *The School of Corpses* (1938), and *The Fine Mess* (1941), which excoriated the Jews in such virulent language that the Nazi minister of propaganda in occupied France believed them counterproductive in their "brutal obscenities." Occupying Nazi generals called the language of the tracts "vicious, brutal slang" even if they agreed with the overall sentiment the author expressed.[50]

A firm believer in the fascist conspiratorial view of history as a sinister carnival of amorphous monsters, Céline called for the extermination of "non-Aryans" and their communist allies on a much larger scale than even the Nazi regime imagined. So unhinged did he become that, as the war turned against fascism in 1944, he speculated at a dinner with the German ambassador to the Vichy government that Hitler had been murdered and replaced with "a Jewish double."[51]

What had become of Céline? Did the horror that he saw and the nightmare his writing evoked lead him inevitably into fascism's embrace? Certainly this did not become the case for Dix, Ernst, Murnau, Lang, or Whale. They experienced the same terror of the trenches, in fact apparently much more of it than Céline did, and created a vision of a haunted world that told unbearable truths without descending into a mad chaos of cruelty, without making other human beings into monsters.

The art of the nightmare, as the fascists well knew, has proven highly unmalleable. Filmmakers, artists, and writers who created the world of horror after the Great War had their audiences and patrons screaming with nightmares of the corpse, the double, the thing that looks back at you in the mirror. But, like Lang in *M*, they forced the audience to stare into the mirror along with the murderers and the murdered, to refuse sentimentality and look deeper into the void that had made millions of corpses.

Céline and his fellow fascists throughout the postwar era savagely smashed the mirror. The distorted image of the world they saw had fragments of truth, fragments they wielded like weapons. To ask what happened to Céline is as much as to ask what happened to the 1930s. The answer can be found only in the crude tendency, one the Great War itself encouraged, to choose chaos over clarity, to allow the emotions engendered by abstract ideas to exclude moral reasoning. In other words, to fall for the same scam Céline himself once warned about in *Journey to the End of the Night*.

There's certainly some pathos in the man who could write with bitter hilarity of wartime authoritarianism and then himself become entranced by authoritarians. Céline had mocked the officer or politician who could give the troops what he called "the big spiel" while they readied to charge across no-man's-land:

> "You no good swine! We're at war! Those stinkers in Country No. 2! We're going to board them and cut their livers out!... All together now! Let's hear you shout... 'Long live country No. 1!' The man who shouts the loudest will get a medal and a lollipop!"[52]

Yet he seemed to be hoping for "a medal and a lollipop" when he joined fascism's absurd parade. "You can be a virgin in horror the same as in sex ... ," Céline says in *Journey*. "And there I was, caught up into a mass flight into collective murder, into the fiery furnace.... Something had come from the depths and this is what happened." Perhaps after his brief time in the trenches, he somehow remained something of horror's virgin. Céline became so entranced by the act of violence that he could not ask about its meaning. He accepted the cruel logic of unexplained carnage.[53]

Something had come from the depths of Céline and an entire generation. The war that educated Céline gave him the same horror as it gave

Breton, Ernst, Dix, Whale, Murnau, and Lang. But the inner madness of fascism urged its believer to take joy in the horror. Hitler would write in *Mein Kampf* that, in Flanders, "horror replaced the romance of battle" but also described a grim "ecstasy," the will sharpened by the "eternal battles" of the conflict. Only the weak, "those who could not stand up under the storm," had been "broken" by the war.[54]

You did not, however, have to spend time in the trenches to believe this hokum or to profit from it. The case of Salvador Dalí in some ways offers an even more reprehensible example than that of Céline, if for no other reason than Dalí's reputation has never suffered any particular damage for his nearly lifelong collaboration with fascism. Moreover, though he seems to have supported Hitler and other fascist leaders with glee, much of his perennial dalliance with dictators can be explained by his own mercenary motives rather than anything like a comprehensive worldview or even that part of the consciousness broken inside of Céline and millions of others.

The painter of dead landscapes filled with twisted human forms and the coproducer of *Un chien andalou* seemingly represents the epitome of fascist conceptions of "degenerate art." Dalí did, in many respects, but his protectors in Francisco Franco's Spain proved willing to overlook his art in return for his acquiescence. Born in Catalonia, Dalí made sure to remove himself from Spain to France at the outbreak of the Spanish Civil War. He left Paris when the Nazis arrived, uncertain of what might become of him, given that his earliest participation in the surrealist movement yielded him a bevy of friends on the left. He likely had little to fear. Most of them, including Breton, had long broken with Dalí because of his fascination with and praise for Hitler.

Indeed, Breton, still known as the Black Pope of surrealism, had formally banished Dalí from the surrealist movement at a meeting held at Breton's famed apartment on the rue Fontane. The reason for the Spanish artist's excommunication: "glorification of Hitlerian Fascism." Dalí's 1939 painting *The Enigma of Hitler* and comments he had made since 1933 on the Jews and fascism more generally had pushed Breton to the limit. Perhaps not surprisingly, the national museum in Madrid that exhibits the painting, Museo Reina Sophia, suggests that the surrealists ended their connection with him because they had "never been comfortable with the brazen way in which Salvador Dalí exhibited his sexual obsessions in public." But their reasons had a bit more specificity, given the difficulty in finding a surrealist who sought to repress sexual desire. What truly infuriated and disgusted them was Dalí's tendency to express erotic attachments to Nazism and Hitler himself.[55]

The idea of a gaggle of surrealists joining together in a synod to formally declare Dalí a heretic may seem ludicrous—until you look into what Dalí said and did with much of the remainder of his long life. He praised Hitler as "the great masochist who would unleash a world war solely for the pleasure of losing and burying himself beneath the rubble of an empire; the gratuitous act par excellence that should indeed have warranted the admiration of the surrealists." In February 1939, on the eve of the war that buried much more than Hitler in history's rubble, Dalí insisted that the basic trouble confronting the world was racial and that all the white races banding together to reduce all the "colored people to slavery" offered the only solution.[56]

This possibly calculated outrageousness aside, Breton and other surrealists had often been angered by Dalí's desire to monetize modern art, a movement Walter Benjamin believed, in its origins, had "attached much less importance to the sales value of their work that to its usefulness for contemplative immersion." Breton made up an anagram for his former friend: "Avida Dollars" (*ávida*, in Spanish, meaning "eager for"). Obviously some jealousy at Dalí's ability to find a "sales value" for his painting so effectively may have influenced their views. But the impossible-to-quantify concept of envy aside, there's little doubt that Dalí went further than any of his compatriots in seeking to derive financial benefit from his work and flaunting perhaps the most central tenet of the surrealists: confronting the self-satisfied with the horror story of the twentieth century.[57]

Dalí found great success in the United States, where his paintings appeared in popular shows at New York's Julien Levy Gallery. Many aspiring American aesthetes viewed Dalí as an accessible surrealist, his paintings offering an opportunity for cowboy American capitalists to show off their interest in the avant-garde. Collectors considered his art an investment in both cultural and financial capital. The California plastics manufacturer Reynolds Morris footed the bill for Dalí's expensive and elegant American excursions and eventually built a museum for his vast Dalí collection in St. Petersburg, Florida.[58]

Dalí even collaborated with Walt Disney in 1946 on a short animated feature called *Destino*, which was darker than anything else the Disney company ever produced. Dalí's imagination conjured one of his characteristic desertscapes, which appears as kin to Eliot's waste land of shattered images. Against this background, a beautiful woman gazes into faces that melt, hot and waxen, to reveal nothingness. Disney funded the project, although the film eventually became too expensive for the pop-culture entrepreneur, who found himself deeply in debt for several years after World War II. He ended production on the project, although it did come to fruition in 2003 (long after the deaths of Disney and Dalí) under the tutelage of French animator Dominique Monféry.

Walt Disney called Dalí "a real swell guy" and, as his own nephew Roy E. Disney has suggested, their mutual love of self-promotion helped bring them together. More may have been at work in their friendship. Disney had powerful anticommunist sympathies, ginned up by an intense fight with his own animators, who attempted to unionize in 1941. His anticommunism drew him far to the right, and there's strong, though not conclusive, evidence that, while never joining, he attended meetings of the German American Bund, a pro-Nazi organization that operated in the United States until the beginning of World War II.[59]

Fascist Italy feted Dalí as well. Maintaining ties in the United States even during the war, he played some role in the firing of his old collaborator Luis Buñuel from the Museum of Modern Art, convincing powerful conservative figures such as Cardinal Francis Spellman of New York to brand Buñuel "an atheist and a communist." After World War II, Dalí made his home in his native Spain, where he openly supported the fascist regime of Franco, whom Mussolini and Hitler had placed in power, saying that the dictator had freed Spain of "destructive forces." On his frequent visits to New York, Dalí made a point of telling the press that he prayed at St. Patrick's Cathedral for the success of Franco.[60]

George Orwell, reviewing in 1944 one of the many "autobiographies" Dalí would produce over his lifetime (this one titled *The Secret Autobiography of Salvador Dalí*), wrote that "one ought to be able to hold in one's head simultaneously the two facts that Dalí is a good draughtsman and disgusting human being."[61]

The Terror

Arthur Machen had never been able to gain anything like literary fame. "The Bowmen" looked for a time like a turning point in his career. He attracted the attention of a number of literary figures, and many of his earlier stories did come back into print. Machen could have decided to turn hack and churn out a bevy of patriotic ghost stories. Instead, belligerently out of step with reader interest, he wrote an abstruse novel, *The Great Return* (1915), about the Holy Grail and what happens when it finds its way to a small Welsh village. He would follow this up with more tales, and expository writing, on the Grail legend in the 1920s, generating almost no interest among readers who had liked his story about warrior-spirits socking it to the Huns.

When Machen did return to the theme of the Great War, he did it very much on his own terms. His 1917 novella, *The Terror*, to my mind his best tale written after the 1890s, told a war story no one wanted to hear. England faced an unexplained horror, one that indicted the war itself.

Machen opened the novella by describing how 1914 generated a lethal kind of excitement, "the thrill of horror and doom that seemed at once incredible and certain." The daily reading of the news by the people of England might make us think about our own reading of the latest obscenities: we are sometimes fascinated and sometimes so horrified we glance quickly at the notifications on our phones and then try to put them out of our minds (until we feel compelled to look again). Rumors abound, scattered bits and pieces of news are shared, delusion and fear spread.

In Machen's story, the explosion of a munitions plant in "a northern district" garners scant attention until a rumor spreads that the dead had their "faces bitten off." The narrator of the tale begins to investigate other such strange occurrences, and his collection of newspaper clippings takes him to the Welsh village of Meirion. Like Wegener's *Golem* and Lang's *M*, Machen's tale contains a scene that seems to foreshadow perhaps the most terrible moment in Whale's *Frankenstein*: "It began with the tale of a little child who wandered out into the lanes to pick flowers one sunny afternoon, and never came back to the cottage on the hill."[62]

The girl disappears, her body not found. Some suppose that she fell from the high cliffs. But then a father and son are found beaten to death. A doctor driving his coach along the main highway comes across the bodies of an entire family, "their skulls battered seemingly by some heavy instrument." The death toll mounts, news comes of similar occurrences happening across the country. Many become convinced that it's the work of "concealed German agents." The press fails to make connections between the events. Some take this lack of information to mean that the government has covered up a wide-ranging conspiracy of foreign saboteurs.[63]

One of the villagers doubts the wild theories of Germans striking from underground rat holes but confesses bafflement about the numerous strange deaths: "People were being killed in an inscrutable manner by some inscrutable means, day after day, no one asked 'why' and 'how'; and there seemed no answer." The narrator can only explain it in the language of collective terror, the language used to describe the war itself. People died, people continued to die by new and strange methods, and no one knew why. The survivors of the massacres, or the people who find the bodies, are like the shell-shocked, deeply damaged by the war: "They were like people who had seen something so awful that they had gone mad."[64]

The reasons for the terror are both mundane and horrible in their implications: animals have caused the deaths, yet there is more to it than that. A lesser writer would have handled the ending badly, maybe ludicrously. She or he would tell us that an escaped circus animal had savaged the victims and somehow blew up a munitions plant. Maybe German agents had unleashed some dangerous circus animals (undoubtedly these beasts would have come "from Africa"). Machen does something subtler, and it's some rather high-octane nightmare fuel not unlike the inexplicable savagery of Alfred Hitchcock's avian terrors in *The Birds*.

It's not that an animal, or a group of them, has been tearing humans apart. Nature itself, in all its primal power, has risen against humanity. The gentlest animals, known for offering their undeserved friendship to us, have gone mad because of the hatred and fear of the Great War. The conflict itself has become a virulent poison to them. In a somewhat controversial claim for 1917, perhaps an unlikely one for Machen the romantic monarchist, "the fury of the whole world at war, the great passion of death that seems driving all humanity to destruction" has "infected" even the animal world with "rage and wrath and ravening." Our war, in which we used our technological prowess to practice sadism unknown among the most predatory animals, deranged the course of nature itself and caused it to turn against us.[65]

Machen never wrote anything again that contained the unsettling power of *The Terror*. He went back to writing, still without generating much public interest, about the Grail. After the nationalist fantasy of "The Bowmen" (which he actually mocks in *The Terror*), he'd made a definitive statement about the war and its obscene meaning. The conclusions seemingly frightened even him. Meanwhile, Machen's contemporaries continued to create tales of the weird, often responding to the times but often badly misreading them.

Race and the Weird Tale

H. P. Lovecraft hated his marriage and hated New York City. He left both behind in 1926, though he remained ostensibly married to Sonia Greene until 1929. He insisted he felt exhilarated by his return to Providence, Rhode Island. He had already expressed his horror of the alien and the immigrant in tales written during the New York period, including "He" and "The Horror at Red Hook." He never ceased to regard his unhappy time in New York City in racist terms. In June 1933, he wrote to his longtime friend James Morton that, "A hideous example of what Hitler is honestly—if crudely—trying to prevent is the stinking Manhattan pest zone!"[66]

Horror in the United States, at least until 1931 and Universal Studio's release of *Dracula* and *Frankenstein*, continued to have its primary outlet in the pulp magazines. *Weird Tales* became the conduit for most of this material. The magazine, the only one of its kind until the 1930s, published the work of Lovecraft and other notables such as Clark Ashton Smith, whose artwork and short fiction reveals the links between surrealism and horror. This group also included Robert E. Howard, the creator of Conan the Barbarian.

What some had begun to call "scientific fiction" appeared in John W. Campbell's *Astounding Science Fiction*, later published as the hugely popular *Analog* magazine. Campbell's magazine, and the stories he wrote, generally dealt with intergalactic wars and visits to alien landscapes. Horror frequently played some role in these stories, however, and Campbell's novella *Who Goes There?* (1938) became the inspiration for the classic Howard Hawks sci-fi/horror film *The Thing from Another World* (1951), which in turn influenced another horror classic, John Carpenter's *The Thing* (1982).

For at least some of these pulp writers and editors, fascism proved a fascination and a temptation. Lovecraft's correspondence reveals fulsome praise for fascism throughout his adult life and a better understanding of how his politics changed toward the end of his life. Robert E. Howard's heroes of sword and sorcery battling supernatural horrors are almost parodies of the fascist Übermensch. Campbell maintained a lifelong commitment to ultra-right-wing causes. A distinctly fascist cast appeared in much of the fiction published in his magazine, particularly in his emphasis on "alien" outsiders and praise for the racially pure tough guys who fight them. Acclaimed fantasy author Michael Moorcock famously assailed the work that appeared in *Analog* and related the tale of how Campbell responded to the 1965 Watts riots by suggesting that the event represented the natural outcome of the emancipation of enslaved people, whom Campbell called "worker bees." They rioted, he insisted, because they had become "leaderless" without their masters.[67]

Certainly not all horror writers felt drawn to fascism and its virulently racist tendencies after the Great War. A rather large number actually went very far to the left in their politics during the 1930s. Frank Belknap Long, a contributor to *Weird Tales* and a protégé of Lovecraft's, joined the Communist Party USA and, in so doing, gave his mentor much distress. A number of early science fiction writers had ties to left-wing groups, some of which worked closely with the CPUSA. In fact, these connections led to an FBI investigation of famed sci-fi author Isaac Asimov (best known for *I, Robot* and the *Foundation* series), whom agents close to J. Edgar Hoover believed had spied for the Soviet Union.[68]

Moreover, the influential writers and editors of horror certainly didn't corner the market when it came to fascist sympathies. In the United States, as the example of Walt Disney shows, support for Mussolini and Hitler's program gained significant support from powerful friends and fellow travelers. Certainly no mass movement toward fascism emerged in Depression-era America, but interest in the European right's message sometimes shaded into praise for fascist ideals and open support for Europe's most successful fascist dictatorships. Charles Coughlin, a Catholic priest in the Detroit area but also one of the most popular radio personalities in America during the 1930s, ranted against the administration of Franklin D. Roosevelt, claiming it had been hived with secret communists. In 1938, Coughlin became allied with the highly anti-Semitic Christian Front and, in the early years of World War II, parroted Nazi propaganda.

The maestros of pulp horror did, however, have at their disposal something other supporters of fascism did not. The emergence of horror as a cultural phenomenon gave them the ability to create convincingly lived-in worlds of heroes and monsters. Too often their fiction celebrated the Manichaean fantasies of fascism, underpinned by their own worldviews.

Robert E. Howard had a limited interest in international politics, though he certainly had a deep emotional and aesthetic investment in imagining race as the key to history. One of his earliest Conan tales, "The God in the Bowl," imagines his barbarian hero coming in contact with the decadent corruptions of urban civilization and proving himself superior to them. He appears as a racialized superman from the beginning as a guardsman takes note of his "broad shoulders, massive chest, and heavy arms," set off by "a pair of dangerously blue eyes."[69]

His racism often reveals itself in his fiction, but Howard, unlike Lovecraft, had little use for the continental dictators no matter how frequently he sounded a bit like them in the virtues he praised. He saw in figures like Mussolini a threat to what he claimed as his primary value: "individual liberty." During their long correspondence, Howard criticized Lovecraft for his support of the Italian dictator, commenting that Mussolini gave him a "sickening and nauseating feeling." Howard also saw behind the rank hypocrisy of Il Duce's 1935 justification for the invasion of Ethiopia. Some of his final correspondence to Lovecraft castigated his Providence correspondent for his "sympathies for the Fascists" and called Mussolini a "damned rogue."[70]

Lovecraft had a deeply racialized view of history that always led him to praise the "Britannick" or, more generally, "Nordic" peoples as the master race. In a circular letter to several correspondents in October 1921, he described himself as "kin to the giant chalk white conquerors of the cursed effeminate Celts ... the son of Odin" and, in a line that could have appeared in Giovanni Gentile's work, noted that "as I grow older I respect art the less and power the more."[71]

Lovecraft openly praised FDR during the 1930s, and much has been made of his utter admiration for the new president. His support for the New Deal certainly appears like a radical political turn for someone who admitted that he had once favored "the concentration of [economic] resources in a few hands, in the interest of a stable hereditary culture." A closer took at Lovecraft's attitude, however, suggests that he did not experience a turn to the left, but rather a deeper appreciation for, and perhaps understanding of, the promises of fascism. He feared that the Great Depression had revealed an "unemployable" population that if not "fed and amused . . . will dangerously revolt." He "deem[ed] both democracy and communism fallacious for western civilization" and expressed a preference for "a kind of fascism." He elsewhere called his ideal political program "a fascistic socialism."[72]

Lovecraft first wrote admiringly of Mussolini at the time of Il Duce's rise to power. He expressed his pride in being "a reactionary," given that he saw "the rise of democratic ideals as a sign of cultural old age and decay." He sometimes seems to have found Hitler personally ludicrous, but faintly mocking his mustache—his "lip-blot" he called it—constituted the far limits of his criticism. However, when it came to saving "Aryan" cultural traditions he declared himself "a red hot Nazi" until and if Hitler's Germany went to war with Great Britain. This, of course, doesn't speak well of him either. Lovecraft shared the Nazis' own lack of desire to fight England, a struggle they accepted as a necessary step toward their desire to seize *Lebensraum* (living space) from the Slavic *Untermenschen* (subhumans) and crush monstrous Bolshevism to the east. Lovecraft had no reservation concerning these goals.[73]

A letter to Howard in the fall of 1933 reveals Lovecraft's willingness to view Nazism as perhaps a useful, if at times extreme, measure to stave off decadence. He asserts that "the naïve ethnology of the Jew-baiting circus" and "the destruction of books" are foreign to the tastes of America and much of western Europe. "However," he continued, "it remains to be seen whether these peculiar differences represent unmitigated evils." Lovecraft admitted he would forgive Hitler much, "even that moustache," if he could prevent a "collapse into communism."[74]

Both Lovecraft and Howard suffered from the delusions of warrior dreams. Neither had participated in the Great War, but both fetishized combat. In the passage where Lovecraft declares himself "kin to the chalk white giant conquerors," he laments that he never attended West Point to pursue a military career. Howard had been too young for the Great War, but, given his obsession with bloodshed, battle, and barbarism, he would have likely attempted to join the doughboys. The end of his teenage years found him pursuing a rigorous regimen of boxing, weight lifting, and wood chopping. He transformed himself from a skinny, bookish kid into the burly physical specimen he idealized in his fiction. In a 1933 letter to Lovecraft, he sounds too much like the fascist dictators he despised when he praised "the original Aryan type" of the barbarian who took pleasure in "the slashing and mangling of human organisms."[75]

Lovecraft's vituperative racism appeared in both his correspondence and his tales. Although he seems pathological at times, we would fail to take Lovecraft seriously if we confined his notions about race to the realm of psychology and personal experience. He had, from his reading, developed a systemic philosophical view of the world that understood history as a story of decline and fall. Rot and decay came to higher cultures, described by him as the "culture streams" of Aryan, Nordic, or Anglo-Saxon peoples, when an infestation of an "alien element" occurred.

Lovecraft made himself into a perpetual motion machine of reactionary ideas. He may have morbidly pondered how human feeling and action meant less than nothing on a cosmic scale. But as he floundered in his racist imaginings and horror tales of ruin and rot, his despair perfectly embodied what those with a fascist mind-set sought to inculcate: they understood how often despair and obedience are lethal allies.

"The Waste Land Grows"

T. S. Eliot, unlike Lovecraft, sought to escape his nihilism in conservative religious faith. Many, perhaps most, of the era's artists, filmmakers, writers, photographers, and poets took a hard left turn in their politics in the 1920s and '30s. If they despaired of the next world, they chose a revolutionary optimism in response to this one.

The poet of the dead lands took a different course. His conversion to Anglicanism came in 1927. In the same year, he applied for and received British citizenship. The boy from St. Louis, Missouri, began calling himself a "royalist." His comments on this have often been noted, but the absurdity of it has been too frequently ignored. He had declared his allegiance to a crown that represented pageantry rather than power, a symbol that oversaw a dying imperial regime. Eliot's conversions of religion and nationality read like the empty gestures of his hollow men, the wounded generation of the Great War. Prayers and kisses meet only broken stone.

A few years later, upon being offered a prestigious professorship at Harvard, Eliot took the opportunity to separate himself from his wife, Vivienne Haigh-Wood. Her own story darkens considerably at this time. She nurtured rage of various kinds toward Eliot, once interrupting one of his public readings while, bizarrely, wearing a uniform of a British fascist organization. In 1938, her brother committed her to the Stoke Newington Asylum, where she died in 1947.

Eliot's right turn took him into the morass of 1930s anti-Semitism. His 1934 series of essays *After Strange Gods: A Primer of Modern Heresy* worried over the role of Jews in the Western world, particularly those who had left behind their traditional faith. He sounds like Lovecraft when he tells his Virginia audience (the essays had originally been a 1933 series of lectures at the University of Virginia) that "the chances for the re-establishment of native culture are perhaps better here than in New England. You are farther away from New York; you have been less industrialized and invaded by foreign races."[76]

Defenders of Eliot's politics, and there are many, often note that he allowed this book, as Kevin Jackson puts it, "to fall out of print." Jackson claims Eliot reached this decision because he became "uncomfortable with the tenor of some of its passages." This is as much to say that the rise of Nazism made such views impolitic.[77]

He did not go as far, at least in his public persona, as did his mentor and friend Ezra Pound. Pound frequently wrote of his own horror at the Great War. He pursued an inquiry into its causes that took a much more political and economic turn than Eliot's poetic vision of calamity. Like many on the left, Pound decided that capitalism had been the root of the war. Unlike the hundreds of thousands who found in this a reason to join the Communist Party or one of the proliferating socialist parties in western Europe and the United States, he concluded that the Jews represented the capitalist class. Pound fell rather quickly into the embrace of fascism.

Pound moved to Italy with both his wife, Dorothy, and his paramour, the concert violinist Olga Rudge, in 1924. Both women became pregnant around the same time. Pound farmed out his child with Olga to a poor Italian family. Pound's wife's child became Omar Pound. Sending Omar to live in London with Dorothy's mother, Pound declined to see the young man until he turned twelve, and then only briefly. Meanwhile, he became utterly entranced with Mussolini as the new avatar of modernity, a way to escape the abattoir of the Great War.

All of this—probably no spoiler alerts needed—ended badly for Ezra Pound. Pound met Mussolini in 1933 and giddily explained his *Cantos*, a cycle of poems essentially impossible for nonspecialists to understand, with their obscure allusions and passages in Mandarin. Mussolini responded to Pound's description during the brief meeting by saying that it was *divertente* (amusing), yet the curt dismissal of his life's work overjoyed Pound: he took it as approval from a man he thought embodied the spirit of the age. He soon began writing puff pieces for Mussolini and for Oswald Mosley's fascist, highly anti-Semitic journal *Action* in Britain.[78]

Pound commits himself ever more fully to fascism in the years to come. In his poem "Hugh Selwyn Mauberley," Pound had famously written of soldiers during the Great War: "There died a myriad . . . For an old bitch gone in the teeth / For a botched civilization." He fell in love with the horror of decay and bought into the tale of terror chanted by fascism's bards.

But, as had been the case since the dark heart of the Great War itself, other artists told their monster tales to caution and warn about the dangers of looking too long into the abyss. These artists saw the original root of the word "monster" (the Latin *monstrum*, meaning "omen" or "portent") and sought to put them on screen and page as signs of wonder, marvels—portents of danger.

Chapter Five

Universal Monsters

Now all roads lead to France
And heavy is the tread
Of the living; but the dead
Returning lightly dance.

—EDWARD THOMAS, "Roads" (1916)

"I give you, the Monster!"

Ernest Thesiger wrote a memoir in 1927. The book dwells far more on his experience as the child of a well-to-do family and his early life on the stage than on his experience of combat. He mostly wanted to entertain his readers with stories about his life in the theater, meeting the world-famous French actress Sarah Bernhardt ("queen of the pose and princess of the gesture") just as he'd hoped to do since he was a boy, and generally giving a sprightly account of the Edwardian era, when an older version of England died forever. However, the future star of some of James Whale's most significant horror films could not, despite some morbid attempts at levity, escape the effect the Great War had on his psyche, even in his writing.

When the war came, Thesiger attempted to join a Scottish Highlander regiment. In a sly suggestion of his later interest in what the era called "female impersonation" he wrote, "I thought a kilt would suit me." He could not convince the recruiter with his feigned Scottish accent, and the officer sent him to another regimental headquarters, where he "came away a few hours later a private in His Majesty's army."¹ He specifically tells the reader that he has no wish to describe the weeks that followed his arrival in France in November 1914. He notes little fighting at first, only "wading through seas of mud" and how "the rain never stopped." A brief respite around Christmas had Thesiger the consummate actor convincing French matrons to cook his meals, for "tomorrow I go to the trenches and will be killed." He repeated this day after day, calling it "the trump card I always produced when I couldn't get my food cooked for me."

Thesiger did find himself in the trenches by New Year's Eve, only to discover that all the earthworks had flooded. His regiment had to build a new line in the bottomless mud, a common experience on the western front. A deserted if nearly shell-ruined barn offered a place to rest nearby. Waking up from what sounds like a comfortable night sleeping in straw after a day of dredging mud, Thesiger recalled that he had some Christmas candy, a gift from across the Channel. Sitting in the unusual quiet of the morning, he had just shared a piece with a companion when "we heard the noise like that of an approaching express train." A shell crashed into the barn, splintering what remained of the erstwhile shelter. Yet another "ominous crashing sound" signaled another direct strike.

Thesiger remembers briefly wondering if he had, in fact, died. The moaning of his comrades brought him out of a semiconscious state, and he realized that he had somehow survived the bombardment. He also quickly discovered that he lay splattered in blood with his hand "swollen to the size of plum-puddings" and all his "fingers hanging at impossible angles."

In his dazed state, he looked to his friend (whom he does not name in the memoir) and began to wonder why the man had left his boots. No soldier in the Great War ever abandoned his boots, even if fleeing for his life. A confused Thesiger attempted to pick them up with his broken hands now hanging limp. He took a closer look and realized that his friend's boots were not empty at all: "In each boot a few inches of leg remained. That was all that was left of him with whom a few moments before I had been sharing chocolate." He fled the scene. "I had seen enough—I made my way out of that charnel house," leaving behind "the bodies of twelve of my friends."²

Nearly two decades later, American audiences of James Whale's *Bride of Frankenstein* watched Thesiger raise a glass in a charnel house to toast the empty sockets of a skull. "I give you, the Monster!"

Brutalized Bodies

The turn toward horror in continental European film, the arts, and the fiction of Britain and America emerged even as the consequences of the Great War continued to shamble across the landscape of the world. Fascism had already struggled, and won, against a liberal democratic version of modernity in significant parts of Europe by the 1930s and became a live option in the political culture of nations throughout the Western world. Unrelenting violence had been endemic in Europe since the alleged end of the war, but an even greater conflict loomed in the wake of fascism's meteoric rise. Hitler's Germany and Stalin's Soviet Union had begun to take the measure of each other like fighters edging out of their corners for the first round.

By 1935–1936, Mussolini's Italy had invaded and laid claim to Ethiopia despite weak protestations from the crumbling League of Nations. Mussolini then joined Hitler in providing war matériel for General Francisco Franco's fascist forces seeking to overthrow Spain's newly elected, left-leaning republic. Stalin, a few months late to the game, provided the forces of the republic with arms, while volunteers raised by Communist Parties around the world went to fight in Spain, most famously the "Abraham Lincoln" and the "George Washington" brigades from the United States.

The slaughter in Spain very quickly became some of the worst seen in continental Europe since the early 1920s. Hitler hoped to use the struggle as a testing ground for the Reich's new Luftwaffe (air force). On April 26, 1937, the German Condor Legion under the command of Wolfram Freiherr von Richthofen, joined by a small number of Italian warplanes, thunderously broke the quiet over the town of Guernica, a Basque village in the province of Biscay. Richthofen wrote in his journal, four days after the bombing, that the attack resulted in the village's "complete annihilation" while also insisting that most of the town had been away on holiday. In fact, it had been a market day, with most of the inhabitants at ground zero of the bombers' attack. Hundreds of civilians died, the exact number likely never to be known. We do know, however, due to research by the historian Xabier Irujo, that the German air force commander Hermann Göring had planned the attack as a birthday present for the Führer. Logistics delayed the assault slightly, and Göring had to make a belated gift of the carnage.[3]

Pablo Picasso's mural *Guernica* (1937) famously displayed the outrage, its frightening imagery of an obscured death's head, suffering innocence, and suppurating wounds. Dora Maar photographed the progression of Picasso's work and, in later conversations with her, art historian John Richardson realized that her photography—a craft about which Maar had already taught Picasso a great deal—contributed much to the confrontational rendering of the horror. *Guernica*'s ultra-matte palette gives the painting the spectral immediacy of one Maar's photographs.[4]

The phrase "interwar period" makes it sound as if the world took a deep breath between 1918 and 1939. In truth, the Italian incursions into Africa, Japan's invasion of China, and Hitler's seizures and annexation of territory in central Europe are only part of the story. We have seen that between 1918 and 1924 civil wars and revolutions raged across the continent, including a little-known conflict in Finland that killed 1 percent of the entire population. The United States, flexing its muscles after almost two decades of seizing territories in the Caribbean and the Pacific and entering the Great War at a strategic moment, continued to intervene in Latin America. In fact, American forces began an occupation of Haiti that lasted from 1915 to 1934. The destruction of the old Russian, Hapsburg, and Ottoman Empires transformed their former territories into violent frontier regions. In the bloodletting that ensued, the distinction between combatants and civilian populations remained as meaningless as it had been during World War I.

How exactly did the Great War produce these conflicts? One answer, much debated among historians, goes by the evocative name of "the brutalization thesis." In this understanding of what happened after 1918, the savagery of global murder left behind such severe psychic wounds that violence on a massive and heretofore unknown scale became part of the muscle memory of political and cultural life.

Although historians continue to argue whether or not such an interpretation explains all the political catastrophes of the years after 1918, artists, authors, and filmmakers took no time for debate and sought to brutalize audiences with images of death that made the world confront what it had done and what had happened to it. Sometimes these images came with implicit political content. Just as often, the art of horror offered no message but the dead body itself. The corpse became unruly, raged at its fate, hid inside doubles and mirrors, reanimated or rose again, and rampaged around a world suddenly more violent and deadly than it had ever been before.

Haunted Houses

Director Paul Leni refused to go to the dentist despite entreaties from friends and the head-splitting pain of his toothache. Eventually, he claimed the pain had subsided, and perhaps it had as the nerves in his gums became necrotic. He contracted sepsis and died at his Los Angeles home on September 2, 1929, at age forty-four.

The director had not come to America primarily because of his fear of Germany's far right. Leni had been born in Stuttgart but had spent much of his career in and around Berlin, first as a student and artist of avant-garde painting, then as a set designer in the film industry. His macabre taste on display in *Waxworks*, and the younger Carl Laemmle's belief in the profitability of such films, prompted Carl Laemmle Sr. to invite Leni to Hollywood and place him under contract with Universal Studios.

The two made an odd pair. Both were German, Laemmle coming to the United States long before the Great War. He opened a successful haberdashery in Chicago and then an even more successful theater in 1906. Although he loved movies, he also tended to think of them as consumer products rather than art, once famously saying that both Hollywood and Mr. Woolworth's department stores had identical business plans. Had he ever talked with the scholars of the Frankfurt School, they would have found him bafflingly agreeable to their theories about American popular culture.

If films represented just another kind of big business, then the success of his *Phantom of the Opera* impressed the former retail salesman enormously. Laemmle constantly worried about a public backlash against horror films, but he knew, or at least his son and namesake convinced him, that Germany's haunted screen had been churning out some of the most successful of these sorts of pictures—thus his invitation to Leni to come to America in 1927.

Experimental efforts like taking on Leni and creating the American horror film probably would not have happened without Carl Laemmle Jr., known to everyone affectionately simply as "Junior." Stories abound about Junior's playboy reputation, with an entire subgenre of anecdotes from screenwriters who found him easily distracted by phone calls with his bookies and girlfriends. His reputation aside, it's unlikely that Universal could have had the success it did without Junior. The younger Laemmle encouraged his father to produce the international hit *All Quiet on the Western Front.*[5]

The prosperity of the United States certainly shocked Leni after what he had experienced in postwar Germany. He did not know, of course, that what looked like a muscular system of industrial production had the shakiest of foundations, with U.S. banks (as they do today) investing their customers' funds in stocks likely to reap huge profits for captains of industry.

The year 1927 gave few hints that the house of cards would collapse a few months after Leni's death. The studio he had come to work for had become something of a director's dream since the elder Laemmle had purchased a ranch north of Los Angeles in 1913 that would become what he called, with little exaggeration, "Universal City." The enormous back lots could draw on warehouses brimming with every conceivable film prop while filmmakers worked on editing in eight projection rooms. Many of the actors and camera crews actually lived at Universal, and Universal City had its own hospital, school, fire department, and police station. When Laemmle Sr. first invested in the studio, workers broke ground thirteen miles outside of downtown L.A. The grounds remained so rural that a working farm existed on the site. The tradition of giving tours began immediately: for five cents, the public got a walk around the back lot, a box chicken lunch, and the chance to buy produce from the farm.[6]

Leni's first project for his new employer tapped a vein of horror that Hollywood simply had not explored in any meaningful way. *The Cat and the Canary* (1927) brought very continental terrors to American audiences in a film that marked the beginning of a revolutionary change in how the silver screen imagined haunted places. The film told a tale, soon to become a Hollywood standard, of an elderly spendthrift harassed by his relatives, all of whom gather at the estate like carrion birds after his death for the reading of the will. Frightening goings-on occur in a scenario that would replay itself in remakes of Leni's original and in later classics like William Castle's *The House on Haunted Hill* (1959) and *13 Ghosts* (1960). These imitations of Leni's idea themselves would receive remakes (in 1999 and 2001, respectively) that employed more contemporary technology without departing from the basic plot.

The Cat and the Canary departed in some ways from what had already become the silent era's tradition of rationalizing the supernatural, a sort of Scooby-Doo approach to metaphysical phenomenon in which the ghost turns out to have been a greedy cousin after the heir's fortune. Leni mixed and matched elements of this scenario. There is indeed an evil cousin pretending to be a deranged lunatic on the loose, but the possibility of a ghost, a spirit more than a bit vengeful, looms threateningly in the shadows.

Leni's establishing shot shows what the title card calls "the grotesque mansion" of Cyrus West on a hill overlooking the Hudson River. This shot, one that the director returns to several times throughout the film, almost seems a joke tied into the origins of horror on the wasted landscape of Europe. The West house looks nothing like the Hudson Valley mansions built by the financiers of the Gilded Age. It's Dracula's castle and the looming tower from *Nosferatu*, teleported to America.

Shadows leak from every corner of Leni's moody set, engulfing the rooms in nearly every scene. Even the sympathetic characters we hope will live through the ordeal cast malevolent shades wherever they walk, and Leni's off-kilter camera angles make them appear even more menacing. The audience never gets their balance throughout the film, which moves at breakneck speed from the death of the patriarch to the gathering of the cousinage to the persistent threat of the house, in the form of madness, melancholy, and the possibility that, as the house's caretaker persistently warns the guests, the living may not be the only inhabitants.

American audiences saw something definitively new in Leni's work, and the cinematography of *The Cat and the Canary* remains genuinely disturbing even today. A long, steady shot down the length of a hallway features the curtained coverings of the old house billowing with unnatural life, while a white mass against the wall could be a chair with a dust cloth or a shrouded corpse. Leni superimposed images that created, for an American film of that era, startling spectral effects, including the ticking mechanism of a clock that shimmers over the group gathering for the reading of the will. Only in part because of the technically complex photography, it looks more like the participants are settling in for a séance than for a legal proceeding.

Inexplicably, some film historians and silent film fans see in *The Cat and the Canary* Hollywood's tendency to mix scares and giggles in the 1920s. There are certainly some Rosencrantz and Guildenstern moments in the film, though that much can be said for most horror films from *Frankenstein* to *Halloween*. But *The Cat and the Canary* never laughs off the possibility of the supernatural or provides us with a full explanation of all that goes on in the West mansion. We never learn, for example, why the clock strikes midnight for the first time in twenty years when the reading of the will begins or why the glowering picture of Cyrus West falls of its own accord from the wall.

Ultimately, *The Cat and the Canary* has little to do with Harold Lloyd's *Haunted Spooks* (1920) or Buster Keaton's *The Haunted House* (1921), both the earlier films having some spectral laughs while making use of their headliner's gift for physical humor. Leni's film leaves open the possibility of some supernatural events hanging in the fetid air. He also confronted American audiences with monstrous twins born of the Great War: bodily disfigurement and mental breakdown. A "dangerous lunatic" has escaped a local asylum. Several times throughout the film, we see a curled, grasping claw reaching from secret panels and from behind beds, with one scene in which the abnormally distended hand reaches over the bed of female lead Annabelle in a sequence that will remind modern horror audiences of Freddy Krueger's deadly hand in *Nightmare on Elm Street*. Some 1927 audiences would have remembered the shadowed claw of Nosferatu and his monstrous and misshapen, though uncomfortably human, form.

When at last we see the murderer's disguise, it's distinctly silly. One eye pops wide, oversized and seemingly lidless, and the teeth look like the tusks of a miniature boar. However unconvincing this might be today (and even in its silliness it's a little unsettling given our contemporary obsession with clown horror), the age of the prosthetic limb would have been affected by it much more strongly.

Leni's frightening evocation of ghosts and his at least partially inde-terminate explanation for some of the events at the West's mansion fit well into the era's renewed interest in the paranormal and the possibility that the human body represented more than what the Great War had made it seem. Could the body perhaps be more than an empty puppet, easily shredded by Maxim guns?

But here the fear of the dead took an unlikely turn. The terror of the corpse as the husk of a human being, a dead doll, made the idea of the ghost rather comforting by comparison. Dread of the corpse helps explains the refusal of some of the more well-known funerary and memorial art of the Great War to represent the human figure. The cemetery and the abstract obelisk take up much of the memorial space along western Europe. At the Ypres salient, touring paths thread for miles through cemeteries dotted with white headstones reading "A Soldier of the Great War: Known Only to God."

More common than representations of the body, and the terror that sits on its haunches waiting behind such representations, are so-called utilitarian memorials. The Menin Gate on the eastern side of the town of Ypres stands as a giant arch, not so much an *arc de triomphe* as an arch of death imbued with the language of sacrifice for monarch and empire. The names of 54,389 British and commonwealth soldiers are engraved on the giant monument, though not a single sculpted human figure can be found. Several miles eastward, near the front lines of the Battle of Passchendaele, the famous cemetery of Tyne Cot contains a monument to Australian troops molded in concrete around the actual pillbox they lost their lives defending.

Commemorative art such as this, the fruit of a desire to transform the landscape of the war into a memorial of an event rather than represent the in-dividual soldier, carried over into a lack of interest in recovering the remains of the beloved dead. The rapid disappearance of this impulse seems espe-cially astonishing, given the now exotic-seeming efflorescence of Victorian-era death rituals. In the half century before the Great War, much of western Europe had engaged in morbid sentimentality to such a degree that the fu-neral had come close to acting as a form of popular entertainment. Photo-graphs of the dead, open displays of the corpse, and highly sentimentalized mourning rituals (including the collection of the hair of the dead frequently twined into a macabre kind of jewelry) had all become commonplace.

Most of this culture of mourning collapsed overnight during World War I. Although there are notable examples of some who sought to challenge the British government's ban on returning the dead for "proper" burial, most of the British public readily acquiesced. Perhaps even more interesting, neither the French nor the Germans made a significant effort to find and bury the remains of their individual beloved dead, even though the effort, while difficult, would have been more practical than for the British. The British dead remained "known only to God," while thousands of French headstones that dot the landscape from Verdun to the Channel starkly assert "Unknown." No one wanted the return of the repressed, the return of a million dead, the corpses at the door. *J'accuse.*[7]

Dreaming of the friendly ghost certainly offered a comforting alternative. In the year after the armistice, Sigmund Freud noted with some shock that the primal horror of the dead communicating with us had become a fascination. He wrote with despair, "In our great cities, placards announce lectures and undertake to tell us how to get in touch with the souls of the departed." He seemed both saddened and at something of a loss to explain this, particularly since the trend had shown itself among even "the most able and penetrating minds of our men of substance."[8]

Spiritualism, a phenomenon most associated with the Victorian era, certainly experienced a resurgence during and after the war. The sudden popularity of the séance appeared with such force that the Vatican felt the need to issue a decree against it in 1917. Numerous Protestant pastors and their synods issued similar warnings.[9]

Theological critiques had little effect on the many figures from art and politics who took part in the movement in the postwar period. Sir Arthur Conan Doyle, whose son Kinglsey; brother, Innes; and brother-in-law E. W. Hornung had all died in the final, pointless months or shortly thereafter, became the most famous enthusiast of the séance. Doyle eventually became as well-known to contemporaries for international lecture tours promoting spiritualism as for creating the world's most famous detective.

The undoubted popularity of séances, mediums, and books about spiritualism during and following the war cannot fail to impress and, to some degree, surprise us as it did Freud. Why relinquish so many of the funerary rites of the last century but maintain the interest in contact with the souls of the departed in a movement that had its roots in the 1840s?

The answer seems to be that the fascination with the dead took on a very different meaning than it had in the nineteenth century. The assurance that the dead had moved on to their next abode rather than a desire for continued interaction with them marked the new fascination with spiritualism. In a perhaps counterintuitive way, then, the interest in hearing from dead loved ones offered assurance to the middle- and upper-class patrons of the séance that their loved dead would not return. Their bodies remained across the English Channel, unidentified in a mass grave; their souls remained on the other side of the Great Beyond.

Evidence for this new, safe way to imagine the dead appears in an incredibly popular English book by Sir Oliver Lodge, *Raymond, or Life and Death*, which appeared in a dozen editions between 1916 and 1919 alone. After presenting the war record of his son Raymond, Lodge provided readers with a series of supernatural messages from the beyond. These messages asserted that the war dead resided "in a better place" and, importantly, that they were kept safely in that other place and would not impinge on the world. Communication with the beloved dead, Lodge asserted, did not mean communion with them, as spiritualism had so often promised in the past.

After all, what might the dead really say to the living in the aftermath of the useless conflict? What horrors did they have to communicate? Might they not come to accuse? The Ouija board had been patented in the United States in 1891 as a parlor amusement, but it was during the Great War that it first acquired its reputation as an occult object whose use could bring about dangerous consequences. Chicago's Pearl Lenore Curran became a celebrity during the war years for her use of a Ouija board and the claim that she could contact a seventeenth-century woman named Patience Worth. The Ouija board, of course, became a frequent prop in later horror films, beginning with *The Exorcist* in 1973, an association that would only increase its reputation as diabolical instrument rather than board game.

In the era of the Great War, thinking of the dead as emanations of light and love in a happier place provided much more comfort than the realities of what had become of the bodies of the dead—or in many cases the living.

Paul Leni became, along with Lon Chaney, one of the figures who brought the fear of the disfigured body to the American screen. In 1928, he directed Conrad Veidt (Cesare from *Caligari*) in *The Man Who Laughs*. Given its setting in the seventeenth century, *The Man Who Laughs* might seem far removed from the mud and steel of the Great War. Based, like *The Hunchback of Notre Dame*, on a novel by Victor Hugo, Leni's film asked Americans to ponder the same questions about the relationship of bodily disfigurement and violence that Chaney's films posed.

The film tells the harrowing story of Gwynplaine, a child of a noble family kidnapped by a foreign criminal underworld that carves children into human oddities and sells them to the traveling circus. Gwynplaine, portrayed by Veidt, has a permanently grinning rictus sliced into his face, the eerie perpetual smile becoming ever more unnerving as the film becomes darker. (The creators of the Batman villain the Joker used Veidt's character and look as a direct inspiration.) The subject matter of the film did not prevent it from being a hit with audiences. Universal quickly had Leni working on a companion piece to *The Cat and the Canary* that would become his final film, bearing the ominous title *The Last Warning*.

Jack Pierce, soon to work his dark magic with the makeup of James Whale's Monster in *Frankenstein*, transformed Veidt into the face of the modern world. The facio-dental disfigurement of Veidt's character alluded to the most startling of injuries caused by the war. Gwynplaine begins the film as both a sympathetic character and the film's monster, not unlike the *gueules cassées* (broken mugs) in the French media. Although the setting in seventeenth-century France might appear to dilute any thoughts the audience might have of the Great War, the costume drama spends enough time visiting torture chambers, showing various kinds of refugees, and exploring how camera angles can make a disfigured human visage generate both horror and empathy to remind even the most insouciant of American moviegoers about the recent horrors visited on much of the world.

Had Leni sought treatment for his infected tooth and lived past the age of forty-four, he might have made the Universal lot even more interesting in the coming golden age of monsters. He did have an admirer in James Whale, who shared Leni's fascination with set design and the arts. In fact, Whale sometimes called *The Man Who Laughs* not only his favorite film but also, in an even greater compliment to Leni, the film he most wished he had directed.[10]

"It's alive!"

The Monster hurls his maker from the top of the windmill as a howling lynch mob screams for his blood. Dr. Henry Frankenstein falls and hits one of the blades of the windmill like a ragdoll before flopping to the ground. The Monster, made from parts of corpses and brought to life via lightning and a "ray of life," grunts with inarticulate horror as the mill burns around him, set aflame by the mob. The camera pulls back with no accompanying score as the mill collapses in on itself. The credits roll.

This scene, soundless but for the crackling of fire and despairing screams of the Monster slowly dissipating on the wind, ended James Whale's *Frankenstein*. At least that's what the audience at the Granada Theatre in Santa Barbara, California, saw when the film premiered on October 29, 1931, just in time for Halloween. Whale and his romantic partner David Lewis attended this first showing, along with Carl Laemmle Jr. Neither Colin Clive (Henry Frankenstein) nor Mae Clarke (Elizabeth) appeared, as both had already started work on other films. No one actually invited Boris Karloff. Nobody at Universal, Whale included, thought the public would much care about the man who grunted and groaned behind the monster makeup.

During the screening, viewers got up and left and then returned for more. At the film's sudden, quiet conclusion, the audience sat for a moment in stunned silence. David Lewis later commented that "it was an alarming thing" and "pretty strong stuff" in 1931. No applause followed the test screening, and no one said much to either Laemmle or the director as they quietly filtered out of the theater.[11]

Junior seems to have utterly misunderstood the response of that first audience. "Jesus God!" David Lewis reports him exclaiming. "We've got to do something! This thing's a disaster!" Though assured by some that he had "the hit of the year," he kept talking about how people had walked out. A likely irritated James Whale had a better read on the audience reaction and knew that the story of a murderous patchwork of corpses had hit the viewers where they lived. Whale had perfectly captured the age's corpse-terror and given it back to them, many times squared.

The studio remained unconvinced and wanted changes before the film's national release in six weeks. The holiday season in the 1930s, unlike today, tended to be box office poison. This, combined with Laemmle's doubts, meant Whale had to fight to keep the film he had made. He lost part of that fight. The studio demanded that a new, soporific ending replace the bleak image of the mill collapsing in silence. In the quickly filmed epilogue, we learn that Dr. Frankenstein has inexplicably lived and will marry Elizabeth. The final scene has stage actor Frederick Kerr, who played Dr. Frankenstein's father, raising a glass to toast "the house of Frankenstein," an unintentionally chilling bit of dialogue given the subsequent history of the Monster in the modern imagination.

Whale later made a comment that suggested he thought the studio's offer to make a version of *Frankenstein* must be a joke. But there's no real evidence that this meant he disdained the idea or saw it, and his other important horror films, as a distraction from his real work. In fact, in at least one version of the story, after Junior gave him "carte blanche with respect to the sundry projects on Universal's slate," Whale chose *Frankenstein* from the pile of possible projects. Whatever the case, he certainly threw himself fully into the making of the film, having a number of discussions with David Lewis about the nature of the novel. According to Lewis, out of these discussions came the idea of creating a monster that might elicit the audience's sympathy. Whether or not the film succeeded in that on its original release remains an open question.[12]

Like Dr. Frankenstein himself, Whale developed an obsessive concern over the creation of the Monster and his setting. He became something of his own art director. He wanted very much to give the film the shadowy look and mise-en-scène of *Caligari*, a film he screened repeatedly during the making of *Frankenstein*. One of the film's editors noted that various versions of the script had sketches drawn by Whale. They contained details as specific as how the arches and drapes should look in Castle Frankenstein and in the mad scientist's *Nosferatu*-influenced tower, lab, and lair.

Whale also passed along a number of conceptual images of what the monster could look like, though we'll likely never know the proportion of

Whale's influence on the visage of Frankenstein's Monster in relation to that of effects artist Jack Pierce. Pierce has become legendary among fans of Universal's golden age of monster films, and many partisans argue for his undoubtedly enormous influence. I don't think we can say for sure whether Pierce, as he later claimed, actually pored over anatomical texts to help him shape Boris Karloff's makeup, but he certainly had experience crafting a sympathetic physiological horror after working on Conrad Veidt's face in Whale's beloved *The Man Who Laughs*.

Although we cannot know exactly how much Whale contributed to the physical look of the Monster, it's an image that, along with the mushroom cloud, became one of the most recognizable and layered icons of the twentieth century. But we do know that he, in a very essential way, made the monster out of his direct confrontation with death in the Great War and his years of trying to bring variant versions of that experience to stage and screen.

Since the story has been told over and over again, modern viewers are likely to forget, in a way that 1931 audiences would not have been able to get out of their minds, that we are watching a field of corpses stumble about the stage. We are seeing a thing of unimaginable horror, a kind of living graveyard that became the ultimate death doll, the most memorable cemetery automaton, in an era that produced so many for screens in Europe, America, and around the world.

Frankenstein's monster can still provoke the chills that every audience and reviewer discovered during its original screenings with some clarity about what we are watching. Bela Lugosi's *Dracula* echoed religious horrors, curses, and taboos from the distant past so strongly that the vampire has remained a creature lurking in the shadowy parts of our consciousness for the last century. Frankenstein and his Monster became much more. Boris Karloff's monstrosity stumbles across the imagined European landscape like a moving mountain of the dead. An industrial process created the thing. Dr. Frankenstein's lab seems as much factory as lab, just as the war had been a mechanism that made corpses by the millions.

Whale achieved his macabre intent in at least two ways. First, the use of light and shadow throughout the film followed what he had absorbed from German and German-American directors like Leni. Whale shot much of the

film in darkness, making near-perfect lighting absolutely necessary. He succeeded in creating an ominous-looking world of stark shadows against high
walls. His success with this came in part from Leni's influence and what one
employee of Universal's screening rooms remembered as his frequent view-
ings of Lang's *Metropolis*, Wiene's *Cabinet of Dr. Caligari*, and other essential
films of Germany's haunted screen. The final film used Weimar cinema's
tendency to bring together the clashing elements of harsh lights, thick darkness, and ominously moving shadows that appear uncannily detached from
the characters who throw them.

Whale combined his use of shadow with the image of the death skull,
another version of Otto Dix's "Skull," appearing in varying forms throughout the film. In the opening scene, one that left many audiences unnerved,
a statue of a hooded skeleton holding a sword presides over the burial of a
corpse, along with a much more traditional crucifix. This image, accompanied by the sickening thud of dirt on the coffin and then Dr. Frankenstein
and his assistant, Karl, digging up the body, proved stomach-churning.

We're at the gibbet in the following scene, the corpse dangling like a
broken doll as Dr. Frankenstein has his assistant cut it down. In a later scene
at the Goldstadt Medical College, a specimen of a human skeleton hangs,
casting a giant shadow on the wall as Fritz steals the brain that will bring
the crazy quilt of dead bodies to life. Skulls decorate the desk and shelves
of the office of Dr. Waldman, Frankenstein's mentor. Dr. Frankenstein
keeps a skull on the desk beside his bed. Our first look at the Monster, the
way Whale shoots the scene from fragmented angles with jump cuts, suggests that we are looking at pieces of bodies. The director has taken us to
the trenches, where Whale had learned that bodies are transformed rather
quickly into disassembled and mismatched parts.

Unlike Mary Shelley's loquacious Monster, who recites long passages of
Milton and wonders aloud about the nature of revolution based on his reading
of eighteenth-century radical texts, Whale's Monster grunts and growls, generally menacingly, during the hour-and-ten-minute running time. Whale's
direction accounts for Karloff's ability to communicate, without speaking,
a language of dread, confusion, or anger. A number of witnesses on the set
recall the director working with Karloff and making the gestures he believed

the Monster would make. Whale wanted to bring his mound of corpses to life, or perhaps more appropriately, living death.

Almost seven decades after audiences first saw the Monster, it's nearly impossible for Whale's design, Jack Pierce's makeup, and Karloff's angry melancholy to have the same effect. Show almost anyone the battered-looking square head with two electrodes protruding from the neck, and "Frankenstein" will automatically register, the Monster and the maker's name forever mixed in the chaos of creation and destruction. He's been remade for a number of films, and he walks again every October as one of the most popular Halloween costumes of all time. He's been placed on cereal boxes and used to sell hamburgers. We'll never have the 1931 audience's experiences when Whale used a series of quick cuts and angled shots to show us his puppet made of corpses. But we can begin to understand the moment's eerie chill when we consider a period in which nothing else produced as much horror as the dead body in all its implied threat.

Colin Clive as Dr. Frankenstein played almost as much of a role in reactions to the film as the Monster did. Whale apparently saw the doctor as the central character, far more important than Karloff. Although his manic scream "It's alive! It's alive! It's alive!" justly remains one of the most famous moments in film history, contemporary viewers are perhaps too familiar with overacted mad scientists to feel the anxious, strained edge that Clive gives to the entirety of the film.

Before *Frankenstein*, most American audiences knew Clive as Captain Stanhope from James Whale's film version of R. C. Sherriff's play *Journey's End* (1930). The film garnered close to the same interest in Britain and the United States as did *All Quiet on the Western Front*, made the same year. In that era, the two films had a relationship perhaps a bit like *Platoon* and *Full Metal Jacket* for post-Vietnam American audiences.

Clive proved absolutely wrenching in his portrayal of Stanhope. In the original play and film, he incarnates the British soldier teetering on the edge of a complete nervous collapse. Stanhope attempts to hide this by drinking heavily to steady himself and insisting that his men, often against better sense, do their duty. In one particularly powerful scene, he breaks down and cries with another soldier just after accusing him of shirking and suggesting

that the soldier's alleged illness can't be worse than "being shot for deser-
tion." Film historian James Curtis sees the characters of Stanhope and Frankenstein connected in that both are "on a collision course with fate, tortured
by personal demons and powerless to prevent [their] own destruction."[3]

In other words, Stanhope as played by Clive appears as the ghost at the
feast of war commemoration. He embodies the horrifying truths about the
conflict that all the sentimental doggerel about the British Tommy and his
sacrifice tries to hide from us; the "poppy porn" that still infests the remem-
brance of the war dead.

Noël Coward called Whale's production "a nasty little vilification of the
war" that he believed offered a much-needed antidote to sentimentalism and
inspired his own play *Post Mortem*. The tragedy of Raleigh, a young officer
led by Stanhope, capped the film's message and joined it firmly to some of
Whale's decisions in *Frankenstein*. Stanhope and Raleigh have a troubled
and complex relationship, set off in part by Raleigh's grief over the loss of
his friend Osborne, whose dead body lies somewhere twisted in the barbed
wire of no-man's-land. Stanhope, having known Osborne far longer and
doing his best not to feel anything, finds Raleigh's grief grating. The film
ends, however, with news that Raleigh has received a spine injury and has to
be moved into the officers' dugout, where much of the claustrophobic film
occurs. Stanhope comforts him as he dies, though in the final scene the tortured captain rushes forth to take part in an assault just as a shell collapses
the dugout and buries Raleigh in the rubble.

The catastrophic entombment of Raleigh appears again in the flaming
collapse of the windmill that buries Frankenstein's Monster, a scene Whale
chose as the most appropriate end for his film. Indeed, the Monster dies en-
tombed again, this time with his Bride, in the explosive collapse of Dr. Frankenstein's tower in the 1935 *Bride of Frankenstein*. Whale never fully let go of
the image, played out again and again on almost all fronts of the Great War,
of bodies being buried beneath the carnage of trenches, the living and the
dead sealed beneath the collapse of thousands of pounds of dirt and concrete
from shells and sap mines.

Clive captured the unsettling energy of Stanhope nearly perfectly, perhaps in part because of his own demons. The actor likely would be diagnosed
today with some form of anxiety disorder. During the 1930s, he became in-

famous for self-medicating with heavy drinking, often on set. This may have actually aided his portrayal of Stanhope, who also appears terrified, angry, and drunk. Audiences who, about a year later, then saw Clive as the deeply tormented Dr. Frankenstein, sweating, eyes darting fearfully, seemingly running in terror even as he leads a mob to destroy his dangerous creation, could not help but remember the tragic, broken Captain Stanhope.

Earning some ill will from critics at first, *Frankenstein* proved a huge success with the American public. A film exhibitors' paper described it as "a thriller," adding, "Women come out trembling, men come out exhausted. I don't know what it might do to children but I know I wouldn't let my own go to see it." The reviewer said he would not forgive the Laemmles or James Whale for showing little Maria's drowning: "It carries gruesomeness and cruelty a little beyond reason or necessity." Whale had reversed Wegener's tale of the Golem by having the Monster kill the little girl rather than accept salvation from her. However, before we decide we prefer Wegener's sentimental ending, we'd do well to note that the man who made it also made Nazi propaganda films in the 1930s, even if he seems to have been personally ambivalent about the regime.[14]

Comments about the "weird" subject matter of *Frankenstein* did not keep box office receipts from being enormous almost from the day the film opened nationally. Whale had a peculiar hit, and, from the Laemmles' perspective, the money might continue to roll in from even more monster films. The film did well in Germany, where theaters screened it on the eve of Hitler's rise to power. It quickly became branded as degenerate art soon after. Fascist Italy banned it, while in England the censors appear to have edited it into meaninglessness.

The Old Dark House

Whale continued to explore the macabre even as he churned out films on a number of different subjects. His once forgotten film *The Old Dark House*, produced in 1932 but considered essentially a lost film until the late 1960s, showed the influence of Leni's *The Cat and the Canary* while somehow managing to include both more campy humor and more terror of the empty-eyed corpse all at once.[15] For *The Old Dark House*, Ernest Thesiger worked with Whale as the aristocratic and self-admitted criminal Horace Femm, one of two siblings who actively despise each other while keeping their ill father and maniacally murderous brother locked away in various upper-story rooms. Boris Karloff appeared in the form of the frightening, lumbering, inarticulate butler Morgan. The character, threatening throughout and any audience's early pick for the most dangerous character in the house, very much resembles Frankenstein's Monster. Karloff arguably manages to appear even more menacing despite the absence of electrodes protruding from his neck.

Whale's film has a group of young people seek refuge at Femm's tormented old dark house in the middle of a deadly storm with rain coming down "in buckets," a phrase the characters keep repeating until it becomes a running joke. Serving the young guests gin ("I like gin," Horace Femm preens suggestively), the Thesiger character's signature cattiness and sarcasm leads him to toast "illusions," which, he adds, probably seems a foreign idea to his young guests. No one responds to Thesiger's comment except for the character of Penderel (Melvyn Douglas). He's well aware of the nature, and the dangers, of illusion and says so. Femm responds, "Of course, you are of that generation battered by the war." Later, in perhaps a parody of his own and other veterans' tentative feeling about discussing the war, Whale opens a scene with Penderel talking to his love interest with the lines "Well, and then the war ended, so that was that." Whale leaves it to our imagination what sort of horror Douglas's character has just related.

Death of all kinds occupies the center of the film, from visual imagery to off-handed references. Other times, Whale makes the point more plainly. In one of the most memorable scenes Whale directed, Gloria Stuart (who later worked with him as the female lead in *The Invisible Man*), who plays the character Margaret, dresses for dinner in a shimmeringly beautiful gauzy gown. The mirror doubles her sex-drenched youthfulness for the audience to admire. Horace's unloved sister, Rebecca (played by Eva Moore), meanwhile, delivers a hellfire-and-brimstone sermon to the young woman, saying that her unblemished flesh will rot down to its bones. She grabs Margaret's gown in her bent and clawed hand and wheezes, "That's fine stuff, but it'll rot." Pointing her finger and then laying her hand on the exposed skin between Margaret's throat and breasts, Rebecca adds, "That's finer stuff still, but it'll rot, too, in time!"

One of the oddest decisions made by Whale, and it's perhaps due to the uncredited work that R. C. Sherriff did on the script, concerns how the film splits the image of the World War I veteran between the heroic Penderel and the monstrous Morgan. Penderel embodied what patriotic poetry had chosen to see as the flower of British manhood, the sentimentalized veteran, handsome and brave. Yet even he admits that the war has taken away his sense of purpose, his belief that there's any real meaning to things. Morgan displays a darker version of the man who has seen too much. He's psychically and physically mutilated, his scarred face matched by his inability to speak except in a gibbering stammer not unlike Karloff's more famous Monster. Like Captain Stanhope in *Journey's End*, Morgan drinks heavily (notably, so does Penderel) and becomes violent; indeed he's clearly shown trying to rape Margaret. It's as if Whale and Sherriff took the character of Captain Stanhope and divided his disturbing characteristics between Morgan and Penderel, a split image of the same horrors.

We unfortunately have really nothing from the director himself regarding how the war shaped his vision of horror. Whale never spoke openly about the relationship of his experience of the war to his horror films, but this should surprise exactly no one. He seldom spoke about the war at all. Whale never gave interviews about his experiences on the western front or as a prisoner of war even in relation to his three major World War I films. Moreover, the concept of a director's "vision" for a film had little meaning in Hollywood in the 1930s. This would have been particularly true at a studio such as Universal, whose chief executive viewed filmmaking as something akin to Henry Ford's assembly line.

There's little reason to argue over what Whale's monster films are "really" about, given his silence on the matter. I certainly wish he'd been as loquacious about the meaning of his work as Fritz Lang, even taking into account Lang's tendency to tell different stories about his career at different times. Whale may have proved as mute as his Monster on the subject but his choice of themes spoke volumes. His horror films dwelled on the twin terrors of mental illness and physical disfigurement, blending them in a way terrifyingly recognizable to audiences who had seen, and often tried to forget, the maimed and mutilated returning veteran. The creature, seen first wrapped in the bandages that suggest the zombie soldiers of Gance's *J'accuse*, seemed like the dreaded return of the war corpse. Frankenstein's Monster was no ghost, no friendly spirit, no departed beloved soul returned to tell its loved ones that all was well in the great beyond. He was a whole world of corpses, sewn together by madness, another automaton that confronted audiences with the ultimate fear of the empty nothingness of death, the body as a "broken doll."

The thing created by Dr. Frankenstein—sad, violent, angry—moved like a surrealist collective of body parts. The Monster became a reminder of the torn and shredded dead that lived in the nightmares of the soldiers who had, for example, been at Gallipoli and watched while a field of corpses bloated in the hot sun of the Dardanelles. They had sickened at the smell until a one-day truce had to be called in May 1915, a brief respite in which soldiers buried bits and pieces of their comrades so that they could resume the slaughter the next day without the unbearable stench.

Whale created his monsters at a time when the mutilated dead and the bandaged, shattered face had become an icon of the age. Gance had of course recognized this with *J'accuse*, while Leni in *The Man Who Laughs* and most of Lon Chaney and Tod Browning's collaborations of the 1920s had further explored the ugly spectacle the war had made of the human body. Erik the Phantom had been in 1925 the ultimate "broken mug," complete with a mask that resembled the prosthetics that covered the era's grotesque wounds.

Whale's monsters, and a number of related films made by Universal, took the horror of the bandages even further. In 1934, Whale created another of the era's horror masterpieces, *The Invisible Man*, which made a monster of a bandaged man who also suffered delusions and complete derangement. Numerous attempts had been made to bring the story to the screen, but all had failed, in part because H. G. Wells, author of the novel adapted for the film, had disapproved of them. By the time Whale made the final version, no fewer than five treatments and six screenplays had been proposed. One had made a direct connection between the Great War and the events in the original novel by setting the tale amid the Russian Revolution of 1917. This version featured an invisible monster created as an act of vengeance by a scientist whose family had been killed by Bolsheviks.

Whale's own treatment dealt obliquely with the themes of the war, imagining a disfigured scientist who seeks invisibility to hide his mutilated face. His experiments drive him to become a mentally unstable murderer. The idea of mental instability remained and made Whale one of the first Hollywood directors to combine horror with the concept. The Great War stumbled, ranted, murdered, and raved on the back lots of Universal.

Whale became only one of the directors producing stories of corpses moving across the wasteland. Karl Freund, who had worked on principal photography with Wegener in *The Golem* and Lang on *Metropolis*, joined the growing number of central European exiles in Hollywood. His 1932 production of it makes of Karloff a shambling icon of death once again. This time Karloff appeared in an even more mordant atmosphere, croaking out dialogue as a long-dead Egyptian priest returned to the twilight regions of the living.

This film made no direct allusion to the Great War, but the creature became one of the era's numerous death dolls, its movements replicating the behavior of the shell-shocked. Its success encouraged Universal to use both of its monster stars, Karloff and *Dracula*'s Bela Lugosi, in one of the more shocking films of the 1930s. *The Mummy* did make direct reference to the Great War, along with other themes it's almost too incredible to believe made it into a film of that era.

The Black Cat (1934) borrowed the title of one of Edgar Allan Poe's better-known stories, although, with the exception of an actual black cat that occasionally wanders through a scene and frightens Lugosi's character, it's hard to find any connection to Poe's original tale. The film's director was Edgar G. Ulmer, an enigmatic figure who spent his boyhood in Vienna and worked in some capacity with F. W. Murnau. What exactly Ulmer did during his apprenticeship under Murnau, and in the Weimar film industry more generally, remains hazy. He frequently made now-disputed claims that he had been an uncredited set designer for *The Golem, M,* and *Metropolis*. Whatever his precise background in film, Ulmer certainly brought the moody and surreal look of the films he claimed to have worked on in Europe to his first major Hollywood venture.

Karloff, fresh from *The Lost Patrol*, in which he played a Great War sergeant driven to madness, became a different kind of psychological victim of the war in Ulmer's film. Karloff plays Hjalmar Poelzig, a brilliant, deranged, and shell-shocked architect who lives in a bizarre Bauhaus version of the old dark house he built on an unnamed Great War battlefield where he suffered an unexplained trauma. In this castle, a set heavily influenced by Wegener's haunted vision of Prague, he conducts cultic rituals with his followers. Ulmer became one of the many fascinated with Aleister Crowley's "magick" during the 1920s and '30s and modeled Karloff's character partially on him.

Dracula's Bela Lugosi appears as Dr. Vitus Werdegast, a psychiatrist and veteran visiting his former battlefield comrade. We learn rather quickly that the two have an infinite depth of hatred for one another born from the Great War. Werdegast has come to visit the surreal house of horrors because Poelzig abandoned him to die of his wounds in the very wasteland where his house now stands. He has arrived, as was not uncommon in old dark house films, to exact revenge. In a nod to another common trope of such stories, a young (in this case newlywed) couple has arrived for a night's stay in Poelzig's castle and ends up being forced to take part in the gruesome proceedings.

The similarity between the old dark house genre and *The Black Cat* ended there, and the script, especially the original one, took a vicious turn. The film became the first of five that Karloff and Bela Lugosi worked on together, and it's the strangest by far. We learn that not only did Poelzig leave Werdegast to die on the battlefield; he also murdered the psychiatrist's wife and then married his daughter, eventually killing her as well. Seduction of both mother and daughter and a subtext of necrophilia appeared in Ulmer and screenwriter Peter Ruric's early drafts of the film.

The young honeymooners serve as pawns in the game the two demented veterans play against one another. The new bride becomes an object of desire for Poelzig, with the suggestion that he and his followers will use her in a cultic ritual. The theatrical release, which went through so many cuts that it runs only about an hour, makes Werdegast into at least an antihero who seeks to save the young woman. But, again in Ulmer's first draft, he seeks to rescue her from Karloff's clutches only so that he can possess her first. While the film that made it to theaters may have dropped this idea, it still ends with Poelzig being flayed alive while the avant-garde confection of his house tumbles to the ground after being dynamited by Werdegast, sap-mined like hundreds of points along the trenches of every battlefield of the war. Yet another collapsed earthwork in the wasteland.

Lugosi's own experience in the war had an uncanny similarity to that of the unlucky Dr. Werdegast. Lugosi's service in the Austro-Hungarian army always receives the briefest of mentions in discussions of his life and career. The possibility that these experiences served as the defining element in the various vampires, mad scientists, and murderers he played onscreen has seldom been explored. Even his son, Bela Lugosi Jr., in a 2006 essay for a celebration of the Universal Studio's famous monsters, simply writes his father "volunteered for service when patriotism called" and "received the equivalent of a purple heart." After the war, he left Hungary because he "took an active role in an actors union" and "found himself on the wrong side of the ruling party." All of this is technically accurate, but the story of Lugosi's war experience is both more interesting and more gruesome.[16]

Lugosi had served as an infantry captain and for a time in the imperial army's elite ski patrol corps on the eastern front. He suffered three wounds, though war neurosis apparently gave him his discharge and possibly saved his life. Reports as to what happened to him vary. There has been some unsympathetic speculation that he pretended mental instability. There's no evidence that he did not suffer like millions of others. Lugosi seldom spoke at all in specific terms about the Great War, but he did tell Anna Bakacs, an actress and a romantic interest in the 1920s, that he once burrowed underneath a large pile of corpses to save himself after the Russian army overran the Hapsburg trenches.[17]

The themes of *The Black Cat* seemed to make Lugosi a bit more loquacious than usual about the war, even though Edward Ulmer's widow has described the actor as generally "unapproachable." Perhaps she referred to the odd story that has circulated about Lugosi, known for his reserve on set, occasionally telling the cast that he had been "a hangman" for the Austro-Hungarian army and that the experience had left him feeling thrilled and guilty. He seemed to perhaps be joking, but no one could be sure of that or even what the joke might be.[18]

Watching *The Black Cat* today, and knowing about the strict censorship that James Whale's films faced, it's something of a wonder that even the highly expurgated versions of Ulmer's strange film ever made it into theaters.

In fact, it did receive plenty of attention from the Motion Picture Production Code office, which in 1930 had established guidelines for acceptable versus unacceptable content in movies. In discussing the film with Ulmer, Joseph Breen, who administered the code's restrictions for the Motion Picture Producers and Distributors of America, insisted that the film use "shadow and silhouette" to prevent the scene of Poelzig being skinned alive from appearing "too gruesome or revolting." Following the Weimar-era masters he admired, Ulmer certainly drowned the film in shadow, though whether this kept the "gruesome" and "revolting" nature of the film to a minimum remains debatable. The American public certainly took to the truly bizarre film either way, making it Universal's most profitable film of 1934.

"The air itself is filled with monsters"

It's utterly true, if something of an understatement, for the dean of American horror historians, David J. Skal, to note that "a central point of *The Black Cat* is that the First World War has not yet been resolved." Universal released the film as Hitler tightened his grip on Germany, and within months his regime instituted the Nuremberg Laws. Fascism, fueled by the savagery and sense of shame engendered by the war, competed with renewed efforts by the United States and its allies to secure a neocolonial global order.[19] "The air itself is filled with monsters." When Elsa Lanchester spoke this famous line in *Bride of Frankenstein*, the greatest horror film of the era, she said more than she or the screenwriter knew.

Universal Studios held no monopoly over the making of horror films in the 1930s and early '40s, especially after producers came to regard them as quick and easy moneymakers. Many of these low-budget affairs, written by screenwriters and shot by directors who had received only limited influence from the great talents of the Weimar years, nevertheless picked up on the themes of mental illness and bodily disfigurement that stalked American and European culture.

Warner Brothers, for example, produced *The Mystery of the Wax Museum* (1933), a film that echoed the themes of the Universal monsters and reached back to Leni's *Waxworks* of the postwar era in Germany. The theme of the human body as the death doll proved as troubling in this film as in Universal's *The Black Cat*. In the gruesome tale of a murdering maniac who seeks to transform his female obsession into a puppet, *Wax Museum* contains a fairly obvious suggestion of necrophilia. Lionel Atwill's disturbing character wore makeup that suggested severe burns, as if he'd nearly been immolated in a trench set ablaze by a flamethrower. Censors, ignoring recent human history, called it "the most nauseating" portrayal of the human face they had ever seen.[20]

Not all of the rival monster films came from small studios with equally tiny budgets. Merian C. Cooper made perhaps the most iconic monster of the 1930s (other than *Frankenstein*) for RKO Studios: King Kong. Appearing in 1933, *King Kong* followed predecessors such as the 1925 classic *The Lost World* by imagining a prehistoric monstrosity threatening modernity. Both films play in a peculiar fashion with Fritz Lang's themes in *Metropolis* and imagine the modern city under threat, in fact the city as steel-and-concrete superego thrusting its pretensions skyward with little thought to the forces that make it work and could destroy it. *King Kong* places an embodiment of the primordial age on the urban landscape, as if Lang's Moloch had broken loose and left Metropolis in ruins. In *Kong*, explosive violence replaced the heart that bound together "the head and the hand," the city's capitalist class and proletariat in Lang's confusing political parable. In place of comity between oppressed and oppressor in modern city, there's only the destructive power of the monster and the effort to destroy him.

The urban terrorscape had, of course, been of concern to numerous writers and artists shadowed by the war. The idea of the city as necropolis appeared again and again in poem, film, and fiction. This tendency seems an eerie presage of the ruined cities of the 1940s that the destruction of World War I had hinted at.

Kong's famous ascent to, and equally famous fall from, the top of the Empire State Building drew rather directly on the director's experience of the Great War. Cooper, an aviator during the conflict, still suffered from severe burns he had received after being shot down over the Argonne. He created the sequence of biplanes battling the monster with fellow Great War veteran Ernest B. Schoedsack, who had worked with the Signal Corps and had his eyesight badly damaged.

Dracula himself began to show up in a number of horror pictures produced by companies other than Universal. Bela Lugosi, perpetually unhappy
with the often unfair billings he received at Universal, starred (or at least
made an appearance) in numerous horror and mystery flicks in the 1930s
and '40s, most of them forgotten now. He just as frequently returned to Universal but, in an unfortunate irony, his efforts to show the studio that he had
not tied his career to the Laemmles had the effect of causing him to be seen
as disloyal, resulting in fewer and fewer meaningful parts.

In 1932, Lugosi appeared in perhaps the most interesting role, and
the most intriguingly horrifying film, of his career outside of *The Black
Cat*. Paramount Pictures' *Island of Lost Souls* retold the disturbing tale of
H. G. Wells's novel *The Island of Dr. Moreau* (1896) in a fashion that circled
back to the surrealist horrors of Max Ernst in response to the Great War.

Surrealism had responded to the ferocity of the Great War by blending
men and machines, or the human and the animal, in disconcerting fashion.
Ernst certainly excelled at this, exposing naked and desperately vulnerable
human flesh, and conjoining it with fur and feathers. *Island of Lost Souls* did
much the same, with Charles Laughton playing the cold, insane technician
of science. His demeanor contrasted enormously with Colin Clive's frenzied
interpretation of Dr. Frankenstein, while still achieving the inhuman effect
that audiences had come to expect from such figures. Although Wells wrote
the original as a kind of Swiftian satire of Victorian England, the motion
picture played on the terrors of technology that made the line between the
human and the animal disappear in the fog of war and violence. The men
who crafted poison gas and built the Maxim gun to shatter the body would
be willing to do anything.

Laughton's heartless Dr. Moreau relentlessly pursues the possibilities
of gene splicing in his "house of pain," the place of surgery where animals
endure all the possible horrors of scalpel and suture. It stands as a symbol
of human willingness to inflict "vile horror" as Edward Parker, the unlucky
castaway who finds himself on the island, describes what he sees there.
Parker learns that Dr. Moreau has taken all conceivable animals and made
them into miserable hybrids burdened with human desire and consciousness.
But, it's made clear, they have not transcended their previous state. In a bleak

estimation of human values, this has made them less than what they had been before.

Lugosi has a rather small role in the film, but it's utterly pivotal to the story's direction. He's covered in fur and unrecognizable under makeup, but he stands upright in his role of Sayer of the Law. In ritualistic fashion, he leads the village of Dr. Moreau's malformed monstrosities in a kind of ritual utterance of "the Law" by which they live—they will not eat meat, they will not shed blood—all proclamations followed by a kind of antiphonal response, "Are we not men?"

The paradox inherent in "the Law" on Dr. Moreau's hellish island is that this generation knew that human beings certainly did shed blood and, unlike the animal world, did so driven by ideology, nationalism, and their own fears rather than out of an evolutionary imperative to eat flesh for food. The film uses this obvious fact, and the Sayer of the Law recognizes that Dr. Moreau violates his own precepts. The creatures stitched together from the corpses of human and animal, an army of Frankensteins, rise against Moreau in an orgy of violence. These tormented hybrids, the film darkly suggests, truly become human when they acquire the taste for murder.

Lugosi worked with a number of studios in roles that called for dangerous and often deluded men of mystery. So-called poverty row studios, small production companies in size and budget that produced B pictures, churned out these movies, often in imitation of the more successful genre films of the Big Six (Universal, Warner Bros., Paramount, RKO, 20th Century Fox, and MGM).

The 1943 film *The Return of the Vampire* sadly encapsulates Lugosi's trajectory from master of horror to prop piece in monster pageants. It also speaks unwittingly about the Great War's shadow continuing to hover behind the haunted screen. Although campy and absurd, the Columbia Pictures production makes the subtext of horror films for most of the interwar period into a blindingly obvious allegory of the times. Lugosi plays a vampire who sucks the blood of London for much of the Great War. Armand Tesla, as he's called, receives the requisite stake through the heart just as the conflict comes to an end in the autumn of 1918. The Luftwaffe strafes the city during the Blitz of World War II and reawakens the monster. Crawling from the wreckage, the vampire and the war begin its killing spree anew until yet another bomb buries him alive. Awakened by the first Great War of the century, the corpse had waited for a humanity to outrage itself again to rise and do his nightly wet work.

The silliness of the plot—some of Lugosi's most dramatic lines in the film elicit giggles today—doesn't mask the real-world horrors that gibber in the shadows. In this film, the last time the former infantry commander played a vampire except for the pure comedic value, Albin Grau's vision of the "cosmic vampire" who "sucks the blood of millions" remained even if in attenuated form. The vampire lived amid war and slept while it awaited war to again ravage the world.

Unlike the Great War, which had stunned humanity with its ability to turn human beings into corpses, the century's major conflict that opened in 1939 did not create the same level of reflective horror in art, cinema, or literature, even though it caused a number of deaths incalculable in comparison to 1914–1918 and to any major conflict since. Many in western Europe and America felt themselves so dumbfounded by the second great slaughter of the century that they numbly watched adventurous reenactments of its great battles instead. The horror film, once almost painfully allegorical in its efforts to biopsy the meaning of massive violence, became a playground of escapism and even humor. The new horror would be shaped by what the century began to call the Second World War, a century that in America at least frequently displayed a bizarre optimism with seemingly no relation to what had actually occurred.

The era before World War II had, however, given birth to one last great masterpiece that told a story that no one wanted to hear. Millions willingly watched in terror anyway.

The Bride

James Whale loved the idea of the knock that comes in the middle of the night, a portent to everyone warm and safe inside. He used it in his Frankenstein films, in *The Invisible Man*, and in transmogrified form in *Journey's End*, the greatest of his war films. The quiet of the trenches in the latter film—and all accounts suggest that they sometimes did have an exhausted silence about them—would suddenly explode in a hard rain of shells or machine gun fire, shattering nerves and leaving men in a state that suggested both drowsy abstraction and nervous fidgety horror.

In *Bride of Frankenstein* (1935), the knock at the door pulls Dr. Frankenstein from his bed, on his wedding night no less, to meet fellow mad scientist Dr. Pretorius, played to the hilt by Ernest Thesiger. Together they will do more than manufacture undead automata from the fragments of corpses. They will, as Dr. Pretorius exclaims, inaugurate "a new world of gods and monsters."

The greatest of Universal Studios' horror films of the 1930s ended the cycle of reflections on the Great War that began in 1919–1922 with *J'accuse*, *The Cabinet of Dr. Caligari*, and *Nosferatu*. James Whale's *Bride of Frankenstein* offered a final meditation on the trenches. Whale had debated producing a sequel to *Frankenstein* not because he disdained the horror genre, as its sometimes suggested, but simply because he had killed the Monster and, had the studio let him have his way, he would have killed the maker as well.

However, he began to see some possibilities in making what became his masterpiece. He suggested to David Lewis and other friends that he would make the film "a hoot"—that is, a satire, a comedy of horror. Novelist Christopher Bram describes *Bride* as a comedy about death. This phrase captures much of what Whale hoped to put on screen. Death stalks everyone, embodied in the Monster who has become much more murderous in the interim between the two films. In fact, he shows himself capable of both random acts of violence and even what we might even call domestic terrorism. He retains our sympathy when we watch the film today, as Whale seems to have wanted, although, as with the original *Frankenstein*, it's unlikely 1935 audiences felt anything but terror when watching the Monster.

The era's bone-deep obsession with physical abnormality and disfigurement appears throughout the film. The Monster has emerged out of his experience with the burning windmill with more scars than we saw at his creation, filled with rage at his unasked-for plight. He kills in his first appearance in the film, savagely murdering the parents of Maria, the child drowned in *Frankenstein*. Whale has an owl watch somnolently as they die. Una O'Connor, a frequent player in Whale's work, screams her way through the story, first in a scene in which the Monster, the blood of Maria's parents still on his hands, looms above her.

Thesiger's Dr. Pretorius appears in the film completely mad and utterly gay and fully in love with death while obsessing over its ambiguous boundaries. In one of the film's most memorable scenes, Thesiger tells the body snatchers, who have just rifled the corpse of a young woman that will provide the raw material for the female Monster, to leave him be so that he can take his dinner in the crypt. "I rather like it here," says the actor who had once watched as his fellow soldiers' body parts exploded around him.

The scene becomes one of the strangest, and most meaningful, moments in all the lore of Frankenstein that has appeared since 1818. Dr. Pretorius enjoys a veritable feast in the crypt of roasted chicken, bread, and a bottle of wine. We hear him before we see him as Whale's camera peeks through the shadows. He's laughing uproariously at the fleshless skull that sits on the tomb he has made a table. Raising a glass he toasts the skull, "I give you, the Monster!" he cries out, laughing until he cries. The Monster is not what Dr. Frankenstein made on his table; death is the only real monster, and it's a hoot.

The Monster, Frankenstein's pile of corpses, appears to Dr. Pretorius for the first time after this peculiar moment. Pretorius receives the scarred and mutilated image of death with all the nonchalance of a person receiving a pizza delivery. In their exchange, the tipsy mad doctor shares a cigar with the shambling horror and talks of life and death. "Love dead. Hate living," says the Monster in yet another of the film's infamous lines. "You are wise in your generation," replies the world-weary Pretorius. Is this the mad scientist or is it Ernest Thesiger remembering the shell exploding in the barn? Whale lets him be both in this scene and lets the Monster embody, in his loneliness and death-longing, the horror of the twentieth century.

Colin Clive also returns as Dr. Frankenstein. Whale ordered that cast and crew watch Clive closely to make sure that no flasks or bottles went with him back to his dressing room. It's not clear Whale succeeded. Clive once again acts out Captain Stanhope raving as mad scientist, careening wildly between the manic and the frighteningly subdued.

Whale planned to blow them all up at the end of his joke on the world. The lonely murderous Monster continues to kill for the sake of killing. He had murdered the parents of little Maria out of blind rage and hurled the mad doctor's assistant (still not bearing the name Ygor) off parapets for no clear reason. Overall, the Monster in *Bride* racks up a body count higher than Freddy Krueger in the original *Nightmare on Elm Street*.

The doctors are by now fully out of their minds when Elsa Lanchester appears at last, a kind of art deco masterwork of elegantly placed scar tissue. We don't meet her until the final moments of the film. She comes into the world chirping and screeching like an angry bird, refusing to play Bride to the Monster. Whale had originally hoped to have Brigitte Helm in the role, the young woman who portrayed the android Maria in Lang's *Metropolis*. As interesting a connection as this would have made, today it's impossible to imagine anyone but Lanchester, with her daimonic, elven features, taking the role of the Bride.[21]

The Monster in Whale's original shooting script, now rejected by the only creature from which he could possibly find love, utters another of the film's most famous lines to his makers and his presumptive mate. "We belong dead," he sighs with the generation of the Great War, a generation appearing shocked to have made it out of the trenches while inwardly so shattered that they never left them. The Monster pulls a lever, and of course it seems a design flaw that the lab contains a single switch that destroys the entire tower when activated. The whole kit and caboodle blows sky-high like a bunker in the Ypres salient undermined by sappers.

The studio didn't care for this, wanting both a Hollywood ending and the possibility of more sequels from the profitable franchise of monsters. Pretorius, the Monster, and the Bride all seem to die in the explosion, but Dr. Frankenstein and Elizabeth live, the romantic strains of the marvelously composed soundtrack rising as they embrace. Apparently Elizabeth has forgiven her new husband his penchant for gravedigging and monster-making, and the couple disappear into the happily-ever-after.

You have to have a heart of stone to love the ending of this otherwise brilliant cinematic feat. Whale had pulled off a hoot, to be sure, but he had not been able to fulfill his ambition to create a real comedy of death by successfully killing off all the characters. Much like the 1931 *Frankenstein*, the studio opted for a more hopeful conclusion than a burning cataclysm. Studio executives worked under the impression that the audience needed to leave the theater happy; just as significantly, they believed, rightly, that the Monster's tortured existence could make them more money in the future.

It seems entirely appropriate that the studio responsible for *All Quiet on the Western Front* also produced *Bride of Frankenstein*. Much has been made of the homoerotic subtext of *Bride*, but, truthfully, it's so glaring to most audiences today that it's now part of the formal presentation of the film rather than its subtext. If there's an underlying message, not openly discussed but the assumption behind every scene, it's the Great War. In some respects, it's Whale's greatest World War I epic.

Colin Clive, just thirty-seven, died two years after the successful opening of *Bride of Frankenstein*. His drinking had brought on catastrophic kidney failure. On the set of his last film, *The Woman I Love*, all his scenes had to be filmed by noon. Otherwise he would already be too inebriated to continue. In some scenes of that last film, he's being physically held so the director could make a few over-the-shoulder shots.

James Whale thought much of Clive but did not attend his funeral service or burial. He didn't care for funerals or cemeteries. When David Lewis needed to attend a service at Forest Lawn, Whale supposedly said, "Oh stop it! Keep away from that place!"[22]

Mountains of Madness

H. P. Lovecraft would have none of it. He may have thrilled to *Phantom of the Opera* and longed to see *The Cabinet of Dr. Caligari*, but the golden age of Universal Studios monsters left him cold.

Lovecraft wrote his great, and final, masterpieces during Universal Studios' classic run of horror films. In 1931, he completed a draft of "The Shadow over Innsmouth," the tale that today creates almost as many new Lovecraft readers as "The Call of Cthulhu." It's a story of a town full of monsters and a sea teeming with creatures that rise to threaten human frailty, its depths like the cosmic depths that, in his best stories, echo back human pleas for meaning and create the purest chill of horror. Of course, many readers just find in it a story of a desperate struggle to escape from some fish people that has a bit of a surprise ending, and that's okay, too.

The year 1931 also saw *At the Mountains of Madness* seep out of Lovecraft's pen, the closest he ever came to writing a novel. He used the long form to slowly unwind the tale of an expedition of Miskatonic University geologists and archaeologists to the Antarctic. There they find, preserved in limestone and ice, "huge specimens" of barrel-shaped creatures with star-shaped heads. The scientists quickly proceed to vivisect the creatures, but their dispatches to base camp soon stop and the remainder of the expedition quickly discovers that something has left their comrades mangled into unrecognizable shapes, many of them looking as if they had been carefully "incised" in a way that suggested the removal of whole masses of tissues. It looked, in other words, like a battlefield.

The narrator explains to the reader that the expedition had told the world little of what happened next and blamed the deaths of their fellows on the effects of the violent Antarctic winds. But he writes that now there are new exploratory parties planning to make their way to the frozen wastes. He fears that "if not dissuaded, they will get to innermost nucleus of the Antarctic and melt and bore till they bring up that which may end the world we know." So the narrator begins the longer explanation of the city built into vast mountain ranges at the bottom of the earth, a "cavernous aeon-dead honeycomb of primal masonry" and "a monstrous lair of elder secrets." It's a story more frightening in its implications than the 1930s wanted to hear, even as the nations of the earth seemed determined on their own apocalypse.[23]

At the Mountains of Madness, like much of Lovecraft's other work, reads as if it could only have been produced after 1918. The mysteries that lie beyond mountains of ice are dead cities that tell of a history in which humans played no meaningful role. Human beings had been born after the creatures from the vast darkness embarked on "elaborate experiments after the annihilation of various cosmic enemies."

Lovecraft's vast mythology concerns a war that long ago ravaged the world, a war beyond human comprehension in its destruction and even its implications—in so many ways like the way most people looked uncomprehendingly at what had happened between 1914 and 1918, or the horrors that had emerged since.

As he had been able to achieve in the skin-crawling scenes from "Herbert West—Reanimator" and "The Dunwich Horror," Lovecraft wrote a nearly perfect scene of physical horror. Still unknown to most of the world at the time, he created a dysmorphic summation of the body horror the mangled corpses of the Great War placed in the minds of artists and filmmakers. The moment that drives at least one member of the Miskatonic expedition insane, the appearance of a creature known as a Shoggoth, puts even masters of modern body horror to shame. The chilling epiphany begins with a malodorous whiff of something not quite like gasoline, a fetor emerging out of the abyss. In their descent into the darkness, they encounter the blackness of a "slime-spewing protoplasm" that seems part virus moving upright and part every nauseating encounter with gore ever imagined. Running to escape, one of the surviving party loses his sanity, shell-shocked into insensibility by the sounds and smells and sights of violence older than imagined time.[24]

At the Mountains of Madness has become the inspiration for a whole subgenre of horror in frozen wastelands (John Carpenter's *The Thing* owes much to it) and has come close, several times, to being adapted into a film by Guillermo del Toro. Lovecraft did not see it published for almost five years, though it came out in truncated and serialized form as a trilogy in the science fiction pulp magazine *Astounding Stories* between February and April 1936. S. T. Joshi's research into the original publication suggests that, along with other alterations, perhaps a thousand words had been cut from the story, leaving it something of a confused mess.[25]

By the time Lovecraft saw the slapdash publication of the tale, he had become very ill, indeed much more so than he let on to his small but hardy band of correspondents and admirers. Beginning in 1936 until his death in March 1937, he suffered irremediably from intestinal cancer, apparently long untreated. He was forty-six.

Although he had given up on literary fame in the early 1930s (a rejection of *At the Mountains of Madness* by *Weird Tales* represented an especially severe blow), he had not stopped writing. His final years saw the production of his most disturbing and imaginative tales—including the time-travel epic *Shadow Out of Time*—which leaves us wondering what he would have produced given time.

He could not see that film had, in any way, crossed into the nightmare lands he knew so well. A much more devoted moviegoer than he ever admitted in his letters, he did let it slip now and again how much he often enjoyed movies, voicing special admiration for Charlie Chaplin and Douglas Fairbanks. Unfortunately, he never had the chance to experience the work of Murnau, Wiene, or Lang, and may not have even seen the American work of Leni.

He did see, at some point in the 1920s, Wegener's *Golem,* and his pedestrian reaction makes us wonder what he would have made of the other horror classics that came out of the Great War. He loved Gustav Meyrink's novel, and his criticism of the film version seems utterly adolescent; he liked the book better. Whale's work he called "the alleged *Frankenstein,*" and he grumbled that other than making him drowsy, it simply evoked sympathy for the harm done to "Mrs. Shelley's" work. He saw *Dracula* one night in Miami, Florida, and couldn't bear to sit through its spare running time. He chose instead to walk out into the "fragrant tropic moonlight" rather than see Lugosi's performance come to what he called "its full term of dreariness." *The Invisible Man* may have been the only film of Universal's golden age he enjoyed, describing it as "genuinely sinister." Given Lovecraft's feelings on the matter, it's almost a relief that he apparently never saw *Bride of Frankenstein,* or at least left no record of his impressions of it.

Lovecraft, with his great disdain of communism, would have been horrified to learn that his attitude toward film mimicked that of the Marxist thinkers of the Frankfurt School. When Lovecraft grouched in 1934 about "the utter and unrelieved hokum of the moving picture," he sounded rather like these scholars who worried that the "culture industry" had made revolutionary fervor all but impossible.

T. S. Eliot would have shared Lovecraft's (and the Frankfurt School's) general sense of junk culture, but not because he feared it would desensitize the masses to revolutionary possibilities. Eliot, on some level, thought that passing entertainments were just fine for the proletariat, who should remain proletarian.

Eliot produced very little poetry from the 1930s until his death in 1965. His early reflections on the Great War the world caused some, with reason, to see him as a prophet of the wasteland. His oracular status has continued while his anti-Semitic, and at the very least crypto-fascist sympathies, have largely been forgiven.

The same cannot be said for his mentor Ezra Pound. Pound's hearty

embrace of Mussolini and fascism, a position that may have come as much
from increasing mental illness as reactionary politics, completely unraveled
the poet's tenuous hold on reality. Unlike Eliot, who sought to soften (and to
hide) his anti-Semitic ideas when Great Britain and then the United States
edged toward war with the Axis Powers, Pound crossed from sympathy and
admiration into unadulterated treason after the war began. He, in fact, be-
trayed humanity as well as the Western democracies.

Not only did the deeply cultured poet continue to write nasty little essays for fascist journals that appeared in Britain up to 1939, but he also made
radio broadcasts for Mussolini's government both before and during the war.
Once the United States entered the war, his broadcasts on Rome Radio became unhinged; he insisted that the conflict had all been a conspiracy started
by FDR, whom Pound, undoubtedly thinking it clever, called "Jewsevelt."
American courts eventually indicted the poet for treason, and he went on the
run after Allied forces began the invasion of Italy in 1943.[26]

Marx's famous comment about history first playing itself out as tragedy
and then as farce could serve as the motto for the fate of Ezra Pound. On the
lam from advancing American and British forces, he was captured by Italian
partisans, who let him go after two days. They were apparently some combination of deeply annoyed with him and unconvinced of his importance.
He eventually turned himself in to American authorities and faced trial. A
Washington, D.C., court decided that he belonged in a mental institution
and placed him in two different asylums over the course of twelve years. Released in 1958, he returned to Italy, gave the Fascist Party salute to the small
crowd that greeted him, and proceeded to live rather well off family money.
He suffered bouts of depression until his death in 1972.

Eliot remained a supporter of his mentor and indeed arranged to have
him win the prestigious Bollingen Prize for Poetry while in prison. Both
poets of horror had their politics, and their sensibilities, violently wrenched
toward the fantasies of the right. Eliot created images of horror that haunt
us while, perhaps sensing the drift of things, stayed (mostly) out of politics.
Pound's literary and personal life appear, in contrast, as one long, sustained
attempt at cleverness. He didn't succeed, and rather than becoming a ba-
rometer of the world of horrors, he became a horror himself. Whatever one
thinks of his poetry, and the experts (of which I am not one) seem divided

as to whether he was genius or a fraud, he certainly became a impresario of fascism's Gothic pornography.

Of all the authors we've examined who lived through the war years, Arthur Machen continued to maintain the most uneventful life. He gave his solid support to the British war effort, and his own brand of Celtic Christian mysticism immunized him against the racial mysticism of the far right. He had given up the writing of horror tales however and, in fact, did little writing between the late 1920s and his death in 1947. His family fell on financial hard times when the interest in his work waned at the end of the Great War. The literary community continued to hold him in high regard, and, in 1943, a group that included Bernard Shaw, fellow writer of supernatural tales Algernon Blackwood, and T. S. Eliot himself raised a financial subscription for him.

He died in genteel poverty after the defeat of Nazi Germany. He regretted that "The Bowmen" had helped fuel the legend of the Angel of Mons his whole life, but, for a long time at least, his reputation remained wedded to the tale and the legend. Today he's not much read and primarily known as a chief inspiration for H. P. Lovecraft. Hopefully the growing appreciation of Lovecraft over the last few decades and Stephen King's frequent mention of Machen's work will bring his terrifying vision to the wide audience it deserves.

Director Richard Stanley, known for some of the landmark films of the weird produced over the last twenty years (*Hardware*, *Island of Dr. Moreau*, *Dust Devil*) developed a special interest in Machen. In 2004, he wrote a review essay on the author that related how locals at the Kings Arms pub in Amersham still remember him and his "inexhaustible supply of baffling anecdotes."[27]

Escape

We like to tell tales of decline and fall whether we are talking about historical change, art forms, or our own lives and the lives of others. This has certainly been true of the golden age of horror. After the first cycle of classics—*Dracula*, *Frankenstein*, *The Invisible Man*, *The Mummy*, and above all *Bride of Frankenstein*—along came the allegedly derivative sequels *Son of Frankenstein* (1939) and *Dracula's Daughter* (1936). Universal gave us *The Ghost of Frankenstein* (1942), which didn't include a ghost at all, and then *Frankenstein Meets the Wolf Man* (1943), the first of what have been called "the monster mash" movies. The studio followed with *House of Frankenstein* (1944) and *House of Dracula* (1945), both promising that the favorite monsters of the 1930s would be "ALL TOGETHER!" Sadly, audiences seldom received the payoff. The directors of both films seemed unable to keep Dracula (played now by John Carradine) alive after about the thirty-minute mark.

There's certainly no real comparison between these films and what Universal succeeded in doing, mostly with James Whale's guidance, in the 1930s. But it's a much more mixed bag than critics have sometimes perceived. *Son of Frankenstein* perhaps deserves a second look. In the last picture in which Karloff appears as the monster, the absurd geometry, dreamlike atmosphere, and staircases that seem to float without support place us back in the fever dream of *Caligari*. A world on the brink of another, greater war calls back to the moment when horror film made its first, halting attempt at suggesting the world had become all madness.

Covered oddly in furs, Karloff's Monster stamps around, seeming to have lost the scars that had further mangled him in *Bride* and made him even more an icon of this age of disfigurement. The film sometimes seems a rather clever joke about itself, an attempt at what today we would call metanarrative. Basil Rathbone, who plays the eponymous son of the late Dr. Frankenstein, complains that the name of the maker and of the Monster have become confused—people call the shambling horror by the name of Frankenstein. It's true then and true today—a meaningful confusion that asks us to think about what we mean when we label something a monster. In the 1930s, as the authoritarian right used the language of horror to talk about entire ethnicities, the question became more important than ever.

Karloff brought in the audiences, and Universal Studios, now no longer under the control of the Laemmle family after severe financial difficulties in the mid-1930s, pressed on with more sequels. Along the way, they managed, with the help of German émigré Curt Siodmak, to make at least one horror classic. Released in 1941, in fact the week after Japan's attack on Pearl

Harbor, *The Wolf Man* provides an example of how war and horror culture became desperate to separate themselves from one another.

The Wolf Man is a near-perfect film on its own terms. A compact story that nevertheless makes us care about the characters very quickly, it starred the son of the late Lon Chaney, Lon Chaney Jr., as the titular lycanthrope. It feels like one of the films of Universal's golden age in part because it introduced a new monster to American entertainment—almost all the alleged werewolf lore assumed by filmgoers since 1941 comes from this picture. Indeed, Siodmak publicized the film by insisting he had done research into folklore related to European werewolves in order to make the movie. In fact, he made it all up out of thin air: the werewolf transforming under a full moon, the pentagram, and even the notion of silver causing death. In this film it's the top of a cane, and later it becomes the much more practical silver bullet, although future directors would complicate things again by sometimes making it "a silver bullet to the heart."

Siodmak had developed a successful career as a novelist in Weimar Germany, with ties to the film industry through his more famous brother, the director Robert Siodmak. Both had left Germany after Hitler's rise to power; Curt made the decision to move to America almost immediately after listening to one of Goebbels's radio rants. Robert became one of the great noir directors of the 1940s, *The Killers* and *Criss Cross* being the best and best-known of his films, although he would direct one of his brother's horror fantasies, *Son of Dracula* (1943), which today seems a bit like a noir mystery with a vampire tossed in for fun.

Curt Siodmak became known for fantasy and horror, and he was an early adopter of the idea of science fiction, which he rightly sensed would become the next big thing. *The Wolf Man* and its success came at a peculiar turning point in American history and launched a career that included successful genre novels and screenplays. Siodmak would always chuckle over how he had utterly convinced a generation (and some in the generation of the "monster kids" to come) that the most famous lines of his film were presented as a verse that came directly from "Gypsy" folklore:

Even a man who is pure in heart
And says his prayers by night

May become a wolf when the wolfbane blooms
And the autumn moon is bright.

"Everyone knows about werewolves!" gave the audience an intentional joke in a line from the film's female lead Evelyn Ankers. In fact, absolutely no one knew about werewolves, so Siodmak could make up his fantasy as he went. (Audiences and critics skipped the 1935 film *Werewolf of London*, now seen as a classic.) To paraphrase David J. Skal's clever point about the popular film, it takes place in a 1940s England where everyone seems to have a wealth of knowledge about lycanthropy but not a single person knows (or talks) about the catastrophic war with Germany.[28]

Indeed, the world that Siodmak constructs feels more like a fairy tale out of time and place. It seems far from the realities of Hitler's triumph over France, England itself bracing for an amphibious assault and enduring the fury of the Luftwaffe, Japan overrunning much of the Pacific, and the United States going, against most Americans' wishes, into the war. The world of *The Wolf Man* is all gnarled, ancient trees and fog combined with a fantasy castle and a quaint village that could be Anywhere, Europe, pre-1939 or perhaps pre-1914, a train of fortune-telling Gypsies riding into town (one of them played by Bela Lugosi) to add the exotic and picturesque. It is, Siodmak once admitted, his dream of a lost world, destroyed by the First World War and its consequences. A child's memory.

A few attempts have been made to link the sudden interest in wolf men to either the earlier tendency of surrealists to combine the animal and the human or even the Nazi fascination with the wolf, indeed the werewolf, as a symbol. Truthfully, there's more whimsy than world war in this film, a movie that is, to use the term too many horror films are often charged with, truly escapist. Americans poured into theaters to see the flick. They could briefly forget that their Pacific fleet had been crippled, permanently for all they knew, while Japan threatened Hawaii and the entire West Coast.

This tendency toward escapism grew in American filmmaking. Unlike the oblique horror that touched the raw nerves of a generation that experienced the Somme, Ypres, Gallipoli, or Verdun, the horror films of this era turned the very places the war raged into the kind of make-believe worlds that Walt Disney would soon make of American history itself in Disneyland, founded in 1955.

When Hollywood did want to make a film about World War II, the industry created simple stories with films like *Sands of Iwo Jima* (1949) telling tales of unmitigated heroism amid simple morality plays. Another fantasy slipped into films like *Sands*. It's one of the movies that left many Americans with the "memory" that John Wayne actually served in the military, a peculiar effect that's a version of Ronald Reagan becoming convinced that he personally witnessed the liberation of the Buchenwald death camp because he had edited footage of it from his stateside post. Today a similar phenomenon exists, with Clint Eastwood, whom many believe to have served in either the Korean or Vietnam War because of his tough-guy roles and military fantasy films. In fact, Eastwood tried to keep out of Korea by entering Seattle University in 1951. He ended up drafted into the U.S. Army anyway, but he spent the war in America as a swimming instructor and lifeguard in the Seattle area.

While the world witnessed horrors on a scale not even imagined between 1914 and 1918, Hollywood's fantasy horror became an almost paint-by-numbers effort, mixing in the expected atmosphere, actors, and even outcomes. *House of Frankenstein* (1944) might have been a particular low point in this period. It promised much and failed to deliver while giving a rather depressing role to Boris Karloff. Karloff returned, not as the Monster, but as yet another one of the era's mad scientists hoping to continue the work of Dr. Frankenstein. He escapes imprisonment for his gruesome crimes and becomes the impresario of a traveling carnival's "Spook Show" (a term for a popular type of entertainment in the 1940s that gave audiences an experience somewhere between a live performance and a haunted house) in which "the bones of Dracula" are the main display. Dracula has become a literal sideshow, and in the course of the film he briefly animates only to be dispatched by the sun in a spectacularly silly fashion.

The very next year—timing that gives some sense of how quickly Universal churned out these moneymakers—*House of Dracula* not only signaled an end to the monster-mash sequels to the classics but also indicated that the new horror film would move in a new direction. The 1950s in America have been called "the age of anxiety," though of course that could be said of most any age, including our own. The dawn of the atomic age—when Americans lived, in the words of Paul Boyer, "by the bomb's early light"—should be remembered as the time when people both contemplated the end of human history as a daily possibility and, after some slight dithering, accepted the U.S. government's promises that it would never happen.

House of Dracula actually foreshadows some elements of most 1950s science fiction/horror, in which the formerly mad scientists worked to bring good to humanity, sometimes using their skill to exterminate creatures, generally radioactive, they themselves helped create. The film features a similar motif, a scientist laboring to solve Count Dracula's centuries-old "disease of the blood." He also works on some unnamed cure that will heal his nurse. In an interesting turnabout from the hunchback assistants of the rest of Universal's horror catalog, a female actor took the hunchback role. Other than a not-very-convincing hitched arm and shoulder, she fits the heteronormative standards of beauty for the era.

What's most notable about these films in 1939, 1944, and 1945 is that while the world exploded in a war whose body count stunned even the veterans of World War I, there was not a *J'accuse* produced, or even a *Nosferatu*. The best historical and cultural explanation for this concerns the idea we have examined previously of unending war rather than of what sometimes, from this distance, is called the interwar period. The historian Robert Gerwarth has most closely examined this idea, pointing out that civil wars, revolutions, and mercenary armies of the defeated stalked the landscapes of Europe and the Middle East, setting off "cycles of conflict" that boiled over into Africa, Asia, and the Pacific world long before September 1, 1939. Seen in such a light, the Second World War represents a continuation of a "Great War" that opened in August 1914 and, as I will suggest in the conclusion, did not reach resolution in August 1945. In fact, the consequences of the conflict continue to unfold even as I write these words, almost a hundred years after the guns fell silent on the day of the armistice.

So it's not that World War I had been met with great seriousness by artists and filmmakers producing the world of horror while World War II produced either cartoonish war fantasies or serious realist efforts to come to grips with the meaning of what had happened (Roberto Rossellini's

"War Trilogy" for example). It's rather that Europe, in particular, had been stunned to silence or to mumbled gestures toward making sense of the horror of several decades. The horror movie as art form did revive in the European context, but it took years of reflection and recovery for it to do so; it did not erupt out of the immediate and blinding shock of war in the way such movies had in 1918.

The Gothic monsters of the early 1930s did not walk the American landscape after World War II. Horror took something of a breather while the country boomed with a degree of economic prosperity it, and global history, had never before experienced.

In 1948, Universal Studios produced *Abbott and Costello Meet Frankenstein*. In quick succession, comedy flicks had the duo meet the Mummy, the Invisible Man, and even Dr. Jekyll and Mr. Hyde. These encounters, exercises in pure slapstick without the hint of real danger or death, today feel as eerie as *J'accuse* or *Nosferatu*, if for very different reasons. The pratfalls and pretended terror are completely removed from the death camps, the slaughter in China, the bloody Pacific campaigns, the tens of millions dead in the Soviet Union. All forgotten as audiences laughed out loud at Bud and Lou facing off against childhood terrors.

Mad Science

Josef Mengele finished medical school in 1931, the same year that Universal Studios released *Frankenstein*. In 1937, the young physician joined the Nazi Party and the SS after he began work at the Institute for Hereditary Biology and Racial Hygiene in Frankfurt, Germany. Mengele's lab stood near the former home of the Frankfurt Institute and the headquarters of the firm IG Farben, which produced Zyklon B, the insecticide used to murder the Jewish people in the gas chambers. In Frankfurt, Mengele began his infamous experiments on twins, although before the war he apparently followed generally established research protocols. Auschwitz gave him an unlimited number of victims of Jewish and Roma heritage to vivisect in his mad-scientist lab. He tore the eyes from his victims. He gave them a form of gangrene that affects the face and mouth, and he observed their death. He joined other doctors in selecting victims for the gas chamber as the train cars emptied (though he actually did not take the role of leading SS medical authority, as is commonly supposed). Survivors of the camp remembered him more than the others because of his particularly icy demeanor, the rumors about the sadistic experiments, and his tendency to wait near the train depot even during off-duty hours, restlessly scanning the crowds for twins.

This image, the mad scientist at work in a dark place more charnel house than laboratory, had been the ingredient necessary for almost every horror film of the 1930s and '40s. Fritz Lang's Rotwang and James Whale's Dr. Frankenstein certainly account for much of the figure's popularity, even if the madness of Henry Frankenstein reads more like war trauma than a simple moral tale of science overreaching its limits.

But something more worried at the edges of the sometimes silly trope. Dr. Moreau and Dr. Mengele had too much in common when it came to the "house of pain." The horror film, even the horror fantasies of the late 1930s and '40s, somehow understood that the age of mustard gas and the Maxim gun had unleashed something new in human experience, that the desire to annihilate rather than simply force the enemy's surrender had created a dark human future. It had perhaps ended the possibility of a human future.

On July 16, 1945, the New Mexico desert's unearthly silence shattered with a sudden, deafening roar. A mushroom cloud of inconceivably blinding light ascended forty thousand feet in the air. Dr. J. Robert Oppenheimer, head of Project Y, also called the Manhattan Project, later became one of the world's greatest critics of the weapon he'd made possible. "It has led us up those last few steps to the mountain pass," he said, "and beyond it there is a different country." Oppenheimer came to believe he'd been a kind of mad scientist. An avid reader and proponent of Asian philosophy, he often quoted the god Vishnu in the *Bhagavad-Gita*: "Now I am become death, the destroyer of worlds."

Josef Mengele escaped the Allies in 1945 and lived out his life as a free man. Inherited family wealth enabled him to move from Argentina to Paraguay and then to Brazil. He died of a stroke while swimming at a São Palo resort in 1979.

Afterword

The Age of Horror

... I mean the truth untold
The pity of war, the pity war distilled.
Now men will go content with what we spoiled,
Or, discontent, boil bloody, and be spilled.

—WILFRED OWEN, "Strange Meeting" (1918)

Even the dead will not be safe from the enemy if he wins.
And this enemy has not ceased to be victorious.

—WALTER BENJAMIN,
"Theses on the Philosophy of History" (1940)

It is better to live one day as a lion than 100 years as a
sheep.

—attributed to Benito Mussolini,
retweeted by Donald J. Trump from the account
@ilduce2016 (February 28, 2016)

In 1958, Fulgencio Batista, president of Cuba thanks to the backing of both
the U.S. government and the American Mafia, sat in darkness watching
Bela Lugosi in 1931's *Dracula*.[1] The dictator had begun to behave strangely in
what would turn out to be the final months of his cartoonishly repressive re-

gime. Increasingly, he spent his days at his sprawling estate outside Havana eating enormous meals he apparently found comforting. He then would go out into his garden to vomit so he could return to his table, still groaning under the weight of food, to gorge himself even more. Afterward, he would ensconce himself in the mansion's private theater to watch the horror films of the 1930s and 1940s. He did love *Dracula* and its sequels, but he preferred any film starring Boris Karloff.

The work of James Whale and the dread it induced proved surprisingly compelling to Batista. He watched alone in the darkness while the revolutionary 26th of July Movement (once reduced to only twelve men in the Sierra Maestra), led by Fidel Castro, Che Guevara, and Camilo Cienfuegos, came ever closer to toppling his regime and the whole island erupted in a march on Havana itself.

The triumph of Cuba's revolutionary government in 1959 set off a chain of events that led to one of the deadliest confrontations of the Cold War. The United States had responded aggressively to Cuba's revolution, suspecting any Latin American or Asian revolutionary movement with a socialist bent (or the hint of one) as a plot hatched in the Kremlin. This had the effect of pushing the new government in Havana even closer to Moscow, inviting Soviet advisers into the country, and allowing the USSR to place nuclear missiles just off the coast of Florida.

The outcome, the Cuban missile crisis (or Caribbean crisis) of October 1962, found the two superpowers lurching toward a nuclear exchange while the Kennedy administration planned an invasion of Cuba to overthrow its government. Administration officials apparently had been unaware that tactical nuclear weapons—that is, atomic devices for battlefield use—might have been used against American troops on the beaches. The result of the amphibious assault would have been hundreds of thousands of casualties. The United States would have undoubtedly retaliated with its own massive nuclear arsenal, one that far outstripped Soviet capabilities. An apocalypse would have come for the peoples of all nations involved, and a poisoned atmosphere would have brought catastrophic effects for the entire human race.[2]

During the crisis, Soviet premier Nikita Khrushchev sent a deeply personal message to U.S. president John F. Kennedy, asking that the two nations divert from their present course. In extraordinary language for a diplomatic cable, perhaps remembering what two world wars had cost the Soviet people and thinking of his own experience in the hell of the Battle of Stalingrad, he wrote, "If war should indeed break out, then it would not be in our power to stop it. . . . War ends when it has rolled through cities and villages, everywhere sowing death and destruction." Don't make a monster with me, Khrushchev urged Kennedy.³

The historian Eric Hobsbawm called the period that opened in 1914 and closed with the 1990s the Age of Extremes. Military conflict before the Great War, Hobsbawm noted, had specified objectives that, once attained, usually resulted in peace through compromise. The Great War introduced the idea that a nation's conflicts must "be waged for unlimited ends." Nations initiated wars without foreseeable conclusions, and the "unconditional surrender" of an enemy became in the eyes of military leaders the only possible outcome. Today, the concept of anything like a traditional surrender has gone out of style.⁴

The background for this unsustainable state of affairs, not a very old idea on the grand scale of human history, can be located in the two ways the Great War reimagined military conflict. First, the depersonalization of combat, a process begun as volunteers and conscripts from Europe's farms and factories shelled and gassed one another across no-man's-land. Second, the notion that annihilation of an enemy people represents the only legitimate end to war (short of the hostile nation-states' willingness to completely subjugate themselves to the victor). The first new vision of war legitimized the second or at least made it much more palatable. Hobsbawm writes, "Mild young men, who would certainly not have wished to plunge a bayonet in the belly of any pregnant village girl, could far more easily drop high explosives on London or Berlin, or nuclear bombs on Nagasaki."⁵

So, the Age of Extremes. But in truth, an age of horror that looked its rotted death's head in the mirror, even in its art, entertainments, and amusements. Indeed, so many of the Great War's mild young men learned that the bayonet in the belly could be as impersonal as the bomb from the sky. The next generation of young men accepted machine-gunning the helpless after they dug their own graves, sloughing it off as all in a day's work, serving one's country, just obeying orders.

Hobsbawm is correct, of course, that incinerating hundreds of thousands of men, women, and children proved just as easy as shooting and gassing them.

Cuba's Batista obsessively watching Bela Lugosi films born of the Great War makes an idiotic kind of sense as he played out his minor role in the new age of horror.

The horror film, and the wider horror culture, seems today like an insistent, feverish reenactment of the Great War that gave birth to our world. The angry dead of *J'accuse* rose again in George Romero's films, especially between 1968 and 2005. Very recently, they even stumble toward us in the death march of the White Walkers on HBO's *Game of Thrones*. These creatures do not simply touch on some kind of primal, universal fear of the dead; rather, they present the fate of the dead in a specific historical context. They move in oncoming waves, sometimes tens of thousands of decaying corpses on the march. A final charge across no-man's-land, the dead at war again, unable to escape the endless loop of violence in which they died.

The gorefest of the slasher films began in the 1970s and has never really stopped. Blood spurts in red flumes from empty-eyed victims who, in some cases, become collections of body parts. They replicate the death dolls of the 1920s and '30s over and over again, the fear of the corpse that fixated artists and filmmakers and voiced their deepest trauma throughout an era that had created so many corpses that they could never be accurately counted or buried.

The horror has remained with us because the conditions that made for the Great War and its aftermath are still in place. The horror tradition seems to repeat, with more blood shown and changing tropes, the violence of World War I while the results of the conflict continue to unfold in our present.

Billions of people live with two inescapable facts born out of 1914–1918. First, the American empire has a military and economic superiority undreamed of by any tyrant, dictator, or world power before it. This has been true for many decades. Although not perhaps clear at the time, this was the state of play long before the close of the Cold War and the collapse of the

Soviet Union, the United States' only conceivable rival. Woodrow Wilson's conception of America's role in the world not only did not fail; it increased by many thousands of times in ways that he could not have begun to imagine in 1917–1919.

The scholar of international relations Ronald Steel put it this way: "To be a person in the second half of the twentieth century has meant, to some extent, to have made an accommodation to American culture." However, given the outcome of the Treaty of Versailles, this has actually been true for people born since 1919.[6]

Second, an issue inextricably related to the first: there are numerous, often interconnected and double-knotted, problems of violence and ongoing conflict across the globe. These regions—the former Soviet Union, Central and East Africa, the Middle East, and large portions of Central and East Asia—are resistant to American hegemony. Conflicts have ignited over issues where American power serves only as an accelerant. In some cases, the American empire created, or put its imprimatur on the creation of, the very problems it now finds intractable. The vicious cycle has no possible end except more explosive violence leading to even more conflict, perhaps a global catastrophe.

In most cases, the people of these regions suffer the effects of American imperial overreach, even when various warlords, paramilitary organizations, and terrorist networks find ways to strike back at the colossus they view, often rightly, as the progenitor of their deprivation and oppression. Americans themselves, locked tight behind the ideology and practice of "homeland security," have been relatively safe from the full effects of the "war on terror" since September 11, 2001. While it's true that 95 civilian Americans have died from terrorist actions since 2001, many of them killed by individuals acting alone, we need to put this in perspective. From 2001 to 2011, for example, 100,000 Americans killed one another with guns. And, to cite another example, more American veterans committed suicide between 2001 and 2017 than died in combat in Iraq and Afghanistan.[7]

This age of horror began during World War I. Between 1914 and 1918, relatively minor conflicts caused not only the largest war in human history but also unleashed more than thirty years of extraordinary violence across the globe. Historians looking back at the settlement of the conflict in 1919

see the real victors as two late entrants into the Great War that had no real
European concerns at all: Japan and the United States. Japan had announced
itself as a world power in a victory over Russia during a brief (primarily naval) conflict in 1904–1905. It entered World War I on the side of the Allies
to gobble up German colonial possessions in the Pacific and make a landing
at German-controlled Chinese ports, the first stage of a larger ambition of
Japanese military leaders to create a sphere of influence in the region. The
United States also saw the Pacific world, along with all of Latin America,
as its sphere of influence. Since the early twentieth century, the Americans
had held colonial possessions in the Pacific, with the Philippines being the
most strategically significant. Thus the two nations had been on a collision
course since 1918, ultimately leading to war in 1941 with the surprise attack
on Pearl Harbor.[8]

The United States solidified, rather than created, its new role in the
world with the victory secured in World War II. The course of American
empire continued, particularly with the United States holding first a monopoly on atomic weapons and later complete superiority in the arms race that
lasted throughout the Cold War. Viewing the Soviet Union as a threat to
global hegemony, U.S. political and military leaders stoked fears of communism at home. The foreign policy of both the Truman and the Eisenhower
administrations assumed, as in the case of Cuba, that the hand of the USSR
could be found in every effort to end colonialism. This became accepted or-
thodoxy to such a degree that the United States began a commitment, even
as it became embroiled in a conflict in the Korean peninsula, to help France
retain a colony in Southeast Asia known to them as French Indochina but to
its own people as the ancient society of Vietnam.

American involvement in Vietnam (1950–1975) represented not simply a
global public relations disaster for the United States but a true human and
ecological catastrophe for the people of Vietnam, Cambodia, and Laos, as
well as the Americans sent to fight the war. However, it's a stretch to see
U.S. defeat in Vietnam as truly upsetting anything fundamental about the
dynamics of American power. Still, the defeat of the military juggernaut the
nation had created in World War II had consequences more far-reaching
than the humiliation of 1974–1975.[9]

The first of those consequences was the determination that there be no more Vietnams. This did not mean that the United States would become more flexible in its view of the Soviet Union, worldwide socialism, or even revolutionary movements that displayed limited socialist leanings. Instead, it meant that the United States would continue to exert dominance through nuclear brinkmanship, covert operations, and surrogate armies, while committing ground troops only in situations in which the national security state believed it could ensure the outcome of America imposing its will with minimal sacrifice.

These attitudes are related to a second consequence of the American defeat in Vietnam. The Middle East, a region rich in oil, would become the focus of American attention. Here, the defense of Israel, born in 1948 but conceived during World War I with the Balfour Declaration and the decision to divide the old Ottoman Empire into makeshift nation-states, became paramount to ensure at least one dependable ally in the region.

The invasion of Afghanistan by the Soviet Union (1979–1989) gave the United States a putative reason to become deeply engaged in the region. But American interest in the oil fields of the Middle East had a longer genealogy. The cultivation of the Kingdom of Saudi Arabia began as early as the 1930s. This incredibly repressive regime, essentially a medieval theocracy led by the House of Saud, provided America with bases and sent numerous fighters to Afghanistan to aid a U.S.-sponsored effort that, in the words of Ronald Reagan, made the country into the Soviet Union's own Vietnam.[10]

Afghanistan, at least in its modern form, had been formed in the fires of the Great War, one of the first warning signs the British received that their dominance over much of the developing world would soon end. Afghanistan achieved independence from a distracted Great Britain after a brief war in 1919, its third effort. The new country signed a treaty of friendship with the new revolutionary Russian government in the early 1920s, becoming the first nation to do so. By the 1970s, a Soviet-backed socialist government faced a challenge from a Wahhabist Islamic insurgency, supported by men and matériel from Saudi Arabia and the United States.

The catastrophe for the USSR in Afghanistan became one of many factors that led Soviet leaders to attempt reforms in the 1980s. These reforms failed to save the Soviet Union, which fell apart in 1991. In hindsight, the failure of the Soviet experiment held dire consequences for the Soviet peo-

ple, the stability of the region, and Western democracy (an outcome predicted by Hobsbawm as early as 1996). The weakness of the bombastic Boris
Yeltsin, the first president of the newly formed Russian Federation, allowed
for the easy seizure of power by former KGB commissar Vladimir Putin,
who has essentially controlled Russia since the 1990s. (Russia held its last
free election in 1996; Yeltsin turned over power to Putin in 1999.) Putin's
subsequent military adventurism has been a threat to peace for almost two
decades. His regime's recent interference in the elections of many of the
Western democracies, including the United States, is becoming increasingly
well-known even as I write these words.[11]

The consequences of the 1918 armistice that became the 1919 Treaty of
Versailles slammed into the last century like a hurricane making landfall at
high tide, pushing ever more violent waters up the rivers of history, transforming streams into raging cataracts and covering the global landscape with
an ever-rising flood. Looking back over the last hundred years and seeing
the fervent desire for war and the sadistic means in which armies murdered
their way to bitter victory, we have to grimly conclude that the Great War
never ended.

The nightmare continued.

Monsters have lurked and lumbered since the world went gunmetal gray in
August 1914. The years following America's triumph and path to empire are
also the years of a new birth of horror, now in retrospect as important as that
of the 1920s and '30s in the development of new themes that have never quite
gotten beyond the corpses in the wasteland, the endless train of the dead
that marched through Eliot's nightmare city in the twentieth and now into
the frightening twenty-first century.

Stephen King, now for forty years one of the most important influences
on horror films and fiction worldwide, came of age during America's ascent
to the insecure pinnacle of global power in the 1950s. "The real terror . . . ,"
King once wrote, "began on an afternoon in October of 1957." He sat in
a theater and watched *Earth vs. the Flying Saucers* (whose screenplay was
credited to none other than German émigré Curt Siodmak, though it was
ghosted by Bernard Gordon, whose name did not appear in the original

credits because he'd been blacklisted as a Communist in 1947). The 1957 film badly frightened King, with its tale of faceless forces "come only to conquer, the last armada of a dying planet, old and greedy, seeking not peace but plunder."[12]

King also found his way to a floodtide of films, comic books, and horror fiction that tapped the Thanatos syndrome of the age of the bomb. He read everything by Ray Bradbury. Siodmak's best-selling novel *Donovan's Brain*, written after the prolific author created *The Wolf Man*, also impressed King. He dived into Arthur Machen and Lovecraft, at least the version of Lovecraft you could access in the 1950s.

H. P. Lovecraft's work had its first revival in these years. In 1939, his admirer August Derleth, in collaboration with fellow fan Donald Wandrei, established Arkham House Publishers specifically to disseminate the work of the master. They had limited success at first, although Derleth helped secure a deal for the publication of a cheaply printed "Armed Services" paperback edition during the war. Derleth would add to the relatively small number of stories Lovecraft wrote with "posthumous collaborations"—in other words story ideas, or even just titles, that Lovecraft recorded in his daybook and that Derleth turned into fiction of dubious quality. Nevertheless, King and a whole generation of horror fans first met Lovecraft this way, setting the stage for the revival of his work and the entrance of the term "Lovecraftian" into the vocabulary of horror.[13]

Although impossible to know what Lovecraft himself would have made of his current place in popular culture (role-playing games, spin-off novels, video games, films, and comic books), the world these productions have been born into would have made a certain morbid sense to him. "Puny, war-exhausted mankind," as he'd predicted in his 1917 story "Dagon," had finally come to recognize the apocalypse his work imagined. Cthulhu would rise when the stars became right. The monstrous god's time had come.

Fritz Lang, an exile in America from the beginning of World War II until the end of his long life, continued to play with the themes of terror, crime, and the corpse he first developed in the Weimar era. In the world of the 1940s and '50s, however, he dealt less with the technological fears he examined in *Metropolis*, perhaps not wanting to become associated with the low-brow sensibilities of science fiction. He maintained his interest in the idea of criminality, particularly in the attractions of crime that he often weirdly combined with German cinema's fascination with the dead. *Hangmen Also Die!* (1943) and *Ministry of Fear* (1944) represented early efforts in this direction. In *Ministry of Fear*, for example, Lang has a key element in a Nazi plot revealed during a séance.

Lang's 1945 *Scarlet Street* represented a pitch-black entry into film noir, a genre now praised but at the time very much out of step with American sensibilities. The film, starring the old 1930s gangster heavy Edward G. Robinson in a very different role, ends in murder and madness, the voices of the dead echoing in the head of the morally compromised protagonist. Lang had made an earlier, less compelling version of the same tale with Robinson in *The Woman in the Window* (1944). Like all his work in Hollywood, although constrained by studio demands and a public that did not want their assumptions challenged, it comes across as chilly, harsh, and angry at human nature. It also featured horror's fascination with mirrors and, particularly, the Great War's twilight worlds between dream and nightmare, life and death. Lang went on to make more crime pictures in the 1950s, most infamously 1953's *The Big Heat*, known for violence that shocked audiences with its intensity.

Lang had decided by the late 1950s to retire, certainly from Hollywood. He returned one more time to the horror of Dr. Mabuse before he exited the entertainment industry. *The Thousand Eyes of Dr. Mabuse* appeared in West Germany in 1960. Lang once again reimagined the conventions of the Weimar era, including a séance, in a film heavily influenced by the world of Cold War espionage. This became Lang's last picture, although a spy/crime series of genre films based on a "Dr. Mabuse" became popular after Lang absented himself from the director's chair.

Lang retired to private life in California and died of a stroke in 1976. Thea von Harbou had been dead for almost two decades. She briefly spent time in a British prison after World War II but received some plaudits in the German film industry in the early 1950s after many accepted her claim that she never really held deep Nazi sympathies. Harbou and Lang apparently never spoke after he left Germany in 1933. She died in 1954.[14]

André Breton became increasingly involved in the politics of the anti-fascist left, along with many fellow artists. Dalí continued, to the distress of many of his former colleagues, to embody surrealism for the public, especially in Italy, Spain, and the United States. His increasing absurdities and lifelong cozy relationship with General Franco's fascist regime in Spain (Franco ruled until 1975) neither haunted him nor harmed his ability to make money simply by being Salvador Dalí. He remains one of the great, unindicted villains of the twentieth century. Orwell's little-known essay on the artist remains one of the few efforts to point out why he's best consigned to history's well-worn dustbin.

He remains much better known than Max Ernst or Otto Dix, both of whom show up in the occasional art history or cultural history class rather than in popular culture. Ernst married into the Guggenheim fortune after the Second World War and lived in Los Angeles. The marriage fell apart, and he moved to Sedona, Arizona. His presence there, and the book he wrote about it, helped transform the tiny agricultural community into an artists' colony. He died in 1976. Otto Dix, true to form, refused to leave Germany and returned to his native Dresden after the war. His art and his idiosyncratic politics brought him acclaim in both East and West Germany. He continued to paint until his death in 1969. Much of his work in the last twenty-four years of his life focused on understanding his native land's self-inflicted wound. It remains a mystery how the stubborn artist managed to survive the Nazi regime after painting images that parodied the Reich and, in fact, Hitler himself.

Dora Maar's art remains largely unknown. Writers who mention her at all tend to reference her, even in her obituary, as Picasso's muse (a *Guardian* article called her one of his "many" muses). Only specialists write thoughtfully of her paintings and photographs, but I hope what's said of her in these pages will spread interest in her beyond the world of art and cultural historians. Her life's work deserves a full reevaluation and appreciation. The short fiction of Leonora Carrington has recently appeared in a paperback edition that received some attention in 2017, including a review of her life's work in the May 2017 *New Yorker* and in the *Los Angeles Review of Books*. Hopefully, now she'll be remembered as more than Max Ernst's mistress.

Breton, speaking at a rally meant to bring together a coalition of French left-wing groups in 1948, continued his efforts to combine socialism with the surrealist vision. More important for our purposes, Breton made an extraordinary statement about the work of an increasingly well-known writer from Prague named Franz Kafka. Indeed, Breton, who in spite of or maybe because of his pomposity never made such statements lightly, called Kafka "the greatest visionary of the century." He praised both the writer's socialist leanings and his influence on the art of the unreal.

Kafka's old friend Max Brod accounts largely for his postmortem revival. Brod refused his friend's request to burn all his work and instead, in the words of Kafka biographer Reiner Stach, "published as much of Kafka's literary estate as he could find." The results have been as shocking, perhaps much more shocking, than Lovecraft's recent popularity. Today Kafka appears on posters, T-shirts, and coffee mugs. Simultaneously, although *The Metamorphosis* seems to be widely read, canonical for some high schools and nearly every college, few have ventured far into his uninviting work. The term "Kafkaesque" has become, like the term "ironic," used for any situation weird or bothersome. That's not what it means. If you, in truth, ever experience the Kafkaesque, you probably won't maintain the mental stability to survive it.[15]

Kafka continues to have an enormous, if generally ignored, influence on horror. The work of David Lynch has taken direct inspiration from him, particularly in his interest in extreme violence, the malevolence of bureaucracies that seem to have supernatural origins, and the extreme alienation of human beings that often takes horrific physical or psychic forms. Lynch long hoped to adapt *The Metamorphosis*, and rumors of an existing script are numerous. The director paid tribute to his fascination with Kafka's work in *Twin Peaks: The Return* (2017): the office of the FBI director Gordon Cole (played by Lynch himself) contains two outsized photographs: one of a young Franz Kafka, and a second of a gigantic mushroom cloud.

Lynch borrows the terror of the Great War, partially transmitted through Kafka, of the corpse and its meaning. The amputated ear in *Blue Velvet* (1986), the body of beauty queen Laura Palmer wrapped in plastic in the opening scenes of *Twin Peaks*, and his film and television work's interest in numerous doubles, evil reflections in mirrors, and bodies that appear to have no actual identity all would have been recognizable to Murnau, Lang, Leni, and Wegener. His work and worldview have been compared, not entirely convincingly, to the work of Lovecraft as well. At the very least, Lovecraft seems to appear in Lynch's interest in supernatural beings that enter our world through mysterious portals, always with ambiguous motives and an indifference to human suffering that makes them cruel arbiters of the fate of Lynch's characters.

T. S. Eliot seems to live at the height of high culture, exactly where he wanted to be. He would be displeased at the efforts to note how closely his work resembled the themes of what he certainly would consider junk culture. In 2017, religion and culture critic Greg Garrett published a book on zombies in popular culture and mentioned Eliot's *The Waste Land* as an example of early intimation of the zombie phenomenon. He described *The Waste Land* as well-known to "generations of bored students" while also noting that it's a poem "of genuine power and menace." It's hard to disagree with either point. Eliot died in London in 1965. His ashes are buried at an Anglican parish in Somerset, at the time a village that Eliot had no connection to whatsoever, save that his ancestors had apparently lived there before departing for America.[16] He would be immensely pleased to know that he has a stone in the Poet's Corner of Westminster Abbey. He succeeded in making everyone forget that he was from Missouri.

Walter Benjamin, whose work serves as inspiration for this book, has been dead for almost eighty years. He visited Berlin for the last time in March 1933. He came to retrieve his library, stored in an apartment that the Nazis seized from him. The regime had banned his books, including one he published under a pseudonym, a rather dry collection of eighteenth-century letters of Hölderlin, Schleiermacher, Kant, and Schlegel. The book briefly survived censorship when published in 1936 because it bore, for the Nazis, the promising title of *German Men*. However, the Nazis suppressed its small print run in 1938.[17]

By then, Benjamin had taken refuge in Paris. Of course, by the summer of 1940, the city had fallen into Nazi hands, and he fled when the German army entered the city in June. He gave some of the material he hoped to work on further to literary and cultural critic Georges Bataille. The Gestapo seized or destroyed the rest of Benjamin's manuscripts and his books when they tossed his apartment. He and his sister lived in hiding for several weeks in Lourdes and then Marseille. They knew they were not safe in what had become the Nazi puppet regime led by French fascists and collaborators.

Benjamin became increasingly depressed, not knowing what would become of him and even uncertain, as difficult as this may be for some to understand, if he wanted to live with the loss of his irreplaceable book collection. He did not know that friends in New York, admirers in the Frankfurt School, had been working to prepare for his arrival. Apparently Max Horkheimer made arrangements for Benjamin to take a teaching post at the University of Havana. This set up the extraordinary possibility that, in the years ahead, one of the great intellectuals of European Marxist thought would have met a young Fidel Castro and other leaders in the soon-to-be-born 26th of July Movement in their formative period.

This never happened. Becoming increasingly hopeless, Benjamin joined a group of exiles (Siegfried Kracauer among them) in an effort to travel by foot across the Pyrenees into Spain. The United States had granted visas to a number of political refugees, and Benjamin's American friends made sure he received one. (Hannah Arendt notes that the United States did not include Jews in the category of "political refugee.") Benjamin also managed to get a travel visa from the Spanish government that would allow him to cross into Portugal and depart to America via Lisbon. He did not, however, have the required exit visa from France, and the Nazi flunkeys who ran Vichy had no desire to displease Berlin. So Benjamin and his coterie set out for the village of Portbou, rumor claiming it an unguarded entrance into Spain. Franco's fascist regime, also eager to please their Nazi patrons, had closed the border on the very day of Benjamin's arrival. Spanish security forces intended to return them to France the following morning.[18]

That night, September 26, 1940, Walter Benjamin committed suicide while guards stood outside his small hotel room. In a terrible irony, Portbou opened up the very next day for a brief period, and the remainder of his group passed through Spain and on to Lisbon. Benjamin's friend Hannah Arendt passed through this choke point at the Spanish border soon after.

Benjamin had believed, unlike many of his friends and colleagues, that pop culture, film included, could have revolutionary possibilities. But he knew well the Janus face of mass culture: "There is no document of civilization which is not at the same time a document of barbarism." The audience of the great art horror in the 1920s and '30s (or any films) must understand that what they watch has been created within a system of oppression that no human being should have to endure. Even the system that produces great works depends on the labor and support of millions that suffer in myriad ways from this very system.

The quote appears in Catalan and German, written on his tombstone.[19]

James Whale had definitively left the movie business before the beginning of the Second World War.

He had long hoped to pursue another World War I project, this one based on Erich Maria Remarque's novel *The Road Back*, concerned with the lives of German veterans after the Great War. Whale believed this an opportunity to rework some of the themes of *Journey's End* and take the war home. He had the chance in 1937. The film went over budget and fell far behind schedule, and one actor died during an accident on set. The antiwar message of the film meant that it would never get a release in Nazi Germany, and the studio, without Whale's knowledge, attempted to add new scenes and a new ending that, according to James Curtis, left the film "mutilated" and Whale actually hoping few people would see it.

In 1939, Whale worked on his last studio film in apparently a desultory manner, given that he found the script absurd. Titled *They Dare Not Love*, it was an attempt to update *Othello* for the modern era (without examining any controversial racial subjects). Studio executives blamed the failure of the ridiculous movie on Whale.

The years after Whale ended his career in Hollywood seemed at first rather carefree. He had a hit with *Showboat* (1936) and then a catastrophe with *The Road Back*. Universal Studios, no longer run by the Laemmles, assigned him to rescue a bevy of dreadful films (*They Dare Not Love* being an example) in the late 1930s. So he often spoke of how he found relative freedom in getting away from a business that, he claimed, "wanted a Michelangelo every time." He became very interested in news related to the war, involving himself in a number of charities and making one short film for the army that showed possible recruits a pleasant picture of the first forty-eight hours of their new life. He created and directed plays for servicemen on leave that starred old friends from the industry, some of whom had not worked in Hollywood since the silent era. The players also included younger members such as Patricia Hitchcock, daughter of the famous director. Otherwise he took walks, cared for his dogs Sigrid and Cecile, and wrote almost daily to David Lewis after his longtime partner joined the air force in 1942.

Whale directed a Broadway play in 1945 that proved a critical success. However, American audiences at the end of World War II did not wish to think of the grisly murders or ponder themes of disfigurement that appeared in Whale's *Hand in Glove*. Soon after the play closed, he made one short film, a strange, claustrophobic tale heavily influenced by German expressionism called *Hello Out There*. The moody, shadowy story takes place entirely in a prison cell and runs for about thirty-two minutes. It has never been released. Meanwhile, he turned down major film projects, and the offer of being placed on contract with a studio again, even though the offer came from legendary producer David O. Selznick.

In 1951, Whale directed for the last time. He chose a stage play for his final effort, a snarky farce called *Pagan in the Parlor*. The show ran in London, and Whale seized the opportunity to travel in Europe and fall in love with a twenty-five-year-old bartender named Pierre Foegel during a time of strain in his relationship with Lewis. Foegel later came to the States and became a sometime companion to Whale, now in his sixties. Whale maintained his relationship with Lewis even as they chose to live separately. In 1953, Whale had a pool placed in his backyard, a strange decision for a lifelong hydrophobe. David Lewis had recently built one at his new home on Mulholland Drive.

Whale continued to say nothing about his experiences in the trenches during his final years. He did suffer significantly from an anxiety disorder (likely PTSD) that had its roots in the war. This became increasingly apparent to his caregivers after he ceased working. He suffered two strokes in the last year and a half of his life, although, amazingly, he recovered from both. His doctors proclaimed him miraculously healthy, given the combination of his condition and his age. Yet he could not sleep without medication and sank increasingly into what his biographer James Curtis simply describes as depression. Friends noted that he had become increasingly morbid. The nature of many of his films and his well-known sense of black humor perhaps made this less noticeable than it would have been in someone with a sunnier disposition.

Whale committed suicide on May 29, 1957. He had given his nurse Memorial Day off and made sure that none of his friends, lovers, or caregivers would be stopping by. He showered, shaved, and dressed formally, as he often did even for days at home. He took breakfast as usual, went to his studio, and sometime during the morning, wrote a note that said, in part, "Do not grieve for me. My nerves are all shot and for the last year I have been in agony day and night. Except when I sleep with sleeping pills—and any peace I have by day is when I am drugged with pills."

Around one o'clock, he drowned himself in the shallow end of his swimming pool, apparently attempting to knock himself unconscious by diving into the water headfirst. He had often described his fear of death by drowning, refusing to try to swim in the pool's deep end.

Whale almost never spoke about his films in his final years and certainly did not make pretentious statements about "what they meant," even when prodded to do so. This fact makes an incident near the end of his life particularly disturbing and revealing.

Glady Lacey, a friend who had worked in the theater with Whale, remembered that he had taken to staring at himself frequently in the mirror. Mirrors had, of course, often appeared in the German cinema that deeply influenced Whale. They had been portals of horror: a place where one meets the dreaded twin; the death doll; or, most terrible of all, oneself.

Whale had used the frightening possibilities of the mirror combined with one of his own personal fears in his films. The Monster in *Bride of Frankenstein* sees his reflection in the water and growls pitifully and angrily at the death's head that looks back, his scarred hands stirring the face in the pond to fragment and occlude his own face. Whale used a mirror in a scene in *The Old Dark House* in which a beautiful, young Gloria Stuart looks into an ancient mirror and sees her features monstrously distorted. Old Rebecca Femm, her own face reflected in the funhouse glass, has just laid a hand on her supple, dewy flesh and reminded her it would rot.

One day, Whale told Lacey he had taken "a good look at himself" in the mirror and "realized that he had created Frankenstein and that it had become a nightmare to him. That he had launched this horror into the world and that he could not stop it."

"I looked at myself in the mirror," Whale told his friend, "and I suddenly realized what I had done."[20]

ACKNOWLEDGMENTS

I found this work very challenging. There's a lot of death in this book and, unlike my other work, it's less oblique, less a subtext, and more the overwhelming inescapable reality of what human beings have been doing to each other and the world they have lived in for the last century.

Amid all this morbidity, my students have been an unending source of inspiration. Their questions and ideas have helped form my own. I'm especially grateful for the friendship and encouragement of some of our alums, including Blair Mintz, Miah Bundy, and Laura Rashley. The latter in particular has made sure I read things unrelated to the Great War and I hope Laura knows her friendship means even more than the hopefully unending recommendation of poetry and graphic novels.

I am proud to have worked with Counterpoint and their imprint Soft Skull over the years. Executive editor Dan Smetanka brings much needed humor and motivation to me. Thank you to Sarah Jean Grimm, Katie Boland, and all the publicity work of Megan Fishmann for answering my many questions. I appreciate the quick responses from Counterpoint's managing editor Wah-Ming Chang. I also want to note that Janet Renard proved an excellent and precise copy editor who has saved me from many embarrassments. Remaining errors are my responsibility alone.

Deirdre Mullane is an extraordinary agent and a good friend. I don't always feel I have deserved the time she's given me, which makes me admire her all the more.

My parents, Clarence and Joan Poole, are much in my thoughts always. My mom bought me my first book about the Great War and my dad read it to me along with all the other books he introduced me to every night before bed, sometimes books I was probably too young to understand. I appreciate how much this has shaped my life.

Tammy Ingram's own work provides me constant inspiration and I do not know what I would do without her companionship, even when she's rather far away so we must text six times a day.

This book would not exist without Christopher Bram and his novel *Gods and Monsters* (that later became an Academy Award–winning film of the same name).

I dedicate this work to Beth Phillips, for her love and constant support. I am lucky to have a partner who enthusiastically joins me on World War I battlefields and, in fact, has an encyclopedic knowledge of the conflict that dwarfs my own. It's hard for me to imagine completing this work, or indeed getting through life, without her. I love her (and our dogs Jessica and Verna) more than I have ever been able to show.

NOTES

Foreword: Corpses in the Wasteland

1. Adam Lowenstein, "Films without a Face: Shock Horror in the Cinema of Georges Franju," *Cinema Journal* 37, no. 4 (Summer 1998), 37.
2. Clive Bloom, *Gothic Histories: The Taste for Terror 1764 to the Present* (New York: Continuum Books, 2010), 2.
3. Stefan Zweig, *The World of Yesterday: Memoirs of a European* (London: Pushkin Press, 2009), 19. Quoted in Modris Eksteins, *Rites of Spring: The Great War and the Birth of the Modern Age* (New York: Anchor Books, 1989), 147, 301.
4. Sigmund Freud, "Thoughts for the Times on War and Death," in *The Standard Edition of the Complete Psychological Works of Sigmund Freud*, ed. James Strachey (London: Hogarth Press, 1957), 14:287.
5. Walter Benjamin, *Illuminations: Essays and Reflections* (New York: Schocken Books, 1969), 84.

Chapter One: Symphony of Horror

1. David J. Skal, *Hollywood Gothic: The Tangled Web of Dracula from Novel to Stage to Screen* (New York: Faber and Faber, 2004), 88.
2. Anton Kaes, in *Shell Shock Cinema: Weimar Culture and the Wounds of War* (Princeton, NJ: Princeton University Press, 2009), suggests that Hutter seems much like a victim of shell shock. Kaes's book provided me with some material for my reading of Weimar cinema, even when I disagree with his interpretations.
3. Victoria Nelson sees in E. T. A. Hoffman's disturbing tales of automata the philosophical problem of the presence of souls in matter that had worried

Descartes. She finds much the same concern in the work of Bruno Schulz and Giacomo Leopardi. See her book *The Secret Life of Puppets* (Cambridge, MA: Harvard University Press, 2001), 64–73.

4. Rainer Maria Rilke, letter of October 4, 1914, in *Wartime Letters of Rainer Maria Rilke 1914–1921*, trans. M. D. Herter Norton (New York: W. W. Norton, 1940), 18.

5. The exception to the happy ending is, of course, Mina's polyamorous friend, Lucy Westenra, who falls victim to the vampire and gets a stake in the heart.

6. Skal, *Hollywood Gothic*, 88.

7. Quoted in David J. Skal, *The Monster Show: A Cultural History of Horror* (New York: Faber and Faber, 2001), 50.

8. Stéphane Audoin-Rouzeau and Annette Becker, *14–18: Understanding the Great War* (New York: Hill and Wang, 2000), 169.

9. Ibid., 168.

10. Robert Gerwarth, *The Vanquished: Why the First World War Failed to End* (New York: Farrar, Straus and Giroux, 2016), 199–226.

11. Austro-Hungarian document translated by Paul Barber in *Vampires, Burial, and Death: Folklore and Reality* (New Haven: Yale University Press, 1988), 5–9.

12. Skal, *The Monster Show*, 49–50.

13. Ibid.

14. Jay Winter, *Sites of Memory, Sites of Mourning* (Cambridge: Cambridge University Press, 2014), 55–57.

15. Grau's relationship to the occult and Crowley discussed in Gary Lachman, *Aleister Crowley: Magick, Rock and Roll and the Wickedest Man in the World* (New York: Penguin Press, 2014), 262.

16. Kaes, *Shell Shock Cinema*, 92–93.

17. "War Losses (Africa)," *International Encyclopedia of the First World War Online*, encyclopedia.1914-1918-online.net/article/war_losses_africa, accessed May 15, 2016.

18. Casualty counts are taken from Audoin-Rouzeau and Becker, *14–18*, 20–26.

19. Lotte Eisner, *The Haunted Screen: Expressionism in German Cinema and the Influence of Max Reinhardt* (Berkeley and Los Angeles: University of California Press, 1962). Eisner wrote an incredible book and gave it the perfect title. However, it influenced nothing that you read in these pages except to the degree that I generally had a negative reaction to Eisner's conclusions, interesting and thoughtful as they sometimes seem at first.

20. John T. Soister, *Of Gods and Monsters: A Critical Guide to Universal Studios' Science Fiction, Horror, and Fantasy Films, 1929–1939* (Jefferson, NC: McFarland Press, 1999), 7.

21. Jesse Stellato, ed., *Not in Our Name: American Anti-War Speeches from 1846 to the Present* (University Park, PA: Penn State University Press, 2012), 88.

22. Thomas J. Knock, *To End All Wars: Woodrow Wilson and the Quest for a New World Order* (New York: Oxford University Press, 1992), 118.

23. Robert F. Hamilton and Holder H. Herwig, *Decisions for War: 1914–1917* (Cambridge, UK: Cambridge University Press, 2004), 211, 222; and 66th Congress, 1st Session, "Addresses of President Wilson," *Senate Documents* (May–November 1919), 206.

24. Jennifer Wingate, "Over the Top: The Doughboy in World War I Memorials and Visual Culture," *American Art* 19, no, 2 (Summer 2005), 28.

25. "The Bonus Army: How a Protest Led to the GI Bill," NPR News, November 11, 2011, www.npr.org/2011/11/11/142224795/the-bonus-army-how-a-protest-led-to-the-gi-bill, accessed November 27, 2016.

26. Will Murray, "H. P. Lovecraft and the Pulp Magazine Tradition," in *An Epicure in the Terrible: A Centennial Anthology of Essays in Honor of H .P. Lovecraft*, eds. David E. Schultz and S. T. Joshi (New York: Hippocampus Press, 2011), 116–17, 124–25.

27. David Reynolds, *The Long Shadow: The Legacies of the Great War in the Twentieth Century* (New York: W. W. Norton, 2014), 97.

28. Oliver Stone and Peter Kuznick, *The Untold History of the United States* (New York: Gallery Books, 2012), 32.

29. *Selections from the Prison Notebooks of Antonio Gramsci*, eds. Quintin Hoare and Geoffrey Nowell Smith (New York: International Publishers, 2003), 276. Slovenian philosopher Slavoj Žižek often translates Gramsci's statement as "now is the time of monsters," an interpretive translation he seems to have borrowed from a French translation of Gramsci's work. See Ambrose Korn, *Remember Mongo Beti* (Bayreuth, Germany: Bayreuth University Press, 2003), 149.

30. Gerwarth, *The Vanquished*, 9, 10.

31. Sigmund Freud, *The Uncanny*, trans. David McLintock (1919; repr. New York: Penguin Books, 2003), 149.

32. Maya Barzilai, *Golem: Modern Wars and their Monsters* (New York: New York University Press, 2016), 3–4.

33. Ibid., 4.

34. Ibid., 74.

35. Quoted in Eric J. Leed, *No Man's Land: Combat & Identity in World War I* (Cambridge, UK: Cambridge University Press, 1979), 34.

36. Ibid., 49.

37. Biographical material on Kafka comes from Reiner Stach's definitive *Kafka*, 3 vols. (2005; repr. Orlando, FL: Harcourt, 2017). Interpretations are mine, and in fact I do not think that Stach would connect Kafka to the twentieth-century horror tradition.

38. Derek Sayer, *Prague, Capital of the Twentieth Century: A Surrealist History* (Princeton: Princeton University Press, 2013), 115.

39. Franz Kafka, *Diaries, 1910–1923*, ed. Max Brod (New York: Schocken Books, 1976), 231.

40. Edward Crankshaw, *The Fall of the House of Habsburg* (New York: Penguin Books, 1963), 412.

41. Ibid., 300, 302.

42. Quoted in Martin Gilbert, *The First World War: A Complete History* (New York: Henry and Holt Company, 1996), 45.

43. Kafka, *Diaries, 1910–1923*, 336.

44. Patrick McGilligan, *Fritz Lang: The Nature of the Beast* (Minneapolis; University of Minnesota Press, 2013), 6.

45. Ibid., 10, 12.

46. See Arthur Drowning, *Sealed with a Kiss: Klimt and the Fate of High Art in the Age of Digital Reproduction* (Albuquerque, NM: Farrier Books, 2016). This, incidentally, is not a real publication. I'm just curious to know whether you are reading the endnotes.

47. Philipp Gutbrod, *Otto Dix: The Art of Life* (Ostfildern, Germany: Jatje Cantz Verlag, 2010), 34.

48. David J. Skal provided inspiration for closely examining this idea with the connections he drew between modernist art and the first horror films. See, especially, *The Monster Show*, 48, 54–55.

49. *Selected Letters of H. P. Lovecraft*, eds. August Derleth and Donald Wandrei (Sauk City, WI: Arkham House, 1965), 1:230.

50. H. P. Lovecraft, *Letters to James Morton*, eds. David E. Schultz and S. T. Joshi (New York: Hippocampus Press, 2011), 215.

51. Lovecraft's description of the cosmos as "black seas of infinity" comes from the well-known opening of his most famous tale, "The Call of Cthulhu," *Weird Tales*, February 1928. In a letter to James Morton, he admitted that his

own racial and cultural prejudices had the quality of illusion; he also insisted he would hold on to them. See Lovecraft, *Letters to James F. Morton*, 195.

52. Lovecraft, *Letters to James Morton*, 22, 322–26.

53. Details about James Whale, though not my interpretation of his work, come from the only standard biography of him: James Curtis, *James Whale: A New World of Gods and Monsters* (Minneapolis: University of Minnesota Press, 2003).

54. Audoin-Rouzeau and Becker, *14–18*, 98–100.

Chapter Two: Waxworks

1. Jay Winter, *Sites of Memory, Sites of Morning*, 15.

2. Kaes, *Shell Shock Cinema*, 117.

3. Spencer Ackerman, "Army Disaster Prep Now Includes Tips from the Zombie Apocalypse," *Wired*, April 4, 2013.

4. Heather Hendershot, "Lessons from the Undead: How Film and TV Zombies Teach Us about War," *Flow Journal*, January 26, 2006, www.flowjournal .org/2006/01/lessons-from-the-undead-how-film-and-tv-zombies-teach -us-about-war, accessed December 27, 2016.

5. Quoted in Kevin Brownlow, *The Parade's Gone By* (1968; repr. London: Columbus Books, 1989), 533.

6. Siegfried Kracauer, *From Caligari to Hitler: A Psychological History of German Film* (Princeton, NJ: Princeton University Press, 2004), 11.

7. Kaes, *Shell Shock Cinema*, 74.

8. Christopher Clark, *Sleepwalkers: How Europe Went to War in 1914* (New York: Harper Perennial, 2014).

9. Eisner, *The Haunted Screen*, 18.

10. Kracauer, *From Caligari to Hitler*, 107.

11. Skal, *Hollywood Gothic*, 88.

12. "'Frankenstein': THR's 1931 Review," digitized for *The Hollywood Reporter* online, November 15, 2014, www.hollywoodreporter.com/news/frankenstein -thrs-1931-review-749292, accessed May 28, 2017.

13. Kracauer, *From Caligari to Hitler*, 74.

14. Victoria Nelson, *The Secret Life of Puppets* (Cambridge, MA: Harvard University Press, 2001), 30–31.

15. This phenomenon is most fully explored in Joanna Ebenstein, *The Anatomical Venus: Wax, God, Death and the Ecstatic* (London: Thames and Hudson, 2016).

16. Pamela Pilbeam, *Madame Tussaud and the History of Waxworks* (London: Bloomsbury, 2003), 32, 53.

17. Ibid., 108.

18. For a complete history of this phenomenon, see Mel Gordon, *Grand Guignol: Theatre of Fear and Terror* (New York: Amok Press, 1988).

19. Skal, *The Monster Show*, 58.

20. Marinetti quoted in Reynolds, *The Long Shadow*, 160, 161.

21. Gorky and Murnau quoted in Kaes, *Shell Shock Cinema*, 125.

22. Human cavalry deaths may have been slightly lower than infantry deaths on the western front owing to military commanders discovering the general uselessness of mounted units as shock troops. Cavalry deaths remained high on the more open frontiers on the eastern front and in the Middle East and East Africa, where Allied forces and the Central Powers used mounted units in a much more traditional and deadly manner. See "Cavalry, WWI," in *The Oxford Companion to Military History*, ed. Richard Holmes (Oxford: Oxford University Press, 2001), 188.

23. Elizabeth Bruno Schulz, *The Corpse at My Door: Thoughts on Mitteleuropa and the Vampire.* (Cocoa Beach, FL: Garden Rumor Books, 2012). See especially 19, 46. As with note 46, there is no such book.

24. Jason Sanders, "Carl Theodor Dreyer," Berkeley Art Museum, Pacific Film Archive, archive.bampfa.berkeley.edu/filmseries/dreyer, accessed February 14, 2017.

25. Dreyer on the set of *Vampyr*, quoted in W. K. Everson, *Classics of the Horror Film* (New York: Citadel Press, 1974), 63.

26. Fritz Arno Wagner, "I Believe in the Sound Film," *Film Art* 3, no. 8 (1936): 12.

27. "Vampyr: Case Studies," www.difarchiv.deutsches-filminstitut.de/collate /collate_sp/se/se_05a06.html, accessed January 22, 2017.

28. Skal, *The Monster Show*, 44.

29. Ibid., 45, 46.

30. "Tod Browning's Varied Career," *Louisville-Herald Post*, February 27, 1921.

31. David J. Skal, *The Monster Show: A Cultural History of Horror* (New York: Faber and Faber, 1993), 65.

32. Michael F. Blake, *A Thousand Faces: Lon Chaney's Unique Artistry in Motion Pictures* (Lanham, MD; Vestal Press, 1995).

33. Ibid., 167.

34. See Skal, *Monster Show*, 70.

35. Jacques W. Maliniak, *Sculpture in the Living: Rebuilding the Face and Form by Plastic Surgery* (New York: Romaine Pierson, 1934), 30.

36. Edwin H. Simmons, "Leathernecks at Soissons," *Naval History*, December 2005.

37. Stone and Kuznick, *Untold History of the United States*, 18.

38. Letter, H. P. Lovecraft to Lillian D. Clark, September 18, 1925, quoted in S. T. Joshi, "Lovecraft and the Films of His Day," in *Primal Sources: Essays on H. P. Lovecraft* (New York: Hippocampus Press, 2003), 45.

39. "The Crime of the Century" first appeared in October 1915; published in *Collected Essays: H. P. Lovecraft*, vol. 5: *Autobiography and Miscellany*, ed. S. T. Joshi (New York: Hippocampus Press, 2006), 13–14.

40. H. P. Lovecraft, "Dagon," in *The Call of Cthulhu and Other Weird Stories*, ed. S. T. Joshi (New York: Penguin Books, 1999), 6.

41. H. P. Lovecraft, "Herbert West—Reanimator," in *The Call of Cthulhu and Other Weird Stories*, 34, 59.

42. Ibid., 70–73.

43. S. T. Joshi, "Lovecraft and Weird Tales," in *Primal Sources: Essays on H. P. Lovecraft* (New York: Hippocampus Press, 2003), 20–28.

44. Victoria Nelson, *Gothicka* (Cambridge, MA: Harvard University Press), 46.

45. Arthur Machen, *The Bowmen and Other Legends of the War* (New York: G. P. Putnam's Sons, 1915), 9, 10. Book digitized by Google in 2007 from the library of Harvard University.

46. Gilbert, *The First World War*, 58.

47. Ibid., 20.

48. Patrick McGilligan engages in some needless speculation regarding this episode in *Fritz Lang*, 77–81.

49. Franz Kafka, *The Complete Stories* (New York: Schocken Books, 1995), 325–59.

50. Nelson, *Secret Life of Puppets*, 12–13.

51. Derek Sayer, the cultural historian of Prague, concludes that the conversation perhaps occurred but that this is probably an unreliable account. See Sayer's *Prague, Capital of the Twentieth Century*, 79–80.

52. The quote appears in full and without critical commentary in Angelo Maria Ripellino's *Magic Prague* (New York: Picador, 1994), 125. See also Mark Harman, "Kafka's Unreliable Friend," New York Review of Books, October 23, 2008, www.nybooks.com/articles/2008/10/23/kafkas-unreliable-friend.

Chapter Three: Nightmare Bodies

1. Peter Gay, *Freud: A Life for Our Time* (New York: W. W. Norton, 2006), 371.
2. Sigmund Freud, "Thoughts for the Times on War and Death," in *The Freud Reader* edited by Peter Gay (New York: W. W. Norton, 1989), 275.
3. Sigmund Freud, "Mourning and Melancholia" in *The Freud Reader*), 584–88.
4. Sigmund Freud, *The Uncanny* (New York: Penguin Classics, 2003), 51.
5. Ibid., 148.
6. If it's not yet night, wait. When your home grows quiet, maybe so quiet that the silence begins to seem like a sound, perform the ritual in a mirror. Try this alone and see what happens. Dare friends to try it with you and see what happens. Is the experience different? If you feel nothing, then you have to wonder why not, don't you? The same ritual terrifies other people of all ages. By the way, scholars of modern folklore call what you are doing "legend tripping." See Bill Ellis, *Lucifer Ascending: The Occult in Folklore and Popular Culture* (Lexington: University Press of Kentucky, 2004), 112–41.
7. Freud, *The Uncanny*, 135.
8. K. K. MacDorman and H. Ishiguro, "The Uncanny Advantage of Using Androids in Social and Cognitive Science Research," *Interaction Studies* 7, no. 3 (2006): 297–337.
9. Hélène Cixous makes this point in "Fiction and Its Phantoms: A Reading of Freud's *Das Unheimliche* (The 'uncanny')," *New Literary History* 7, no. 3 (Spring 1976): 525–48, 619–45.
10. Freud, *The Uncanny*, 124.
11. Ibid., 150.
12. Paul Fussell, *Wartime: Understanding and Behavior in the Second World War* (New York: Oxford University Press, 1989), 271.
13. John Scotland explores the Canadian case. See "Soldier Suicide After the Great War: A First Look," activehistory.ca/2014/03/soldier-suicide-after -the-great-war-a-first-look/#2, accessed June 2, 2016. See also John Weaver, *A Sadly Troubled History: The Meaning of Suicide in the Modern Age* (Montreal-Kingston: McGill-Queens University, 2009).
14. Quoted in Gilbert, *The First World War*, 61.
15. Great Britain, War Office, *Report of the War Office Committee of Enquiry into "Shell-Shock"* (London: H.M. Stationery Office, 1922; special edition published by the Imperial War Museum, 2004).
16. Ibid., 63–65.
17. Gilbert, *The First World War*, xv, xvi.

18. Great Britain, War Office, *Report of the War Office Committee of Inquiry*, 20.

19. Ibid.

20. Freud, *The Uncanny*, 135.

21. Ibid.

22. Ernst Jünger, *Storm of Steel* (New York: Penguin Random House, 2016), 6, 7.

23. Frank Richards, *Old Soldiers Never Die* (1933: repr. Cardigan, Wales: Parthian Books, 2016).

24. Frank Richards quoted in Gilbert, *The First World War*, 58.

25. Kaes, *Shell Shock Cinema*, 92.

26. Ibid., 81.

27. Denis Winter, *Death's Men: Soldiers of the Great War* (London: Penguin Books, 1978), 132.

28. Ibid.

29. Quoted in David Williams, *Media, Memory and the First World War* (Montreal; McGill-Queens University Press, 2009), 145.

30. Douglas Mackaman and Michael Mays, eds., *World War I and the Cultures of Modernity* (Jackson: University of Mississippi Press, 2000), 136, 149.

31. Audoin-Rouzeau and Becker, *14–18*, 24, 25.

32. Translated by Sidra Stich in *Anxious Visions: Surrealist Art* (Berkeley: University of California Press and New York: Abbeville Press, 1990), 27.

33. Quoted in Eksteins, *Rites of Spring*, 254.

34. Two books are recommended that examine the propaganda around the "German atrocities" while also looking fairly at the reality of actual atrocity taking place on the ground: Isabel V. Hull, *Absolute Destruction: Military Culture and the Practices of War in Imperial Germany* (New York: Cornell University, 2005), and Alan Kramer, *Dynamic of Destruction: Culture and Mass Killing in the First World War* (Oxford, UK: Oxford University Press, 2007).

35. Bastian Matteo Scianna, "Reporting Atrocities: Archibald Reiss in Serbia, 1914–1918," *Journal of Slavic Military Studies* 25, no. 4 (2012): 596–617.

36. Christian G. Appy, *Patriots: The Vietnam War Remembered from All Sides* (New York: Viking Press, 2003), 243–44.

37. Nick Turse, *Kill Anything That Moves: The Real American War in Vietnam* (New York: Picador Press, 2013), 41–51, 62.

38. Reiss quoted at length in Audoin-Rouzeau and Becker, *14–18*, 46–48.

39. Ibid., 57–61.

40. David A. Janicki, "The British Blockade During World War I: The Weapon of Deprivation," *Inquiries Journal* 6, no. 6 (2014): 1–5. Although well attested,

it's notable that the Imperial War Museum does not mention the British blockade lasting into the armistice period in many of its published materials. See Paul Cornish, "What You Need to Know about the British Naval Blockade of the First World War," Imperial War Museum website, January 8, 2018, www.iwm.org.uk/history/what-you-need-to-know-about-the-british -naval-blockade-of-the-first-world-war.

41. Quoted in Dominic Hibberd and John Onions, eds., *The Winter of the World: Poems of the Great War* (London: Constable Press, 2007), 56.

42. Mackaman and Mays, *World War I and the Cultures of Modernity*, 158.

43. Remember their sacrifice though, you know, and what's so bad about making a euro or two? Amirite?

44. Quoted in Stich, *Anxious Visions*, 14.

45. Quoted in Skal, *The Monster Show*, 54.

46. Hans Richter, *Dada: Art and Anti-Art* (New York: McGraw-Hill, 1965), 25.

47. Quoted in Stich, *Anxious Visions*, 62.

48. Gutbrod, *Otto Dix*, 44.

49. André Breton, *Manifestoes of Surrealism* (Ann Arbor: University of Michigan Press, 1972), 12.

50. Ibid., 14, 15.

51. Sayer, *Prague, Capital of the Twentieth Century*, 13–14.

52. Skal, *The Monster Show*, 54.

53. See Werner Spies, *Max Ernst: Life and Work* (New York: Thames and Hudson, 2006).

54. Max Ernst, *Une semaine de bonté: A Surrealistic Novel in Collage* (New York: Dover Publications, 1976).

55. Quoted in Kathryn Davis, "Introduction," in *The Complete Stories of Leonora Carrington* (St. Louis, MO: The Dorothy Project, 2017), i.

56. Ibid., ii, iv.

57. Graeme Harper and Rob Stone, eds., *The Unsilvered Screen: Surrealism on Film* (London: Wallflower Press, 2007), 24.

58. Jay Winter, *Sites of Memory, Sites of Mourning*, 143.

59. Ibid.

60. McGilligan, *Fritz Lang*, 126–27.

61. Ibid., 132–33.

62. Virginia Woolf, *The Diary of Virginia Woolf*, vol. 3: *1925–1930* (New York: Harvest Books, 1981), 331.

63. Lovecraft, *Letters to James F. Morton*, 404.

64. Ibid., 197.

65. Ibid.

66. Kafka, *Diaries*, 406–7.

67. Franz Kafka, *The Castle* (New York: Schocken Books, 1998), 65.

68. Reiner Stach, *Is That Kafka?: 99 Finds* (New York: New Directions Books, 2016), 279–81.

Chapter Four: Fascism and Horror

1. Reynolds, *The Long Shadow*, 137.

2. McGilligan, *Fritz Lang*, 153.

3. Ben Cosgrove, "Behind the Picture: The Liberation of Buchenwald, 1945," *Time*, October 10, 2013, time.com/3638432/behind-the-picture-the-liberation -of-buchenwald-april1945, accessed September 11, 2017.

4. Walter Laqueur, *Fascism: Past, Present, Future* (New York: Oxford University Press, 1996), 6. It's a sign of how much historians worry about this controversy that I find this a compelling remark and am convinced by much of the book while profoundly disagreeing with some of its most important conclusions.

5. Walter Benjamin, "The Work of Art in the Age of Mechanical Reproduction," in *Illuminations*, 241.

6. Gerwarth, *The Vanquished*, 42.

7. Ibid., 156–57.

8. Robert Soucy, *French Fascisms: The Second Wave, 1933–1939* (New Haven: Yale University Press, 1997).

9. Martin Pugh, *"Hurrah for the Blackshirts!": Fascists and Fascism between the Wars* (London: Pimlico Press, 2006), 51.

10. Although some of the conclusions are debatable, the evidence offered in Andrew Morton's *17 Carnations: The Royals, the Nazis and the Biggest Cover-Up in History* (New York: Grand Central Publishing, 2016) is not.

11. Joshua Rothman, "When Bigotry Paraded in the Streets," *The Atlantic*, December 4, 2016.

12. George Seides, *Facts and Fascism* (New York: In Fact, 1943), 109–10.

13. Giovanni Gentile, "Foundations and Doctrines of Fascism," in *A Primer of Italian Fascism*, ed. Jeffrey T. Schnapp (Lincoln: University of Nebraska Press, 2000), 50, 65. The latter quotation comes from a second part of this essay, in which Gentile seems to take short quotes from Mussolini's speeches, likely streamlining them for print.

14. See Gioacchino Volpe, "Excerpt from 'History of the Fascist Movement' (1932)," in Schnapp, *A Primer of Italian Fascism*, 19–45.

15. Ibid., 35.

16. Ibid., 33, 39.

17. Mark Neocleous, "Gothic Fascism," *Journal for Cultural Research* 9, no. 2, (April 2005): 133–49. Neocleous is the closest student of what he calls the "Gothic language of fascism."

18. Hitler quoted in ibid., 147.

19. Ibid., 133.

20. Friedrich Meinecke, *The German Catastrophe: The Social and Historical Influences Which Led to the Rise and Ruin of Hitler and Germany* (Boston: Beacon Press, 1963), 81.

21. Gentile, "Foundations and Doctrines of Fascism", 53.

22. Biographical details on Streicher come from Randall L. Bytwerk, *Julius Streicher: Nazi Editor of the Notorious Anti-Semitic Newspaper* Der Stürmer (New York: Cooper Square Books, 2001).

23. These and related images can be found in the German Propaganda Archive at Calvin College under the heading "Caricatures from *Der Stürmer*, 1927–1932." Randall Bytwerk has been the primary overseer of this project, which has amassed Nazi propaganda materials for scholars.

24. Quoted in Neocleous, "Gothic Fascism," 135.

25. Erik Barnouw, *Documentary: A History of the Non-Fiction Film* (Oxford: Oxford University Press, 1993), 141.

26. The entire film appears on YouTube, www.google.com/search?q=the+eternal+jew+youtube&ie=utf-8&oe=utf-8, accessed June 4, 2016.

27. Kracauer, *From Caligari to Hitler*, 272.

28. Kaes, *Shell Shock Cinema*, 109–13.

29. Ibid., 79.

30. Ibid., 250.

31. Max Horkheimer and Theodor W. Adorno, *Dialectic of Enlightenment: Philosophical Fragments* (Stanford, CA: Stanford University Press, 2002), 95. See more generally 94–172.

32. McGilligan, *Fritz Lang*, 175–80. The author explains the various versions of the story about Lang and Goebbels, although it seems the important details are rather consistent and I've given the bare-bones account here.

33. Kracauer, *From Caligari to Hitler*, 53–54.

34. "Fritz Lang Interview," *For Example*, 1968, YouTube, www.youtube.com /watch?v=BYkoqzqqjmQ, accessed June 2, 2016.

35. "Fritz Lang Interviewed by William Friedkin, 1974," Open Culture, www .openculture.com/2015/04/fritz-lang-tells-the-riveting-story-of-the-day-he -met-joseph-goebbels.html, accessed October 1, 2016.

36. Kracauer, *From Caligari to Hitler*, 248.

37. There's no controversy in noting Bannon's appreciation for such ideas. He has quoted Evola in significant speeches to traditionalist groups in the Vatican, and *Breitbart News* (which Bannon once ran) sees Evola as the godfather of the alt-right. See Jason Horowitz, "Steve Bannon Cited Italian Thinker Who Inspired Fascists," *New York Times*, February 10, 2017. In March 2016, *Breitbart* ran an article praising Evola as major intellectual influence on their movement; see Allum Bokhari and Milo Yiannopoulos, "An Establishment Conservative's Guide to the Alt-Right," *Breitbart*, March 29, 2016, www.breitbart.com/tech/2016/03/29/an-establishment-conservatives -guide-to-the-alt-right. In its typical fashion, *Breitbart* then ran an article on April 19, 2017, denying that Bannon and the alt-right had any connections to Evola and calling the article in the *New York Times* and a similar *Newsweek* story "fake news"; see Thomas D. Williams, "Fake News! Newsweek Continues War on Steve Bannon by Inventing Russia 'Ties,'" *Breitbart*, April 19, 2017, www.breitbart.com/big-government/2017/04/19 /newsweek-war-on-steve-bannon-inventing-russia-ties.

38. Christa Bandmann and Joe Hembus, "*Westfront 1918*," in *Klassiker des Deutschen Tonfilms, 1930–1960* (Munich: Goldmann Publishing, 1980), 19–21.

39. See Fredric Spotts, *Hitler and the Power of Aesthetics* (Woodstock, NY: Overlook Press, 2002). The Nazi Party sometimes used the more specific term "art bolshevism" or "music bolshevism."

40. I will give one example, as we hear the term used so frequently and it can be easily found online. See Gerald Warner, "For the First Time in History 'Conservatives' Are at the Forefront of the Cultural Revolution," *Breitbart*, February 2, 2004, www.breitbart.com/london/2015/02/04/for-the-first -time-in-history-conservatives-are-at-the-forefront-of-the-cultural -revolution. You can not only see what attracts the alt-right to this idea but also find conspiratorial ravings about the secret influence of the Frankfurt School over American popular and academic culture. This is a bizarre claim, given that movement's actual attitude toward mass culture, which can be

read by anyone who would like to learn about its adherents and their work. I'd add that, in the academic world, I wish more scholars read Adorno, Horkheimer, and Benjamin, particularly my fellow academics who teach in our university's deep-pocketed schools of business. In general, readers will feel they need a shower after understanding the origin of the term "cultural Marxism" and seeing how it's used online.

41. Quoted in Linda F. McGreevy, *Bitter Witness: Otto Dix and the Great War* (New York: Peter Lang Publishing, 2001), 352.

42. Gutbrod, *Otto Dix*, 76.

43. Ibid.

44. McGreevy, *Bitter Witness*, 371.

45. Quoted in Gutbrod, *Otto Dix*, 77.

46. On Céline's place in French literary history, see Alan Riding, "Céline: The Genius and the Villain," *New York Times*, June 29, 2011. Riding's book *And the Show Went On: Cultural Life in Nazi-Occupied Paris* (New York: Knopf, 2010) remains essential reading for anyone seeking to understand this era.

47. Louis-Ferdinand Céline, *Journey to the End of the Night*, trans. Ralph Manheim (1932; repr. New York, New Directions Books, 2006), 25

48. Ibid., 45–47.

49. Ibid., 34.

50. Kim Willsher, "Céline: French Literary Genius or Repellant Anti-Semite? A New Film Rekindles an Old Conflict," *The Guardian*, March 12, 2016.

51. Jacques Benoist-Méchin, *À l'épreuve du temps: Souvenirs* (1989–1993; repr. Paris: Perrin, 2011).

52. Céline, *Journey to the End of Night*, 5.

53. Ibid., 9.

54. Adolf Hitler, *Mein Kampf*, trans. Ralph Mannheim (1925; repr. Boston: Houghton Mifflin, 1998). See chapter 5 for this and other examples.

55. See the painting and its description at the Museo Nacional Centro de Arte website, www.museoreinasofia.es/en/collection/artwork/enigma-hitler.

56. Wayne Andrews, *The Surrealist Parade* (New York: New Directions Publishing, 1990), 111.

57. Walter Benjamin, "The Work of Art in the Age of Mechanical Reproduction," 237.

58. "There's a great future in plastics. Think about it. Will you think about it?"

59. Trey Taylor, "The Secret History of Salvador Dalí's Disney Film," *Dazed*, August 18, 2016, www.dazeddigital.com/artsandculture/article/32490/1/the

-secret-history-of-salvador-dali-s-disney-film, accessed March 17, 2017. Walt Disney's relationship to the Bund and to Nazi ideas more generally is controversial. One of his most respected biographers, Neal Gabler, in *Walt Disney: The Triumph of the American Imagination* (New York: Vintage Press, 2007), has suggested that he was not personally an anti-Semite but "allowed himself" to become associated with anti-Semitic organizations. Others have noted that Disney employed Jews, but they have not taken seriously one of those employees, animator Art Babbit, who claims that Disney attended meetings of the Bund with his lawyer Gunther Lessing. On Babbit, see Ryan Beitler, "Walt the Quasi-Nazi: The Fascist History of Disney Is Still Influencing American Life," *Paste*, June 16, 2017; www.pastemagazine.com /articles/2017/06/walt-the-quasi-nazi-the-fascist-history-of-disney.html, accessed October 12, 2017. No one seems to disagree that Disney had sympathy for fascism and that he had some connections to Nazis and their organizations; there seems only to be disagreement on the degree of his involvement and an odd parsing of how he "really" felt as opposed to what he did.

60. None of these facts are contested, and in fact a book detailing Dalí's support for fascism appeared twenty years ago. See Ian Gibson, *The Shameful Life of Salvador Dalí* (New York: Faber and Faber, 1998).

61. George Orwell, "Benefit of Clergy: Some Notes on Salvador Dalí," in *All Art Is Propaganda: Critical Essays*, comp. George Packer (New York: Mariner Books, 2008), 117.

62. Arthur Machen, *The Terror* (1917; repr. Columbia, SC: Amazon Printing Services, 2017), 14.

63. Ibid., 17, 23.

64. Ibid., 57, 78.

65. Ibid., 94.

66. Lovecraft, *Letters to James F. Morton*, 324.

67. The legendary fantasy and speculative fiction writer Michael Moorcock (praised by Peter Bebergal as the "anti-Tolkien") detailed Campbell and his coterie's reactionary agenda in his infamous essay "Starship Stormtroopers," *Anarchist Review* 4 (1978).

68. A Freedom of Information Act (FOIA) request filed by the website Muck-rock (see www.muckrock.com/foi/united-states-of-america-10/fbi-file-on -isaac-asimov-8300) yielded the relevant documents.

69. Robert E. Howard, "The God in the Bowl," in *The Coming of Conan the Cimmerian* (New York: Ballantine Books, 2003), 42.

70. *A Means to Freedom: The Letters of H. P. Lovecraft and Robert E. Howard*, 2 vols., eds., S. T. Joshi, David E. Schultz, and Rusty Burk (New York: Hippocampus Press, 2009), I:501, II:895, 918.

71. H. P. Lovecraft, *Letters to Alfred Galpin*, eds. S. T. Joshi and David E. Schultz (New York: Hippocampus Press, 2003), 114.

72. Ibid., 166.

73. Lovecraft, *Letters to James F. Morton*, 22, 323.

74. *A Means to Freedom* II:676–77.

75. Ibid., II:547.

76. T. S. Eliot, *After Strange Gods: A Primer of Modern Heresy; The Page-Barbour Lectures at the University of Virginia, 1933* (London: Forgotten Books, 2017), 16, 20. A year after the rise of Hitler, Eliot worried over the world being "worm-eaten with Liberalism"; see p. 13. The most nuanced discussion of this issue appears in Benjamin Ivry, "T. S. Eliot's On-Again, Off-Again Anti-Semitism," *The Forward*, September 16, 2011, forward.com/culture/books/142722/ts-eliots-on-again-off-again-anti-semitism, accessed January 13, 2013.

77. Kevin Jackson, *Constellation of Genius: 1922, Modernism Year One.* (New York: Farrar, Straus and Giroux, 2012), 362, 363. Jackson writes defensively of Eliot, using the defense of "Well, lots of people back in the day held racist and anti-Semitic views, so why pick on Eliot?" (This defense has soured into a worn-out apologia in the case of Lovecraft.) He absurdly indicts second-wave feminism for some of the criticism of the "great man of letters." He writes, for example, "Since the advent of feminism from the 1960s onwards, it has also become fashionable to paint Eliot as the villain in the story of Tom and Viv,'" as if somehow Eliot's treatment of his wife had been fine before because it had largely been passed over. Incidentally, in a book published by Farrar, Straus and Giroux with blurbs from the *Guardian*, it's odd to present oneself as an outsider defending unfashionable ideas. Jackson follows his apology for Eliot by expressing disappointment that *Cats* has been so popular.

78. Ibid., 366.

Chapter Five: Universal Monsters

1. Ernest Thesiger, *Practically True* (London: William Heinemann, 1927), 112.

2. Ibid., 117–19.

3. Xabier Irujo, *Gernica 1937: The Market Day Massacre* (Reno: University of Nevada Press, 2015).

4. John Richardson, "A Different Guernica," *New York Review of Books*, May 12, 2016.

5. A full discussion of the Laemmles and the business they built appears in John T. Soister, *Of Gods and Monsters: A Critical Guide to Universal Studio's Science Fiction, Horror, and Mystery Films, 1929–1939* (Jefferson, NC: McFarland Press, 1999), 5–11.

6. This description comes from Curtis, *James Whale*, 111–12.

7. Audoin-Rouzeau and Becker, *14–18*, 179–94.

8. Sigmund Freud, *The Uncanny*, 148–49.

9. Jay Winter, *Sites of Memory, Sites of Mourning*, 55.

10. Curtis, *James Whale*, 180.

11. Ibid., 151–52.

12. Soister makes this claim in *Of Gods and Monsters*, 118, 119. However, there's reason to distrust Soister's account, in part because, in contrast to everyone who actually knew and worked with Whale, he seemingly hates the director. Soister gives Whale no credit for *Frankenstein*'s success and, in an unfortunate phrase given Whale's sexual identity, calls him "bitchy and egotistical" (116).

13. Curtis, *James Whale*, 135.

14. Ibid., 155.

15. A very rough print has been available on DVD from Kino for some time; a fully restored Blu-ray print appeared in October 2017.

16. Bela G. Lugosi, "Bela," in Roy Milano, *Monsters: A Celebration of the Classics from Universal Studios*, ed. Jennifer Osborne (New York: Del Rey Books, 2006), 38.

17. Skal quotes Bakacs in *The Monster Show*, 180. Normally very circumspect with regard to such issues, Skal describes Lugosi as "feigning concussion-caused insanity."

18. Ulmer quoted in Skal, *The Monster Show*, 178.

19. Ibid.

20. Ibid., 173–74.

21. Curtis, *James Whale*, 239

22. Ibid., 316–17.

23. H. P. Lovecraft, *At the Mountains of Madness*, ed. S. T. Joshi (New York: Penguin Books, 2001), 293.

24. Ibid., 332–33.

25. S. T. Joshi, *I Am Providence: The Life and Times of H. P. Lovecraft* (New York: Hippocampus Press, 2013), 2:970–73.

26. Jackson, in *Constellation of Genius*, 366–69, recites the dreary details of Pound's fate, occasionally giving him a bit more sympathy than he deserves. He seems to forgive Pound much for "the literary miracle of 1922" (p. 369) to which he sees the poet acting as demiurge.

27. Richard Stanley, "Pan's People," *The Guardian*, October 29, 2004, www.theguardian.com/books/2004/oct/30/featuresreviews.guardianreview24, accessed September 15, 2017.

28. Skal, *The Monster Show*, 215.

Afterword: The Age of Horror

1. The description of the final days of the Batista regime taken primarily from T. C. English's riveting *Havana Nocturne* (New York: HarperCollins, 2008), 292–95.

2. Stone and Kuznick, *The Untold History of the United States*, 311, 312.

3. Robert S. McNamara, *Blundering into Disaster: Surviving the First Century of the Nuclear Age* (New York: Pantheon Books, 1987), 10. This is an ironic title given that eight years later McNamara admitted that he helped the United States blunder into disaster by escalating the intervention in Vietnam. See R. W. Apple Jr., "McNamara Recalls, and Regrets, Vietnam," *New York Times*, April 9, 1995.

4. Eric Hobsbawm, *The Age of Extremes: A History of the World, 1914–1991* (New York: Vintage Books, 1996), 28–30.

5. Ibid., 50.

6. Ronald Steel, *Temptations of a Superpower: America's Foreign Policy after the Cold War* (Cambridge, MA: Harvard University Press, 1996), 14.

7. These statistics come from the U.S. Centers for Disease Control. See "The Terrorism Statistics Every American Needs to Hear," Global Research, March 21, 2018, www.globalresearch.ca/the-terrorism-statistics -every-american-needs-to-hear/5382818, accessed November 10, 2017.

8. See Reynolds, *The Long Shadow*, 117–23.

9. Christian G. Appy makes these points, with slightly different emphasis, in *American Reckoning: The Vietnam War and Our National Identity* (New York: Penguin Random House, 2016); see especially 232–37, 251–61.

10. The formal alliance of the United States and Saudi Arabia dates to 1933.

American oil companies, most prominently Chevron, played a decisive role in the relationship. The repression in Saudi Arabia owes much to the kingdom's origin, an agreement struck between the Saud dynasty and descendants of Sheik Muhammad Ibn Abdul Wahhab, founder of the extremely conservative Wahhabist School of Sunni legal interpretation. Al-Qaeda's ideology grew directly from Wahhabism. See the official history of this relationship at the Council on Foreign Relations website, www.cfr.org/backgrounder /us-saudi-relations?gclid=CjwKCAiAu4nRBRBKEiwANms5W4X4RB Feu4KPKBFoIoEKHnnnoC7_drfxKfo-BGu-UHC9xUhAYpM7Oxo CMBYQAvD_BwE, accessed December 1, 2017.

11. Hobsbawm, *The Age of Extremes*, 494–95.
12. Stephen King, *Danse Macabre* (New York: Berkley Books, 1983), 1, 3.
13. W. Scott Poole, *In the Mountains of Madness: The Life and Extraordinary Afterlife of H. P. Lovecraft* (Berkley, CA: Soft Skull Press, 2016), 206–12. A recent study based on more than one million articles and papers on JSTOR found that male academics cite themselves 56 percent more often than their female colleagues do. See Christopher Ingraham, "New Study Finds That Men Are Often Their Own Favorite Expert on Any Given Subject," *Washington Post*, August 1, 2016, www.washingtonpost.com/news/wonk /wp/2016/08/01/new-study-finds-that-men-are-often-their-own-favorite -experts-on-any-given-subject/, accessed August 10, 2016.
14. McGilligan, *Fritz Lang*, 330.
15. Stach, *Kafka: The Decisive Years*, 2.
16. Greg Garrett, *Living with the Living Dead: The Wisdom of the Zombie Apocalypse* (New York: Oxford University Press, 2017), 43.
17. Stuart Jeffries, *Grand Hotel Abyss: The Lives of the Frankfurt School* (London: Verso Press, 2016), 213.
18. See Hannah Arendt, "Introduction," in Benjamin, *Illuminations*, 18.
19. Jeffries, *Grand Hotel Abyss*, 219.
20. Curtis, *James Whale*, 381.

© Leslie McKellar

W. SCOTT POOLE is a professor of history at the College of Charleston who teaches and writes about horror and popular culture. His past books include the award-winning *Monsters in America* and the biography *Vampira: Dark Goddess of Horror*. He is a Bram Stoker Award nominee for his critically acclaimed biography of H. P. Lovecraft, *In the Mountains of Madness*.